From the Steeple to the Minaret
Living Under the Shadow of Two Cultures

Hughette Eyuboğlu

Çitlembik Publications 51

Cover art: Bedri Rahmi Eyuboğlu
Cover design: Deniz Akkol
Layout: Tarkan Togo

Printed at Berdan Matbaası, Istanbul, Turkey

ISBN: 975-6663-51-0

In Turkey:
Şeyh Bender Sokak 18/5
Asmalımescit - Tünel
80050 Istanbul
www.citlembik.com.tr

In the USA:
Nettleberry LLC
44030 123rd St.
Eden, South Dakota 57232
www.nettleberry.com

Contents

An Ocean Apart:
A Canadian Wife in Turkey

To Mehmet, my husband and best friend

Acknowledgements

My grateful thanks to Marc Baudouin for the careful reading of part of my manuscript and for many helpful suggestions, and to Lyne Saka for the painstaking and invaluable help in correcting my English. I am especially grateful to my sister Claude for her strong support during the course of this long venture.

Introduction

Writing a book had never been one of my priorities until I read *Not Without My Daughter*. The author, Betty Mahmoody, was an American who had married an Iranian citizen. At one point, she and her daughter became the focus of attention following events that arose from an intricate situation which, as I myself have often witnessed, so frequently occur in intercultural marriages. Her account caused such a reaction that I, a Canadian married to a Turk, could not possibly remain neutral.

While the incidence of intercultural marriages increases at a constant rate, rarely do the spouses find a way of properly preparing themselves for what lies ahead. Heart and soul, we throw ourselves into this adventure of matrimony, as I myself did, hoping for ever-lasting bliss. While some succeed and attain happiness, others fail miserably. Unfortunately, such tragic failures often involve innocent victims, the children. They find themselves hostages caught up in the intricacies of a legal battle* or in the emotional orbit of one of their parents.

Successful emotional adventures, happy marriages don't usually make front page stories, but they do exist. This is why I wanted to relate my story, with its joys and difficulties, simply and truthfully as I have lived it in Turkey, in the country of my husband so far away from my homeland, Canada.

What are the requirements for a successful adventure? Unfortunately, no magic formula for it exists. How did I acquire the

---

* For example, in Iran, the custody of a child cannot be given to a woman.

necessary tolerance, patience and resistance? How did I manage to complete my integretion into these new surroundings and attain a synthesis of two different cultures? Trying to find the answers, I retraced the road I followed beginning from my origins in Abitibi, Province of Quebec. The reality of living in several languages–in this case, Turkish, French and English–has allowed me to discover the richness of other cultures while forcing me to adjust my native tongué to different wavelengths.

The main element of a successful marriage is love. In intercultural unions, you must not only love your spouse, but also all the elements of his country: the people, the beliefs, the customs, the language, the music, the literature, the history, the food, the sufferings, the misery, the paradoxes–in short, everything. The conviction that the values of your own culture are better than those of others cannot be maintained. It should be understood that the choice of values to be applied in the intercultural marriage ensures the success of the relationship.

The desire to introduce Turkey, its people and the life in the country as it really is was the second thing that prompted me to write my book. I am outraged when I read articles or books stuffed with prejudice, deformations and false statements. I would not at all be the least bit surprised if I were to discover that such publications are the work of a group of individuals who expressly have these books written with no other aim then that of harming Turkey. In my opinion, there are limits to what one can write. Turkey does have problems, but it also has a good side. Although it has suffered many difficulties, it certainly should not be thought of as only a negative country. Such defamatory and slanderous publications do not solve any problems. Two English authors, Tim Kelsy in *Dervish* and Jim Pettifer in *The Turkish Labyrinth,* are examples of these tendencies. Quite the opposite, my sole intention in writing this book has been to relate as correctly as possible, via the route of my own experiences, what life has been like in this country by for the last thirty-sevens years.

Chapter I

A Trip to the Past

There I was on the Air France flight to Canada, curled up half numb in my seat. The cheerful, almost pleasant voice of the pilot informed us that we were soon to land in Montréal. He eagerly added for our information that the temperature, on this twenty-forth day of December 1982, was twenty-five below zero! I couldn't help but smile and my first thought was: "At last I won't look odd and out of place in my fur coat; I will be just like everyone else. What a comfort!" This reaction may seem strange, but I had left a sunny Istanbul the day before, scrutinized by the amazed gaze of the other passengers. I was dressed like a polar bear, in my water seal boots and my old fur coat dating from my university years in Québec City. A few hours later, in Paris, under a continuous rain, very much out of season in my fur coat, I tried as best as I could to let the colourful lights and cheerful decorations get me into the Christmas spirit.

The next day, while boarding at Charles de Gaulle airport for the second stretch of my trip, it was then my turn to observe with amusement the flow of elegant, rather scadly clothed ladies. I asked myself what they would do once on Canadian soil in the cold winter without boots, hats and thick gloves. When I was young, we could easily recognise the newly arrived European immigrants by the thin leather shoes they wore in winter. We always thought that they simply must be on the verge of freezing.

Going to Canada is a long trip and my excitement was such that it seemed as though the flight would never come to an end. It was going to be my first Christmas in Canada and my first holiday season with my family since I had left the United States for Turkey in July of 1966–no wonder I was excited! Of course I had seen my family since then, in 1972 and in 1978, but Christmas is really something else. The merry atmosphere, the fever and euphoria experienced by everyone around, is something not easily found in a Moslem country.

The magic of Christmas: What is behind this spell, the tenderness and compassion felt during this period? What do we expect from Christmas? It is surely not the long ago abandoned religious aspect that touches us. Every year, why do we repeat the same customs, take out the same glittering wreaths? Is it a complete ritual to bring back our childhood, the years spent without turmoil or troubles, in the protective womb of the family? Or is it an attempt to recreate the surroundings of that time, when all was enchantment and magic?

I could barely remember the gifts received then except for my white ice skates, autographed by Barbara Ann Scott, the queen of Canadian figure skating. They now hang in a corner of our basement in Istanbul. Another well remembered gift was the Borgona* "fur coat" that I wore for twenty-five years and which is now somewhere in Bosnia with the victims of war. So many preparations made for those few fleeting moments so filled with emotion, moments that remain with us and bring us happiness in the guise of sparkling-eyed children and grandchildren as we remember those days of yore. A nostalgic urge to live once more this atmosphere of days gone by was burning inside of me.

During the course of the journey, half asleep in my seat, I had been day dreaming about, or rather I had been literally living in my thoughts, my stay in the province of Québec–the details of my arrival, the Midnight Mass, even the "réveillon"** to be held in a few hours. Every detail was slowly passing in front of my eyes. Several times I found myself making a list of my gifts, counting my packages, even the extra ones I had brought in case we should have other guests, and envision-

---

* Borgona is a brand name of fake fur coats.
** French name for the meal eaten after midnight mass.

ing Mother's house with the balcony filled with lights, a warm interior without a Christmas tree but instead a lot of poinsettias and decorations of all kinds. I could almost smell the "tourtières"* and the stuffed turkey gracing the lovely table set in Mother's usual perfect style. And in the background, at last I could hear Christmas carols, in French!

What a state of excitement you can be in while preparing for a trip. The creativity of our imagination is such that these emotions, so intense and so powerful, lead us to create an alternative state as strong as reality itself. Once the plane hit the ground, time, until then suspended, began to race by at a tremendous speed. Reality had almost been blurred by the dream...

I remember but bits and pieces of scenes of my arrival at the airport–visions of my sister, her friend Gilles, Mother, my brother Jacques and his fragile girlfriend followed by a sudden feeling of bitter cold and great tiredness.

The family reunion, Christmas and New Year's Day finished, leaving fragments engraved here and there in my memory together with a lingering pain as I sensed a deep split between members of the family and found myself caught in between...

We are already at the beginning of January on one of those very cold days, and I think about Gilles Vigneault's poem and song we once regarded as our national anthem:

My country is not a country; it's winter.

I peek through the frosted window while Claude is completing the last preparations for our trip. We decided to visit the region we had originally come from, Abitibi. It is not common to take a trip up North in the middle of winter, but we still intend to visit our hometown, Malartic, a good 370 miles northwest of Montréal.

During the course of the past years, living in a distant country far from my roots, I had been haunted by my childhood memories: the house where I was born, the school where I studied, the forests, the lakes, the whole scenery of the past. I felt the need to link my past to my

---

* Tourtières: typical meat pie made of pork and spices that's eatern after mass.

current life and wanted to attempt to join together the different threads my life. Claude, enthusiastic about the idea, liked my plans. She made things much easier by proposing that we go together by car. Gilles, who had never seen this corner of the province, would be driving. As a French national who had grown up in Indochina and Morocco, he, of course, could not possibly have any idea of what to expect.

Leaving Montréal in the opposite direction of the morning traffic proved easy enough. The majestic scenery of the Laurentides, the summerhouses, the famous ski resorts and ski trails slowly drifted away and were now far behind us. As soon as we passed the city of Mont-Laurier, the scenery became wilder, the cities more isolated and the cold much more intense. Even the car windows were almost completely frosted over and I was most happy to be wearing my fur coat. Gradually, Gilles began to wonder where we were going. We had the feeling of being the only travellers on the road. Driving through deep, desolated forests, we entered La Verendry Park*, a huge wildlife reserve with no buildings, no signs of civilization, only miles and miles of frozen lakes and snow-covered forest; in short, a huge area of ice and white. About midway through the park we found a small centre with a restaurant, a gasoline station and a few snow-planes on skis parked on the frozen lake. While registering at the entry gate, I noticed a strange look on Gilles' face, a looked that seemed to be saying, "Where are we going?"

Yes, the scenery was wilder, desolate, but so beautiful, so peaceful. I noticed that Claude and I had suddenly become livelier, more dynamic, even more relaxed in these familiar surroundings. I could not help but compare this great silence to the noise of the city of Istanbul. I smiled as I recalled Mehmet's initial reaction on his first visit here in 1960; he was really convinced that we had lost our way on an unknown road leading to nowhere.

The intensity of the cold was at its peak: forty degrees below zero. The sun was shining, the snow was sparkling, a splendid day as they say! At last La Verendry Park came to an end and within a short time we would reach Val d'Or, which meant only another eighteen miles to our destination.

---

* La Verendry is named after Pierre de La Verendry, the famous French explorer who discovered the western part of Canada.

Would we recognise the city entrance? Had it changed a lot? While asking myself all of these questions, my eyes suddenly caught sight of a sign saying, "Welcome to Malartic". I closed my eyes, took a deep breath and thought, "this is where it all started!"

As I was lost in my thoughts, the car slowly went down Royal Avenue, the main street of the town. Suddenly Gilles's voice woke me from my reverie:

"Girls, where do we go now?", to which we quickly replied, "Keep going straight!"

My eager eyes rapidly made an inventory of the buildings I could recognise on both sides. Within a short time we reached the open space in front of the famous parish church of Saint-Martin de Tours. As all good French Canadians, I had been raised a Catholic. Like it or not, this church was intimately connected to my childhood and occupies a large part of my memories. The inescapable monthly confessions our teacher took the whole class to, the Midnight Mass where we sang with such emotion... One must recognise that the warmest aspects of the Catholic Church are its rich repertory of sacred music and the powerful sound of the organ vibrating both the walls of the building and our hearts. It was in the sacristy of this most pretentious church that Mehmet and I were married on the 5 August 1961. At that time in the Province of Québec, there was no other way of getting married. It was also the sanctuary where my father's funeral service had been held a short time before, on 11 June. I deliberately use the term "pretentious" because this place of worship had cost a small fortune and reflected the dream–but mostly the excessive aspirations–of our old ambitious parish pastor, Father Renaud. I do agree that the first years of his apostolate in Malartic were perhaps laborious and a time when he aspired to live in little luxury and comfort, but still. The Stations of the Cross, the Christmas Manger and all the statues in the church were made of antique silver, all paid for by the self-sacrificing parishioners. These might be quite elegant and solemn in appearance, but very uplifting they certainly were not. Even then, my child's mind could not accept that costly fantasy of a village parish priest. It was, of course, still that great era when the ever-powerful Catholic Church

The family house as I found it in 1983

expressed its unquestioned authority, when all good, and to some degree also despotic, parish priests would poke their noses into all matters, intimidating–even terrorizing–their parishioners in the name of the Father and the Son...

Human vanity can be found at all levels, even the spiritual. What is the difference between the women who try to impress us with their new fur coats and ridiculous hats and the parish priests competing to have the most spectacular looking church? Currently living in a period of religious revival and return to Islamic fundamentalism in Turkey, I could not help but smile. The systems are different, the names change, but ultimately everything is the same: at the end of the day, we see that the human race has not really evolved that much through the centuries.

We had now reached Fournière Street. Gilles made a left turn. My heart was pounding, and I felt very emotional after an absence of eighteen years as we arrived at number 300, a two-story white house, the house of my childhood. No visible changes could be detected. The maple tree and the weeping willow had grown a lot, but the yard appeared smaller than I recalled. "Greetings, house where I was born, cradle of my memories, witness of my childhood and youth, so far from my sight but so close to my heart. I have come back to visit you, perhaps the last time, to bid you farewell, as it should be, and to cut the link that binds me here." Is it possible to achieve that? Camera in hand, I took a last picture as evidence, as a remembrance.

I turned around to take a look at my second home, the Dumas family house, the home of Louise, my friend forever. I couldn't believe my eyes; the house was still there but had been painted with strange designs, with dark spots over the white background, like the fur of a giraffe. I had to be dreaming! I took another picture as witness to the spectacle, but later I could never bring myself to send it to Louise.

The cold was extreme and we had to hurry before the sun set. I wanted to see the high school where I had earned my diploma. We quickly returned to our car, which continued to perform wonderfully in that weather. We drove pass the Renaud Primary School and then came to the building, which we were told was no longer the high school. After we had graduated, the education system underwent several modifications and even the terminology was changed, as were the school names. A caprice perhaps, but I wanted to see the huge framed photograph of our class, the Class of 1956-57. Maybe I had an urge to reaf-

firm that I belonged to somewhere, a need to prove that I had roots. How could I define this desire? We were directed to a new school at the other end of the city; perhaps there I could find that relic of the past.

En route to that unknown school, we drove back down Royal Avenue and found ourselves in front of the post office, the building that had been my first link to Mehmet, my Turkish pen pal, my future husband. A bit farther on, we saw the Chateau Malartic Hotel, the subject of many a dream. Every year, just like

Graduation from high school (1957)

Chateau Malarctic Hotel, 1958

Cinderella, we would anticipate the Christmas party organized by the Rotary Club for its members. That was the only time I was allowed to step foot in that establishment. Don't think that that hotel with a very pompous name resembled anything like the four-star hotels of today! The hotel was more an information centre, a meeting place–at all hours of the day–for businessmen, politicians, social club members and most likely secret love affairs. It was the reception centre for all events and for special outings. It was the only establishment in town with a touch of refinement in the food. Needless to say, a lot of alcohol was consumed there, as it appeared to be an integral part of the colonisation of this region. A postcard I bought on this visit some twenty years after my father's death showed his car parked in front of the hotel. I guess he also spent quite a lot of time there.

As we slowly approached the railway track separating the city into two parts, we got a view of the cemetery, its flat stones covered with a thick layer of snow. We were to be disappointed. Since the road leading to the entrance had not been cleared, it was impossible for us to visit the grave where our father had been lying for such a long time. Of course, who could have foreseen that Hughette would come all the way from Istanbul on the third of January for such a purpose. In many ways, winter in Canada can be ruthless.

We finally reached the school building we had been looking for. In spite of it being the holiday season, the door was not locked and inside we even found a few teachers working. Recognising no one, we introduced ourselves and explained our desire to see the photographs of former commencements, especially the one of 1956-57. I could sense some hesitation followed by a polite silence. We were discreetly observed and finally informed that in the bustle of moving so many objects to the new building, some of these pictures had disappeared. I was so disappointed. But surely one does not leave so few traces behind! Dear Hughette, do not search for concrete signs of the past. As long as you maintain them, they exist only in your memories. Don't attach yourself to them and don't try to revive what no longer exists.

The sun was slowly setting, but there was one more place to see: the summerhouse. In a country with only two seasons, the month of July and winter, don't try to understand this love we have for summerhouses. With lakes everywhere, everyone had a favourite spot for such a house. Ours was on the shore of Long Lake, a few kilometres from Malartic. Earlier, when there was no road, it was a deserted area reachable only after an hour of boating. Father struggled hard to have the road built. He was especially convinced of the great potential of the area. He was right; the surroundings of Lake Long have now become a big provincial park.

As we drove along the well-kept road, we saw on both sides a large number of skiers and snowmobiles, in spite of the cruelly cold weather. I must admit that things had changed a lot around there. Having to choose between several roads, we finally stopped near a road leading to the summerhouse. Gilles had no intention of walking around in that cold and so he remained in the car. After a few minutes' brisk walk we passed a huge snow bank and all at once, despite some changes, we recognised it: the famous summerhouse we had been looking for. Nearby, on the frozen lake, fishermen sitting in small huts were fishing through the ice. Dear Lucien Bouffard, your dream did not only come true, it has prospered greatly! Many memories of the white silence came surging back. Father had loved the forest and tranquillity. To him, this place had been paradise. For us, looking for friends and activities, it was not exactly our idea of an ideal summerhouse. But it was there that I spent my honeymoon, our first night interrupted by the noisy visit of a mother bear and her two cubs.

A very amusing memory dates back to my summer vacation in 1960. Every night, Father would put on a spectacular fireworks show in the middle of the forest on the shores of the lake. We owed this extravaganza to the defeat of the National Party in the June elections. As one of the organizers of the party, Father also got to help dispose of the fireworks that were to be used in the party's electoral victory celebration. At that moment, I remembered it clearly; it was to be the last summer he spent at his beloved cottage.

As we walked, we could hear our footsteps crunching in the crisp snow. As the cold weather finally hit us, we pulled our scarves up to our eyes so we could breathe without freezing our faces. We quickly walked to the car and silently left the park deeply lost in our thoughts.

Chapter II

Malartic

As I write these words, my hometown has now been in existence for over sixty years and the current population is at a low of 4,394. Before being officially established, a conglomeration of shacks known as Roc d'Or but called Putainville*, had formed near its present boundaries. With such a colourful name, one can easily imagine that it must have looked like the American Frontier towns we see in westerns. Primitive housing, usually made of logs and lacking running water and electricity, were built on land belonging to the Crown. On the main street stood what would be called the "honest business" buildings, while in the back streets, carefully scattered, were the houses of prostitution where alcohol was also sold illegally. Just substitute European immigrants for the cowboys and the Indians, and add French and English natives, and you have an accurate image of the make-up of this new mining town.

While the provincial police would raid the town once in a while for the sake of appearances, things did not change. As it were, Roc d'Or, a source of human drama and suffering for many, was bound to disappear. I have strange memories of houses being lifted off their foundations and carried away at turtle pace by huge trucks, transporting them this time to a new legal piece of land somewhere. As a child I was quite impressed by this.

---

* Putainville means "city of whores".

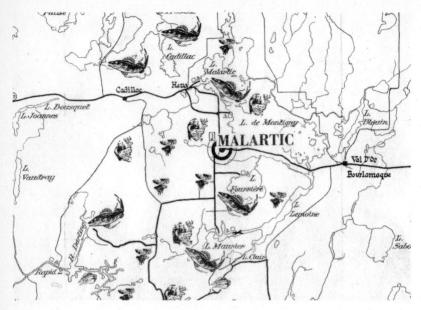

Malarctic and the area. The small insert situated in the province of Québec.

I was born in this new small town in 1940, in a white house built with the help of my maternal grandfather, Omer Germain, one or two years before my birth. The town owed its existence to three gold mines; the first one, the Canadian Malartic discovered in 1922, began extracting gold in 1935. It was followed later by the East Malartic at the end of 1938 and by the Goldfield in December of 1939. The development of the city therefore coincided with the 1930's, the years of the Great Depression when everyone was looking for work.

Geographically speaking, Malartic is in the deep forests of the north-western part of the Province of Québec known as Abitibi. At that time an isolated region along the border of the Province of Ontario, today it is served by the Transcanadian highway. Situated 113 kilometres from the Ontario border, it lies between the cities of Val d'Or and Rouyn-Noranda.

In his unpublished memoirs, former Member of Parliament Mr Jacques Miquelon describes the journey he had to undertake to travel from Québec City to Malartic in 1937. At that time, the roads in northern Québec Province reached only as far as Mont Laurier. Once in

Montreal, one had to drive to Ottawa in Ontario, slowly climb north to Mattawa North Bay, and then Haileybury to finally re-enter the province of Québec in the direction of Rouyn-Noranda. While a mere eighty kilometers from Malartic, in the absence of decent roads, the traveller had to add an extra 240 kilometres via the cities of La Sarre, Macamic and Amos. It was a gruesome adventure: 1,400 km of dusty roads. You could also choose to take the train via La Tuque. This train had earned the nickname of "beef chariot" and the trip cost thirty-five dollars–a fortune at the time for a twenty-four hour journey.

Five years old in front of our house in Malarctic

While the French Canadians comprised the majority of the population, there were also European immigrants and, of course, the elite English Protestants who usually came from Toronto. They formed the core of the professionals working in the mine and the management staff. This privileged group lived in comfortable houses near the mines where they worked. A strict hierarchy assigned these homes to the personnel. Our house, built close to their neighbourhood, gave me contact with English speaking children, unusual for a small town in the Province of Québec. Mother has often mentioned that before I began primary school, my English was better than my French.

Leafing through the pages of a book published to mark the fiftieth anniversary of

A tap dance concert (1947)

With Louise in 1950

the town, I tried to hunt down events I could remember, a familiar face, a name that rang a bell, a story, anything linked to my family. Although a thick book, the harvest was rather poor. While I might have forgotten a lot of things, the authors had omitted the names of many key families that played a role in the establishment of the town. One item in particular caught my attention: "On 25 April 1951, the Rotary Club of Malartic decides to build an outdoor swimming pool." Here was a short sentence that inadequately summarized all of the effort put forth, all of the work Father had done to complete that project. I remember very clearly the first words of his speech he practised at home before the official inauguration: "Thank you... Thank you... Thank you..." In the time between this event and my departure for Québec City in September of 1957, only nine events worth mentioning are listed. Is this not proof that life consists of a lot of minor events leaving absolutely no trace?

Since my departure from Malartic, apart from my childhood friend Louise Dumas, I have seen only a few people from Abitibi. Among them are my former boyfriend Louis Authier and his wife Jeanne d'Arc, a girl from our group. By strange coincidence, I met Helen Coté, the youngest daughter of our lawyer, here in Turkey. She is far younger then I am and was a friend of my sister. Working with a travel agency from our province, she was the guide for a few trips here. Whenever she comes, we talk about our region and the past. She even mentioned smilingly that Istanbul was the only place where she talked about Malartic. During one of her annual trips in 1998, she told me about the impending visit of the wife of our Notary Public, a former resident of Malartic. It is impossible for me to forget this lovely lady because once upon a time, she lent me an opera album that I listened to at leisure in a state of bliss. It was the Fledermaus by Johann Strauss. I must have been twelve or thirteen years old. Despite a lot of work at home, I found the time to visit her at her hotel somewhere in the centre of the city. Seeing someone after forty-five years was rather touching. She asked me if I wanted anything from Canada. I did not know what to say. She promised to send me the memoirs of our former Member of Parliament and Minister of the National Union, a pioneer of Malartic. A few weeks later I received the document and read it immediately. It is a book filled with information and details about the past–just what I needed. What a coincidence! Mr Miquelon* had played an important part in my life by helping me with my admission to the university at Laval and now, so many years later, he happened to be helping me again, just as I began writing my book.

---

* In May 1999, Mr Miquelon organized a meeting of former Malartic people. I attended and got to see many old acquaintances from my youth.

Chapter III

My Childhood

My childhood was like that of any girl from Abiṭibi at that time, except for a period of six or nine months at the end of 1945 and the beginning of 1946. During that time, the reason still a mystery, Father took us to Clova, rank forty-six, a camp of lumberjacks belonging to the Lebel and Murdock Company. The camp was just a dozen houses built on a muddy road close to the railway. On the other side of the tracks was the general store, the social centre of this settlement which was bound to the rest of the world only by the twice-daily train. In our two-room cabin there was a cubby-hole or, to define it more truthfully, a cell with bars on the window and door. Father had been given the responsibility of guarding a high-ranking German officer who had tried to escape from his former detention centre. Who was he? Why and in what circumstances was he entrusted to Father? All these questions still remain unanswered. At the end of this period, as if nothing had happened, we left this rather dreadful place and returned home to our usual life. Except for a trip to Ottawa in November of 1950 and a trip to Montreal and then to Father's hometown in St-Romain near Sherbrooke in 1953, I remained in Malartic throughout my childhood.

Despite being a new town, the education system was already in place and functioning well when I began primary school in 1946. I attended a tap dance and ballet school in this small mining centre from 1945 till 1951, and took piano and singing lessons until 1957. Thus I acquired and developed a sense for music, very unprecedented for an area like this. We must acknowledge the hard work of our leaders during those years. Now living in a country where the Republic has been in existence for the last eighty years, I have the opportunity to witness the difficulties involved in operating a nation-wide network of primary schools. Even in parts of Istanbul, some schools are bare-ly surviving on their meagre budgets with hardly enough money for heating, let alone libraries.

Living simply in a region far away from big cities, we had to be creative in order to fill our days. Sports were very popular

With Claudia in 1949

in the winter and from early childhood I skated a lot and played curl-ing, a game I continued to play as a university student in Québec City. During the years when we had no indoor skating rink in the town, we had to clean the snow off the outdoor rink and my feet were forstbit-ten several times in the process. We would skate every night for at least two hours and often at noon for more than half an hour. We also played a lot of badminton in the school gymnasium.

The many days of rain we endured made our long summer vacations seem endless. On the rare days when the sun did shine and the weather was warm, however, my friends and I would go swimming. However, most days were spent inside the house playing cards, reading, singing together with one of us at the piano or working on our stamp collections. Later, for several years, we organized a summer theatre in the Gagné fam-ily garage. We spent many hours practising new plays, creating new sets and costumes, and finally holding one or two shows for the other neigh-bourhood kids. The entrance fee was two or three cents.

The years of my early childhood were also closely connected to

My maternal grandparents on their
fiftieth wedding anniversary (1958)

those of my cousin Connie Scully, the daughter of Aunt Lucette, my mother's younger sister. Connie's father was Irish and she was always held up to us as the ideal example of a perfectly bilingual child. Since she studied in the English language, once she began school she made new English friends and left our group. Now I know that being perfectly bilingual or trilingual is very difficult, perhaps almost impossible unless you use your knowledge constantly. In everyday life, while one tongue improves, the others seem to lose their rich vocabularies and their grammars are slowly forgotten.

As far as I can remember, my friend Louise Dumas was always there. Some of the events I do not remember are well illustrated by photographs that complete the details. I can't remember how and when we first met, but living in the same neighbourhood and with our mothers knowing each other, we probably met while playing together or while picking blueberries or strawberries in the field not far from our houses.

We were inseparable. I would eat at her house and she would sleep at our house, or vice versa. Louise had four older brothers: Jean, Richard, André and Michel. We would rarely see them; they were either studying in Québec City or working in the woods with their father in the summer. Michel, the youngest and the calmest, was often the innocent victim of our games and endured a lot of teasing from us, his young sisters. But then it was André terrorized *us*. He would devise sophisticated methods to frighten us or simply bother us constantly. He would spy on us unendingly! We could not take a sunbath without being splashed; we could not play ping-pong without his interfering. In short, he was our nightmare come true.

The Dumas house had a fascinating attic filled with magazines of all kinds. There were the old issues of *National Geographic Magazine* that I loved looking at. There were several bookcases filled with encyclopaedias and I used to love browsing through them, too, to the great despair of Louise, who did not share my passion for reading. My favourite section was Tales, Legends and Stories.

Our favourite playing area was on the second floor of the house, in the huge bedroom that belonged to her always-absent brothers. That room became our property, and in this corner where no one would bother us, we created our own universe. Louise's father was a Member of the Canadian Parliament in Ottawa and surely his interest for public affairs was reflected in the conversations at home. In our favourite game, Louise would play Mr Louis St-Laurent, the Canadian Prime Minister of Canada at that time, while I would be Mr Maurice Duplessis, the Prime Minister of the Province of Québec. Our day would be spent sending very important memos to each other, a game filled with humility(!). Later I would learn from my sister Claude that she also played a similar game in which she was the Canadian Prime Minister. Without realizing it, our youth was immersed in politics.

One day at the beginning of Summer 1955, trying to answer the ever-present question, "What are we going to do today besides reading?", we had the brilliant idea of finding

My parents on a late honeymoon in Father's hometown (1937)

foreign pen pals, so we decided to send our names and addresses to the Semaine de Suzette that Louise subscribed to. We wanted to exchange stamps and postcards with youngsters from all over the world. I could never have guessed that a letter from one of those pen pals would completely change my life.

A few weeks later, our post office box was flooded with letters coming from all corners of the world. More than 600 in all arrived during that summer! Vacations were coming to an end and Louise was getting ready to leave for Ottawa to pursue her studies. I chose some twenty letters from different countries and began an extended correspondence with my pen pals. By the following spring, I had eliminated all my pen pals except for an Algerian from the city of Constantine and a young girl from Vietnam. In April, a letter literally covered with different stamps arrived. It had been written by a young man named Mehmet who lived in Istanbul, Turkey. It marked the beginning of an unusual correspondence that ended with the arrival of Mehmet on Canadian soil, in Ottawa, on 25 December 1960.

It was unavoidable; Louise left Malartic for Ottawa where her father lived a good part of the year. Every departure was filled with emotional drama, with tears and sadness and great demonstrations of affection. But slowly our lives took different directions. Louise studied political science in Ottawa; I studied a new profession, medical technology, in Québec City. At one time we had vowed to study this profession together...

At the end of my studies, I found myself in Ottawa where I worked for some twenty months. Louise was then in love with a law school student, Jean-Marc, and they were to be wed some time later. After having lived in various cities of Ontario, they now reside in Toronto. For the last fifty years, in spite of a sporadic correspondence, we still find occasions–either in Canada or in Turkey–to enjoy our friendship.

Besides Louise, I had other friends and schoolmates as well. Perhaps we did not visit each other, but we did spend eight hours a day together at school and two more hours in the evenings attending courses in bookkeeping, stenography and solfeggio. We also spent long hours skating together.

Until my entrance to university, my education was completed in

Malartic. At that time, the education system in the Province of Québec consisted of six years of primary school, three years of middle school and three years of high school. Our school was modern, comfortably heated, with a gymnasium where we could play ping-pong, badminton and basketball. We had access to a fairly extensive library. I still have the notes I took on the biographies of Beethoven and Wagner that I read at fourteen. Since it was a Catholic school, we could not find the works of Voltaire because they were in the Index, the Catholic Church's list of forbidden books. It wasn't until 1962 while living in the United States that I was finally able to read that author, albeit in English.

All the teaching staff were lay, not members of a religious order. Even though I remember very little of what was taught then–may my teachers forgive me–I have very good memories of my school years. I was a good student and after I graduated, I never again saw the other two girls with whom I usually shared the first three places. I do not recall strict discipline, but rather a pleasant atmosphere, one in which we were left fairly free and could develop and use our own initiative without restraints. Surrounded by snow and ice for long months, we took great pleasure in decorating our classroom with great imagination. After some forty-five years I still remember the decorating talents of Diane, my skating partner. We were never criticized for our projects or prevented from executing them; we were even allowed to work sometimes until nine o'clock at night. In reality, school was our second home.

Some of my best memories are of our school choir. It required hours of work. What discipline it required to synchronize all the parts of a piece of music and the various voices! It was a fascinating experience I would have liked to have pursued throughout my life. During these years, I participated in several recitals–ballet, piano and singing–for Mother's Day, Father's Day or other school celebrations. I consider these events very important elements of my education.

Parallel to this classical school education, Mother insisted I learn English well. I am forever grateful to her because the knowledge of this second language has been very useful to me all my life. She encouraged and promoted my friendship with English speaking girls, and later she arranged for Louise and me to join the English Protestant Girl Guide group. This was a rather radical move. It was real misery to have to memorize the regulations, the different knots, etc. in English, a language quite different from the language I learned at school and spoke with my friends. The summer camp in English, with courses in biology and astronomy and the famous theatre role we had to memorize, was, of course, an important step in my road towards a bilingual life. The worst ordeal was having to tolerate two years of piano lessons in English where "do", the first note, is C, not even A!

Mother's insistence was well founded: her sister Lucette was married to an Irishman and her other sister, Jeanne, had a British husband, "a real bloke", from England. In Father's family, two uncles chose to settle in Ontario when their work took them there. This all resulted in a large number of cousins who spoke better English than French. Later, Mother's younger sister and a brother chose to live in the United States, raising their children in the English language.

Another important element of our education was the radio. Access to long play records was limited and television only came later in the fifties. The radio was thus the vital link that bound us to Montreal, to the world of arts, concerts and the theatre. For me a real treat was to be able to listen to the afternoon of opera that came directly from the Metropolitan Opera House every Saturday. Between the different acts we could listen to the conversations that the famous Milton Cross had with his guests. One should also not forget the most important program of all: the hockey game. I would listen with Father while eating my favourite snack: a fried onion sandwich! Radio days, what a miracle they were.

Listening to the radio opened a door onto the world. Today, the role of the radio appears dwarfed and insignificant. The old wooden box had nothing in common with the complex machines of today, with recording devices ready to register, on the spot, anything we wish. Actually, today's hundreds of FM stations and their DJ's broadcast music all day long, hoping to prevent you from thinking straight.

Chapter IV

My Family

At a very young age, we are taught to love all family members; therefore, as a child, we love everyone without understanding and knowing what they are. With time, we slowly notice that certain members of the family get on our nerves. We would never dare express these feelings openly for fear of incurring strong reactions from our parents. The slightest remark would cause a fuss and a litany of unwanted comments.

During my childhood, while the few members of Father's family were far away, Mother's family was very much present. In later years, however, they, too, dispersed to different parts of Canada and the United States. Besides Mother, now ninety years old, of the eight children of Rose Papillon and Omer Germain, only Aunt Jeanne, the youngest daughter living in Florida, and Bob, the youngest son, who lives six months in Florida and six in Canada, are still alive.

Grandmother Rose was born in the United States in Minneapolis, Minnesota. After losing her mother at a very young age, she was brought up in Donaconna, Canada, by her eldest sister. In the middle of the nineteenth century, the precarious economy of the Province of Québec led to a strong wave of immigration south to the United States, since work could be found in factories there. Later, however, most of those workers returned to Canada.

Such was the case with Grandfather Omer. He was born in Winslow, Vermont, but returned together with his family to the Province of

Québec to settle in Donnacona. During the Great Depression, with an extremely high rate of unemployment and a severe economic crisis, he and Grandmother Rose both decided in 1934 to settle with their eight children in the region of Abitibi, at first in the town of Amos, then later in Malartic. Grandfather was a good carpenter despite having lost a few fingers to his craft. A happy fellow, always in good humour, speaking a very colourful French, he enjoyed drinking and then telling jolly "off colour" stories. Possessing inexhaustible energy, he embodied the joy of living. At the age of seventy, as a hobby, he built a small boat for his personal use, but was so successful that he wound up selling it and ended up constantly building new ones that also sold almost immediately. He never did get his own boat.

At the age of seventy-five, he and Grandmother Rose left on a six-month trip to California and Florida. Driving an old car he had painted himself, hat on his head, a huge cigar in his mouth, he had to perch on a big cushion because he was such a short man; one could only see the hat and the nose.

I remember him as the perfect example of how a grandfather should be. On a Christmas night when I was quite young, he gave me some furniture for my dolls: a table with chairs accompanied by a rocking chair and a high chair and bedroom furniture painted in blue with a dresser and a round mirror. How very happy I was!

Father was born in St-Romain in Frontenac County, not far from Sherbrooke. He had lost his mother at a very young age and was brought up by his elder sister, Anna. I have no idea of the circumstances that surrounded his coming to Abitibi.

From the register found on the island of Orléans, my sister Claude has discovered that the ancestor of the Bouffard family in the Province of Québec came from the city of Saint Martin-du-Pont in Normandy, France. Our ancestor's name was Jacques, son of Jean and Marguerite Le Portier. He was born in France in 1655 and died in Canada in 1727. He wed Anne Leclerc in 1680 in the village of Ste-Famille, a parish located on the island of Orléans.

While my Father was not the main figure in my education, a task left almost entirely to my Mother, he remained the pillar of the family, the one to whom I was emotionally bound. He did not talk a lot, but between the two of us there was a bridge that allowed us to communicate without exchanging words. Despite a severe appearance and deep reserve, he showed great tenderness towards us.

Despite his merry appearance, in reality he shunned people, except perhaps for a good game of bridge, a game he had mastered. He spent most of his spare time in the open air, hunting or fishing or simply sitting near a lake observing the wildlife around him. Our summerhouse was some thirty minutes from the town. We could see moose, bears, muskrats and mink. They were part of our daily life. As a teenager, I disliked going to the summerhouse because I craved activity, noise and company. Each time we went there, Mother could placate me only by letting me invite a friend, usually Louise.

The most important time of the year for Father was the month of October, the annual moose hunting period. The word "hunting" most likely evokes in each and every one of us different images according to the regions we come from or the customs that have influenced us. For those not born in Canada, moose hunting most likely does not ring any bells, but for those living in the northwestern part of the Province of Québec, it is a very important happening. Men talk about it for the whole year, never objectively, but always with a lot of exaggeration. Every hunter is a master taleteller.

Hunters spend the entire year getting ready for the event. Their fervour increases during the months of August and September. The hunt is in October and coincides with the reproduction cycle of the animal. While talking, the hunters will never give you a lead as to where their "secret hunting grounds" are. Such precious information should never fall onto the ears of an outsider or a non-hunter. Baggage would start piling up early in father's office: packsacks, sleeping bags, cooking equipment, a portable stove, plates, a two week supply of canned food, alcoholic beverages, guns and ammunition, knives, flashlights and the sacred compass. Day by day the pile would grow, while outside in front of the house the canoe, the outboard motor and the tent were ready to go on duty.

The services of an Indian guide were usually reserved a year in advance. His help was mostly required to ensure that the group did not get lost in the deep forest. He also helped the hunters with the overland portage since the hunt took place in deep forests, where there were no roads, but usually lakes, rivers and streams nearby. There was a lot of walking involved, followed by some canoeing, overland portage and so forth; to put it briefly, it was very exhausting work.

Every time I listened to their conversations, they were always the same stories retold again and again, but each time enriched with new, colourful details. They would recall long sleepless nights spent in the cold and the frost near the shores of a lake, waiting in complete and utter silence for the arrival of the male moose in answer to the mating call of the female. This call was imitated by hunters who would "call the moose" by blowing on a horn made of birch-bark. Many times Father was asked to call a moose at a public function or on a radio program for the benefit of fund drives and charity work. Sometimes the hunters would express the deep fear they felt while sitting in a canoe and seeing an aggressive moose charge at them, or the apprehension felt when seeing a wounded animal escape into the forest, and the thought of losing trace of the animal before it died somewhere in the thick forest. They would then proceed to tell the story of how the carcass of a huge animal was laboriously transported on foot for several miles through the dense forest before they got it to the canoe waiting on some water course. An endless repertory of stories, always begun with the same words: "Do you remember the time when...?"

The excitement would gradually rise to a peak as the final preparations were made, with everyone just coming and going until, at last, the hour of departure arrived. A few moments later, the house would become calm again and life could return to its normal pace. Seven to ten days might go by and then a phone call would let us know "they had killed". Several hours later, Father's car, carrying the head of a moose rising above the windshield, would pull up in front of the house. It was something to see the expression of happiness on their faces as we were submitted to another round of story telling about their exploits. And thus were new tales added to the old ones.

Before being butchered, the moose would be hung for a few days in the garage. I recall the appearance of what seemed like endless tons of meat and the nightmare of a huge liver that we would have to eat for the good of our health! Part of the meat would be distributed to friends

Father at the summerhouse
with his moose head (1959)

while the rest would be frozen or canned.

The second important ritual in Father's life was preparing for Christmas. During this period, he would be completely transformed into someone else, as if he were living his childhood all over again. He would spend hours decorating the front of the house with lights and wreaths of spruce. He would put a nice fir tree in front of the house and then cover it with blue lights*. He would then water the tree several times that day until it resembled a huge lighted icicle. It was a splendid sight both night and day. One winter, when I was thirteen or fourteen, father came home with a huge sheet of plywood. To my great astonishment, he asked me to paint a huge Santa Claus from the waist up with his bag of toys on his back. Inspired by various Christmas cards, I began to work on what would surely become a real piece of art. Once completed and half buried in the snow, our roof exhibited a pink faced red and white Santa Claus with a loudspeaker that played Christmas carols for all to hear throughout the holiday season. To me, this Santa Claus was surely the nicest in the world. In later years while discussing this "masterpiece" with my sister, she immediately commented that it looked rather awful. I thought about this matter a lot and, unable to be impartial, I wondered if Father had put it up for lack of anything better, or not to hurt my feelings, or was it that the magical Christmas feeling just made it look so outstanding to us? Who knows, perhaps my sister was just jealous of my masterpiece!

During the years when I still believed in Santa Claus, Father would do anything to keep my belief alive, even drink the glass of milk and eat

---

*Blue was the colour of his political party, the National Union.

the pastry left for Santa Claus. In case this was not sufficient to convince me, he even tramped the snow on the roof, irrefutable proof of Santa Claus's passage with his reindeers and sleigh.

A brown oval Windsor rocking chair very dear to Father stood in a place of honour in our kitchen. Suffering from backaches, he felt comfortable only in that chair. One after the other, we kids tasted those moments of sheer delight when Father would take us on his knees and rock us with great tenderness. Because of his ever-present back pain, he could not remain seated for long periods of time, which prevented him from coming to the recitals or concerts I took part in or going to the cinema with Mother. He also suffered from migraine headaches and those made him unbearable at times. On those days, we had to behave like little angels. Observing his many efforts to find relief from the deep pain he felt, I enriched my ideas and knowledge of alternative medicine: cupping, original concoctions and some strange curing system based on radiation originating from the patient. God knows what else. The only aspect missing was the religious one, such as a "novena"*.

Father loved singing and when all went well, he would walk around the house humming, always the same songs, but often adding his own words. Among these I mostly remember "Ramona". The most pleasant musical moments we had were spent in the car while travelling somewhere. Our whole repertory of French folk songs would be sung. That was at a time before all cars had radios. During family get-togethers he would lead everyone in singing. First, he sang each verse and then we, the chorus, would repeat it. He was not a great fan of classical music, but I'll always appreciate the great tolerance he showed towards my daily piano and singing practice. I think he avoided being home at those times... He is the one who took me to the store when I wanted to buy my first LP record: Beethoven's Moonlight Sonata and Chopin's Preludes and Polonaises, a real highlight in my life. Later on, he bought a subscription to "The Masterpieces of Classical Music". These records were an important part of my training in music culture. I still have the brochures that accompanied each record of "The Music Treasures of the World". Sometimes I wonder if I ever thanked him properly for the great understanding he showed and

---

*A series of actions and prayers done for nine days in a row.

the support he gave me as my love of music grew.

Father was not a religious person and so did not perform any of those practices dictated by the religion he was born into. This was somewhat courageous during those years in which the priests and the parish priest in our small town enjoyed their authority. Father was a very humane person and kept a close eye on the problems of the community. I recall very well the interest he showed in the immigrants living in our town. He would talk with them and listen to their problems while tasting their different food. Polish pickles and Italian salami were always popular with him. Every holiday season I would help him prepare food baskets for poor families. His greatest project was, of course, the construction of the Rotary Club's outdoor swimming pool. That project benefited children who did not have access to lakes during the summer.

Father was proud of my achievements in school and when the time came to think about university, he supported my plans very generously. He had prepared a budget allowing me a very nice life in Québec City. He never complained about my expenses and in return I completed my studies brilliantly, my way of showing my gratitude.

Both of us got along very well until the onset of my unusual love story with my Turkish pen pal, Mehmet. In later years, Mother told me that Father had had a French pen pal who had come to Canada. However, the meeting had been both disappointing and deceiving and so he wanted to prevent me from having the same difficult experience.

The situation became very painful when, in order to obtain a tourist visa for a visit to Canada, Mehmet needed someone to sponsor him. At that time, Father was recovering from a serious operation and radiotherapy. He just could not bear the idea of an intruder from Turkey. Our love story overwhelmed him. We had very painful, difficult hours during which my determination and my stubbornness brought him a lot of sorrow. Later on, our relationship improved and Father did meet Mehmet. I still feel some guilt for having been the source of such stress during his last days. Father died too young, at the age of fifty. Of the three children he had, I was the only one who was able to enjoy his company for any length of time.

Any description of Mother should first of all pay honour to her great self-control and the great care she takes to maintain her appearance. I

Mother on her balcony in Montreal (2001)

have never seen her in a state of neglect. She has never come out of her room without first having combed her hair and done her make-up; even when ill, her appearance remains impeccable. I don't know how she does it, but she is always an example of impeccable taste. While doing housework even, she wears lovely aprons that don't distract from her distinguished look.

If Mother takes pains with her looks, she also shows the same care and style when drinking tea or eating ice cream. Common gestures acquire some class with her: tea or coffee is served brilliantly in her precious and lovely bone china cups carefully arranged on the table together with her silverware. The cookies are never put directly on the serving dish, but instead are displayed on an elegant paper doily. Ice cream is served in glass dishes, themselves resting on glass plates that have gold borders. All these details attended to with such ease gave us the impression that we were in very elegant surroundings. Impeccable manners would be displayed on the special days when mother would receive her friends for tea. Those ladies would arrive dressed according to the season, in hats of great style. Those were days of pomp and display!

Then, there would be the evenings during the holiday season when her guests, decked out in dresses of velvet with gold or silver glitter, would leave their fancy fur coats on the bed in the master bedroom. With what great delight Louise and I would roll around on those coats of mink, beaver or otter...

The weight of our education rested almost entirely on Mother's shoulders. She was the one who took care of all our needs, be it clothing, cultural life or sporting endeavours. Mother did her best to make sure we got the best education available. Despite difficult financial conditions and being in a small town like Malartic, she found a way for us to take lessons in ballet, tap dance, piano and singing. With great care she would sew the costumes for the recitals: the yellow bird, the dress for the Gavotte–a French peasant dance–, the Dutch dress with the cute bonnet with pointed edges and, finally, the white tutu. How can one define the patience of a mother!

One particularly significant characteristic of my education was a lack of very restrictive or paralysing discipline. What Mother wanted from me was minimal, only obeyance to a few rules of behaviour and respectful adherence to the hours of everyday meals and bedtime. I never felt watched or limited in the choice of my friends. She was very patient and showed great tolerance towards them. She would never complain when, on rainy days, all my friends would fill the living room for long games of cards or other games she herself had taught us.

Every year Mother would celebrate my birthday with an elegant party. I remember how our table would be covered with a lace table cloth reserved for special occasions and laden with the kind of food kids adore: sandwiches, sweets and a birthday cake in which a coin was hidden. The one who found the coin in his or her serving became king or queen of the party. Games with apples were very popular: trying to bite into an apple tied to a string, without the help of our hands of course, or, again with only our teeth, desperately trying to catch an apple floating in a tub. In the photograph albums Mother kept for me, I can see all my birthday parties in chronological order.

Mother had a great passion for the cinema and never missed any of the films shown in our town's two cinemas, one of which showed French films, the other, American. She always went to the seven o'clock showings. This outing allowed me to listen to my favourite radio programs while keeping an eye on my naughty, devilish sister, Claudette.

Grandmother Rose and Mother were avid readers. Since it was difficult to find books in Malartic, an extensive exchange system was prac-

Mother, Claude, Jacques and I (2002)

ticed among the ladies of "high society", usually the wives of professionals, and it became a way to obtain the popular and bestselling books of the day. A neighbour named Manon soon became Mother's close friend. I was always so happy to see that wonderful woman. Her visits were a source of joy for me because she had such interesting things to relate. She had travelled a lot and had attended many cultural events, like concerts and exhibitions, in Montreal as well as New York. She was a constant source of news, always relating her memories in such an expressive way. She made me feel as if I myself had been with her on her various trips. Each of her visits would enlighten me and broaden my horizons, which I felt at times were very narrow.

Mother always had a desire to travel, a strong taste for reading, for music, for all the good things in life. In her fifties, left with more leisure time than she had ever had before, she spent much more time reading, visiting exhibitions and attending concerts. She was able to travel to the United States as well as Turkey, Greece, and other parts of Europe. She became and still remains even at her advanced age a well-informed person, alert, interesting to talk with and always eager to learn new things.

Her great weakness, her Achilles' heel, is her son Jacques, in whom she has placed all her hope. When Father died, Jacques was only six years old and Mother, filled with great intentions in her double role of mother and father, became over protective to an extreme. As a result, my brother grew up never assuming any responsibilities and succeeding only in abusing her good will and generosity. Mother has never complained about his attitude, prefering instead to try and hide it. It did not take very long for my sister, Claude, to become aware of what was happening while I, being so far away, was not really able to properly assess what was going on. I personally became aware of this sad situation when I urgently had to go to Canada in December of 1997 because Mother had complained to me on the phone that she was having great difficulty walking. I was extremely worried about her health at that time because my sister was in Africa for a three-year work contract, and so I decided to fly to Montreal to see what was going on. Mehmet convinced me to take our son Rahmi with me, just in case I should need help.

Upon my arrival, I found myself faced with some problems: Mother had neglected her health and was seriously in debt because of her beloved son. I also painfully witnessed that the magnificent Canadian health system was incapable of finding relief for the rheumatism pain of an eight-five year old lady. For over a month, Mother had suffered from such pain that she could barely walk and her geriatric specialist could only suggest that she use an electric heating pad.

As an honourable citizen of the Third World, I found myself facing a rigid administrative structure that I was totally unable to understand. The system exists, apparently well-organized and always described in the most flattering and impressive terms–but just try to gain access and have the system function, and you will find that it is something else entirely, especially during the Holiday Season! Just imagine, twice I have found myself having to come all the way over from Turkey for the express purpose of organizing medical treatment needed by Mother.

My relationship with my younger sister, Claudette, went through a series of phases over the course of the years. Until the age of twenty, she was simply my sister, Claudette, seven years younger than I. At that time, we were so different that I have trouble understanding how it is that we have ultimately come to acquire such similar ways of thinking.

In her youth, Claude was very active, very spontaneous in her way of talking and would shamelessly produce commentary. Through the years she has remained frank and direct. Curious by nature, she would poke her nose everywhere, would play with anything and everything she could lay her hands on. The moment Mother left the house, she would rush to raid the closets where Mother hid her best dresses and favourite hats. She would put them on and parade through the house trying to walk on high heels. Claude has maintained her love of good clothes and always dresses well.

As a child, she also took wicked pleasure in reading my letters and showed a definite predilection for my stamp collection: she would help herself to all the stamps she so generously wanted to give to the Sainte-Enfance. Our school strongly encouraged the children to contribute either money or stamps to the campaign. It was later discovered that these stamps had been used to enrich the stamp collections of many priests... For every bunch of stamps or every twenty-five cents, we were given a card with the picture of a Chinese child on it and we had the privilege of choosing his or her baptism name. In each class, one could find a board with strings fastened over the picture of a stairway. On the end of each string was an angel, not at all Chinese looking, that would climb one step with every penny given. Ultimate redemption and heaven was attained after a gift of twenty-five cents, or twenty-five steps. This is where Claude showed the first signs of her missionary soul. Since her childhood she has had an open heart and a very generous nature.

Until the age of forty, I lived far from my country and both of us were quite busy with our respective lives–she in Canada, I in the United States and then in Turkey. I seldom returned to the Province of Québec, only every seven years or so. Those brief encounters allowed us to spend but a few hours together, too short a period to develop deep, intelligent contact. Would it ever be possible to reconnect and get to know each other better? I could already sense sparks between us that warmed my heart. I had a profound desire to get to know my sister better.

Finally, once I was over forty years old and my trips were no longer research sessions for the university, I began to have more time on my hands and could afford to use it to establish better contacts with this interesting and bright woman. There I was in front of a mysterious

closed box, filled with secrets difficult to discover, but which I delighted in exposing, one after the other.

I discovered the joys of sharing similar ideas, almost identical tastes,
perhaps expressed differently, but overall very close. I realised that my
best friend was, in fact, my sister and that I had suffered from her
absence. I became aware of the resulting emptiness caused by her
absence. One often learns too late that in order to know people, you
must take the necessary time to learn about human nature. You should
establish your priorities with more wisdom, slow down your pace as you
rush towards professional achievements and choose to nourish your soul
with enriching relationships. It took me much too long to realize this.

Through the years, far from my sight, the young Claudette I had left
as a teenager had transformed into Claude, an accomplished, determined woman, with personal ideas she aimed to apply to the world. She
is from a generation more liberated then mine and this has allowed her
to be more independent, more radical. Both of us appear to be endowed
with a strong sense of intuition, but she can use hers more lucidly than
I, always paralysed by my strong sense of logic, am able to do.

She is as charming at fifty as she was in her childhood. Her childish
restlessness has been transformed into a vigorous energy and a strong
capacity for work, a characteristic feature of her behaviour. Like an ant,
she works arduously and eagerly. All her accomplishments are the fruit
of prolonged and assiduous work. When near her, one can almost feel
the animating flame in her and the energy she generates. This is in deep
contrast to the long and rather severe–almost cold–face of her older sister, a peculiarity I have developed in a country where women must display an impassive face. My energy is most likely as intense as hers,
although mine is not reflected in my movements so much as in my
strong stubbornness when it comes to doing what should be done, a
strong endurance to finalise all ventures. We are both possessed by an
insatiable desire for learning; my way being more theoretical, hers more
practical. Thanks to her knowledge and wide experience, Claude can
provide the spark to ignite that flame required at the beginning of any
project dealing with the well being of a community or group. Her
capacities have made her an excellent and patient helper on the international level, first in Benin, Niger then in Chad and Cameroon, coun-

tries in French occidental Africa, where she worked until August 2002. She is currently working with the Inuits in the northern part of the Province of Québec.

In all her work with individuals or groups, from unwed mothers to drug addicts or commune members, she has aimed at having everyone take control of their lives and responsibilities, and ensuring that they find their identity on both spiritual and mental levels. She is also one of the pioneers in the field of community health for senior citizens in the Province of Québec and in her work in ontology, that is, improving oneself at a personal level.

I spent my first years in Turkey without travelling, without seeing what was happening in the world. When you crave to learn what is happening in the world, living in what is called "a Third World country" with a lack of creativity and novelty and deprived of a stimulating atmosphere, it can be very frustrating. Whenever possible I would leave Turkey, exhausted from a feeling of having been completely drained and filled with a strong desire to recharge my batteries and draw on the unlimited energy of Québec. Of course, by nature just as curious and avid as I am, Claude has had the good luck of living in the most liberal province of Canada where access to knowledge is unlimited. Choosing, learning, understanding and assimilating was her way of life and, perhaps without realising it, she was my periscope through which I viewed the world while pursuing my road in my submarine in deep seas. She became my resource person; it was through her that I glimpsed new horizons which allowed me to broaden and deepen my knowledge in many fields without having to fiddle around losing precious time. Her great experience in community work was very useful to me during the years when I was active in the world of women's nongovernmental organizations (NGO) in Turkey. She is also the person who taught me the basic notions required to design a community pilot project, a first in Turkey.

Her precious help was also felt at a more personal level. She helped me open the doors to a world where I became aware of the energies, the intuitions and the strength of our mental powers, which help us to better understand the events and behaviour of human nature.

My brother is fourteen years younger than myself. He was only seven years old when I married and left home, and was twelve years old when I left the American Continent. I hardly knew him really. He was a blond child with sad grey eyes who barely remembers his father, having lost him at so young an age. His life followed a very different path from that of his sisters. Had he not received the love, or rather the excessive protection, of Mother all his life, I wonder what he could have done or where he would be today.

To me he is a mysterious abyss and, despite some efforts on my part, we have not succeeded in connecting on any wavelength. Over the years, his look has become sadder, almost desperate, and he has shut himself off despite my efforts to reach him. A profound sadness overtakes me when I think of him. Why have we never met as brother and sister should?

Chapter V

Québec and My University Years

In September of 1957, traveling by train, I left Malartic for our old capital, Québec City, to begin my studies at Laval University. Fifteen hours later, I stepped down at the Du Palais train station to begin two wonderful years in that lovely city, very dear to all of us born in the Province of Québec. Steeped in French spirit, this city is closely related to our brief history. I use the word "brief" on purpose because, after thirty-six years of life in Turkey, a country with a long history, I feel I should be modest. Close to the city itself is the Island of Orléans, the cradle of most French-Canadian families and the site chosen by most French settlers to establish their homes. This is the place where my sister Claude traced the origins of the Bouffard family.

The French explorer Samuel de Champlain founded Québec City on a site known to the Indians as "Stadacone". The city developed around "Cap Diamant" and now includes the upper city and the lower city. The oldest part—with its very characteristic architecture—was built within the ramparts. Access to this enclosure is through two imposing gates: the St-Jean and the St-Louis doors. All the streets lead into the Quartier Latin and eventually to the imposing Chateau Frontenanc, a luxurious hotel with a characteristic Gothic silhouette. In front of the hotel, from the long boardwalk of the Dufferin Terrace, there is a splendid view of the majestic Saint-Lawrence River and the City of Levis on the opposite shore. The old fortress is near the flank of the hotel and a bit lower are the famous Plains of Abraham where the colony of Nouvelle-France

Chateau Frontenac in Québec City

was lost to the English in 1763. On the left side of the Chateau Frontenac a steep street leads to the Place Royale, a very tourist oriented, well-restored part of the city. Ancient stone houses have been transformed into restaurants, boutiques and art galleries where you can find the best samples of Amerindian, Inuit and French-Canadian crafts.

Here and there members of the museum staff, dressed in the fashions of the seventeenth and eighteenth centuries, demonstrate how one lived in the "good old times". You may suddenly come across a soldier trying to light up his old pipe or a street vendor with his odds and ends. All this to make you feel as if you were really in the old days of the Nouvelle France colony. How can you not be seduced by such a charming city! Besides, Québec just happens to be one of the favourite cities of our neighbours to the south, the Americans, as well.

In the middle of the cold season just before Lent, as if to shake off the torpor of winter, Québec celebrates its winter carnival. For fifteen days the city undergoes a great metamorphosis. A multitude of monuments, sculptures and palaces made of ice by local and foreign craftsmen decorate the city. The undisputed master of the carnival is of course the "Bonhomme Carnival", a giant mascot presiding over all the activities, escorted by his queen and pretty duchesses, representing each district of the city. A wonderful luminous night parade fascinates all the spectators, young and old alike. One year Mehmet almost froze to death trying to film this parade from a small lookout platform built for our national TV. We could only bring him back to life with a few shots of "caribou", a strong local alcohol drink, and some wild square dancing.

Many activities are planned, such as open air dances that take place outside in every neighbourhood, or the famous canoe race on a Sunday afternoon on the partially frozen St-Lawrence River. Evenings can be spent in big ski centres watching the spectacular descent of skiers holding torches and creating an enchanting wave of colours in the darkness of the mountains. There is a lot of "Joie de vivre" in the air and, supposedly to help keep everyone warm, there is a lot of drinking, not too surprising when you think that all this takes place at temperatures between minus twenty-five to thirty-five degrees Celsius.

In the province of Québec, winters are icy, especially so in the region where I was born. I had experienced dry cold weather, minus forty degrees Celsius and under, but it was in Québec City that I learned about heavy snowfalls and severe storms. Almost every winter weekend of the years 1957-58, the city was systematically lost under a thick cover of snow and isolated from the rest of the province. How many times I went to the cinema on a lovely sunny day to find myself knee deep in snow when I came out a few hours later. Getting to the infamous physiology course held every Saturday morning turned into a battle against the elements, a forced walk in a half a meter of snow through a field swept by wind gusts. On some mornings, when we opened the door to go out, we would find ourselves facing a wall of snow more than one meter high. We had to shovel our way for five or seven meters before we could reach the street, and then we would walk to the hospital–which all made for a wonderful morning of sportive activity indeed! It is the only city where I have ever seen workers from the Red Cross blood bank and doctors coming to work on skis. Many will think I exaggerate, but it is the whole truth, nothing but the truth. I have now been living in Istanbul for many, many years, a city where snow is rather an exceptional occurrence, and I have only admiration for the people living in Québec, people who seem to manage in a country where winter and its trials appear to exist for the sole purpose of crushing them. One should not be surprised that, as soon as winter arrives, thousands of Canadians of all ages fly south.

At that time, the girls of Québec City were very elegant and took great care of their appearances. Coming from a much colder region where the casual look was popular, I was often shunned because of the way I dressed. Remember the years when starched crinolines were very much in fashion? Well-starched and often held out by hoops, skirts would be puffed out in an exaggerated way. I found the idea of going to the cinema and sitting in such garb absolutely ridiculous. Faced with such constraints, once in a while I had to give in and once even found myself wearing lacy gloves in the summer of 1958...

Founded in 1852, Laval University is the first French-Canadian Catholic University in the Province of Québec. During the period of my studies, the administration consisted mostly of members of the clergy. Except for a small number of foreigners, most of the students came from various regions of the province. Generally the students were well received by the locals and many rooms to let were kept at their disposal everywhere in the city. An extremely well organized students' association offered us, at modest prices, all the possible sports and activities imaginable. Our student cards allowed us to take advantage of discounts in many stores and restaurants of the city. I especially remember the Friday Night Special at the Porte St-Jean restaurant, where we could enjoy an evening watching a show and enjoying a glass of wine for $1.25. Our newspaper, the Carabin, informed us about what was going on in town or about the happenings on campus and would complement our schooling with social sciences articles most often written by students. They were the ones who decided if we should boycott the campus, go on strike or whatever. Anyway, under the watchful eye of the Catholic Church, nothing very revolutionary could happen.

Medical technology was then a new profession warmly encouraged by our government and many scholarships were distributed to cover the tuition fees. Thirty-nine of the forty-one students registered were girls, themselves lost among the five hundred young men of the Medical School, where our school was located. Very few women studied medicine at that time. Our comings and goings were subject to comments of all kinds, not to mention the physical difficulties we had threading our way through this solid mass of males!

A few weeks after my arrival in Québec, the School of Medicine left the old buildings of the Quartier Latin to inaugurate its new building on the campus of Sainte Foy at the other end of the city. The School of Business Administration, the School of Land Surveyors and a huge dormitory for students along with its cafeteria had already been there for a few years.

I was very well aware that I was learning a profession I would be able to practice anywhere in the world. The twenty-three months I spent in Québec left me with excellent memories. Those years were filled with a very heavy schedule of classes and laboratory work as well as a year of internship with rotation in the various departments of St-Sacrement Hospital. It was a very happy period when all that was required of me was that I study and learn, my two favourite activities.

I wish here to pay tribute to a brilliant educator and researcher who had a deep influence on my life and on my career, Dr Jean-Marie Delage, professor of Haematology and Therapeutics. From the very beginning, I was impressed by his enthusiasm when describing haematology and its importance in medicine. After all, his voice was so animated and so intense as he described his subject, it was impossible not to be! From then on, this science became the centre of my professional life. Strangely, in my second country, Turkey, I met a similar person, Dr Bülent Berkarda, also an haematologist and a professor in therapeutics, a charismatic person animated by the same flame. We worked together for twenty-three years before I retired.

I lived comfortably on my modest budget and could even treat myself to a few luxuries now and then, like an evening at the theatre, the cinema or even a new dress for a special occasion. This is a period when I saw Gerard Philippe in his interpretation of the great classic *Le Cid of Corneille* and bought a recording of his reading of *Le Petit Prince*, a book by Saint-Exupery that was very popular at that time. These were also the years when Jean Paul Sartre monopolized thinkers with his existentialism doctrine.

During these two years, I met two pleasant girls in our class, both named Lise. We became very close friends and are still in close contact with one another today. The first Lise came from the city of Shawinigan, while the second Lise had been raised in both Québec City and the Madeleine Islands. Her family was one of the warmest and most exciting families I've ever had the chance of knowing. She now lives in Drummondville. By a strange coincidence, Lise's youngest sister, Diane, married the son of our family doctor in Malartic.

It was in Québec City that I became aware of my great interest in different cultures and the attraction I felt towards foreigners. Upon Mother's insistence, I again took up my correspondence with Mehmet, which had been interrupted because of lack of time. In the meantime, during the carnival while I was dancing near the famous Youville Square, caught up in the jostling of the crowd and carried away just as described in Edith Piaf's song, "La Foule" (The Crowd), I met a foreign student originally from Cambodia. It was very cold and we were trying to get into a restaurant to warm up. I studied his smiling face and expressive black eyes with interest. Within a few minutes we were chattering away like two good friends. I joined him and his group for the remaining part of the evening. Such a fraternity reigned among all the students during the course of the Carnival that we shared the impression of belonging to the same family. I have never found this kind of atmosphere in any of the cities where I have since lived.

While having our soup, I learned from my new friend that he had just completed his political science studies in Paris at the Sorbonne University and that his family wanted him to study economics. His dream had been to become a doctor. Naively, I thought to myself that even those with financial means do not succeed in completing the studies they really want... I wondered how a family could be so demanding as to expect their child to study something he did not want, but mostly I wondered how one could be so submissive as to act according to the desires of others. It never occurred to me that other sets of values existed in other parts of the world. We met many times afterwards. His knowledge, his refinement pleased me; his way of thinking and his deep sensitivity, a feature I would later rediscover in the Middle East, fascinated me. He was different, as if coming from another dimension. We were not in love with each other and I knew that some parts of his life were totally unknown to me, but I never asked questions, just enjoyed what he chose to let me know. This was during the period of my internship in the Biochemistry Laboratories of St-Sacrement Hospital.

One day, I was called to the emergency room to draw blood from a patient who had tried to commit suicide. There was no name on the requisition form; I entered the room to draw the blood, a bit curious to see the patient: What a shock, my heart almost stopped. It was he, lying unconscious on the cold bed. The battle to save him had begun and fortunately it was won. Perhaps due to my lack of experience or perhaps because of a deep respect, I never asked him about the cause of this great moment of despair. As he began to recover it became impossible to gain access to his room. He was surrounded by people watching his every movement. He was ushered out of the hospital and left Québec without leaving a trace, as if he had never been there or had never even existed. God knows what became of him, but he is the one who opened my horizons to other cultures during an important stage of my life and taught me that other codes of values very different from ours did exist in this world. I hope one day to visit Singapore, a city that he described as the most beautiful in the Orient.

Leaving Québec was not easy because I felt as though a part of myself would remain there. Many times I have returned to this lovely city either by myself or with Mehmet and our son Rahmi. Despite many changes, the city is always as pleasant to visit as it was to live in and it remains one of Canada's most seductive.

Chapter VI

Ottowa: My First Years of Work

Having completed my studies, I enjoyed a few weeks of vacation in Malartic, then, in September of 1959, took the road to Ottawa, the capital of Canada. Separated from the Province of Québec by the Outaouais River, the city lies in the province of Ontario. Filled with parks and green areas, it is dominated by the imposing Parliament Building which offers an impressive panoramic view of the river. A second point of interest is the Rideau Canal crossing the city and dividing it in two. According to the season, it becomes either a skating rink or a magnificent promenade lined with flowers. In the springtime, thousands of tulips bloom along the canal, as a sign of gratitude, a gift from Queen Juliana of Holland, who took refuge in Canada during the World War II.

During the years I lived there, Ottawa was not a very lively city artistically or socially. The residential neighbourhoods were beautiful and the various embassies sumptuous, but the city itself was gloomy and Sundays were particularly boring because all entertainment centres, restaurants and cinemas were closed. Besides being very dull, Ottawa could best be described as a reserved English City. It was impossible to find the warm atmosphere and the joy of living found in Québec City. If you wanted to do something, you had to cross the bridge into the City of Hull, in the Province of Québec. In the year 2003, following a merger of large towns in the Province of Québec, Hull was given a new name and is now known as Gatineau.

As a new graduate I had no problems finding a job; as a matter of fact, I was faced with the problem of having to choose between several job proposals. I chose Ottawa for purely financial reasons. Salaries were much higher in Ontario than in the province of Québec. I found a place to live in a residence for young ladies where my good friend Louise was also residing. The Jeanne d'Arc Institute was on Rideau Street very near the Ottawa General Hospital where I was to work. This huge thousand-bed hospital belonged to the Grey Nuns; however, on my last trip to Canada, I learned that it is no longer a hospital but a retirement home for the nuns. That institution was a living example of what the Tower of Babel must have been like! Never have I seen so many different nursing uniforms, such a mixture of nationalities working under the same roof and lost in a total confusion of tongues. Never again in my working life was I to work under such culturally mixed conditions. Various political alliances made it possible for medical personnel from Asian countries to work in Canada, giving some of our hospitals the appearance of the United Nations. In addition, the General Hospital at that time had an unusually large number of Indian residents of the Sikh cast, with their colourful turbans. Those turbans were the cause of some extraordinary stories in our emergency rooms because sometimes half-conscious patients, seeing such an unusual figure at their bedside, thought they had reached the Gates of Heaven.

My very first job was in the Bacteriology Department, a branch that I was not really very fond of. However, because the workload was so heavy, it took me but a few months to master this not-so-pleasant branch of medicine. Doctors from the poorer or less developed countries often forgot that we were living in a relatively healthy and sanitary country, with a lower incidence of infections than the city of Bombay!

Never in my life have I searched for so many parasites or spent so many hours trying to hunt down the microorganism of tuberculosis. Finally, I had enough of that and went on to find a new job in Eastview, a suburb of Ottawa, at the Louis-Marie Monfort Hospital. Lise, my classmate and friend from university, was there in charge of the Biochemistry Department. I took over the Haematology Department. It was a smaller hospital with a generally more pleasant atmosphere. The personnel was homogenous, mostly French-Canadians. This state was slightly modified by the arrival of numerous Hungarian refugees who had come to Canada following the Hungarian Revolution of 1956 and the sad events that had upset their country.

My first months in Ottawa calmly passed among the girls of the institute and we soon had formed a circle of friends. Besides Louise, madly in love with Jean-Marc, constantly on the phone and hidden in the wardrobe so she could speak discreetly, there was my friend Lise from Shawinigan, mostly away to her hometown on weekends. Here I also met Nelly, a girl from Switzerland, patiently waiting for the love of her life, a Frenchman doing his military service in North Africa. Unfortunately, that love affair was not to have a happy ending, and so Nelly, after many travels, found her Prince Charming in New Delhi where she married and still lives today. I also met a girl named Yvonne Brodeur, whose French name had been transformed into Bonnie Brothers. She was an easy going girl, an excellent student, and we decided to share an apartment a few months later. At the institute, Bonnie's room was next to Louise's and it had a telephone, a "luxury" not everyone could afford back then. Bonnie was a remarkable piano player and every night, after supper, our group would go to the music room to sing all the songs we enjoyed. Leaving the institute brought an end to these musical evenings that were so dear to me. Later, I searched in vain for a similar group and it was only after forty years that I was able to find this atmosphere once again in the family of a Turkish pianist, a promising talent of the country, Elif Önal.

Other than visiting with friends from one room to another, life was becoming boring in our residence. At night, there was a curfew we had to respect, but in return, the great advantage was to find our meals prepared and served. While certainly not a great gastronomic experience, the important thing was that *we* did not have to cook them! Besides going to the cinema and eating out once in a while, there was not much to do.

A particular thing I remember from this period was my first phone call to Mehmet. Those pretending that the world of communications has not evolved through the years have not lived through such an experience. To begin with, I had to make an appointment many weeks in advance for a phone call to Istanbul to take place on 25 December

10 Sweetland Avenue in Ottawa (1960)

1959. I had to inform Mehmet to make sure he would be available at a specific time, taking into consideration the seven-hour time difference between Canada and Turkey. What an experience! What anxiety! We managed to talk, or rather scream a few words, but not at the given time nor on the expected day! During this infernal waiting period of over two days, I could not leave my room, not even to have a meal, in case the phone rang. What emotions and–of course–what an expense!

Bonnie and I left the institute to rent an apartment near the Rideau Canal on Sweetland Avenue. It was a four-room apartment, including a large room where Mrs Myner, an elderly lady over seventy years old, lived. She shared the bathroom with us. She suffered from a broken hip and so we saw very little of her. While she never went out, we were away all day and we had no idea what she did besides avidly watching TV. We must have provided her with a sense of security.

We led a simple life and since Bonnie was a good cook, I learned a lot of things from her. The major event of the month was her bread baking. I used to watch her with great interest as she mixed all the ingredients and observed how, thanks to the heat in the kitchen, the dough rose after some time. It was, of course, delightful to eat afterwards. Many years later in Turkey, I fondly remembered these days when our "kitchen magician" Şükriye, who has been working for us for the last forty-five years, baked bread for us.

Once her studies in Business Administration were completed, Bonnie began to date a young man who, we were told, was aspiring to the priesthood! Try to understand that! Later on, she married someone else and through the years, she metamorphosed into an extremely devout person. Inflamed by her religious emotions, she joined a reli-

gious sect and the practice of her faith became her way of life. I presume it is reassuring for her, but it has made me realise that the fundamentalist spirit currently sweeping the world is not occurring strictly
among Moslems. Listening to her testimony, I realised that she was
absolutely convinced Jesus Christ would at any moment ring the bell
just to visit her. She is the only person I know who listens to hymns on
her walkman.

At the very beginning of the twenty-first century, I find it fascinating to observe such strong faith in religion. Her behaviour, I confess,
astonishes me completely and I cannot decide if I should be happy for
her or if I should feel deep pity and despair for her. Perhaps I should be
asking myself if I should question my own concept of religion. These
last few years I have received no replies to my annual greeting cards to
Bonnie.

The years spent in Ottawa were transition years; I could feel it. A
kind of routine had set in, and months went by without much happening. The main event in my life was my correspondence with my pen pal
Mehmet, as the tone of our letters slowly began to change, each one
becoming more romantic than the last.

Having achieved financial independence, Ottawa was the city of
"firsts" for me. I bought my first record player and began to collect
records of classical and lyrical music. My first purchase was a recording
of "Swan Lake" and, by happy coincidence, some forty years later, it
was also the first compact disc I bought for Eren, my granddaughter.
My first plane trip was between Ottawa and Val d'Or, the closest airport to Malartic. What comfort and luxury, not having to spend hours
driving through the forests! That trip awoke a desire to travel more
extensively. Slowly, I also modified my hairstyle and my clothes began
to reflect a greater interest in fashion.

The summer of 1960 brought me back to Malartic for the holidays,
but I found Father in poor health. He was seriously considering going
to Québec City for a check-up. The autumn of that year proved to be
a crucial period in my life. Mehmet's father had won a grant entitling
him to six months of travel in Europe, followed by a six-month stay in
the United States. In September, the whole family was getting ready to
leave Turkey. The only thing Mehmet wanted was to come and meet

me, but since he had not yet begun his studies at the university, his parents were somewhat hesitant to send him to Canada. Getting a tourist visa also required the signature of a sponsor.

In September I was informed that Father had gone to Québec City for a check-up and was told that he had to have surgery. I hurried to his bedside because Mother had to remain in Malartic with Jacques and Claude. Father was of course happy to see me even though the circumstances did not allow us to speak much. The operation took place the next morning and truthfully, I did not really feel worried. What could possibly happen when one is in love and life so wonderful? Early the next morning, waiting for the return of Father from the operating room and convinced that all would go well, I was totally surprised by the visit of the surgeon who abruptly informed me that he had just performed the resection of a malignant tumour on Father's kidney. Completely shocked, I could only utter a few words at that moment, but almost collapsed after he left the room. I really had not expected such dramatic news. I did not know what to think, how to react or what to expect, but I felt that the situation was serious. Several years later, as I worked in an oncology department for seventeen years, I often recalled this particular scene, because in Turkey, only very rarely do cancer patients learn the nature of their disease. Which approach is the best? The correct answer is most likely related to the behaviour of individuals from different cultures. A few hours later Father was back in his room and the long and painful waiting period began. The next morning he was informed of his condition and he asked me not to say anything to Mother. He was scheduled for radiotherapy after which he would return to Malartic, where he would then undergo periodical check-ups. Not familiar yet with this disease, I felt a bit relieved, or frankly I wanted to feel relieved, for the dissonance it caused in my life was not at all in tune with my "life is wonderful, I'm in love" state of mind.

I left Québec City to return to work and, as expected, Father was home a few weeks later, his treatment completed. In November, I took a short trip home to inform my family that I was in love and wanted to meet Mehmet at all costs. This meeting would take place either in Canada if Father agreed or else, if my family objected, I would fly to Europe to meet Mehmet. The atmosphere in our home became rather

Telegram informing us of Mehmet's
arrival in 1960

tense and a very unpleasant confrontation took place between Father and myself. Never had I argued with Father with such ardour and never had I shown such stubbornness.

Everything came to a happy end, but at what cost! Most likely it would have been better had I not behaved in such a way, but being in love often occurs in a period of one's life when a lack of experience is added to a profound obstinacy, leading one to force things as if time were pushing relentlessly. Remembering these events is most painful for me. One of the rare fights I had with Father occurred during the most critical period of his life, when what he needed most was love and support, not a family crisis.

With Father's precious signature and his agreement to sponsor Mehmet, I left for Ottawa and sent the document to Paris where Mehmet was impatiently waiting for his visa. A few days before Christmas, I was informed that everything was proceeding on schedule and that he would be flying to Ottawa on Air Canada on 25 December. How can I describe the happiness, the emotions and the fears that filled me until his arrival? Following this first meeting, would the magical state persist or would all my dreams fall to pieces like sand castles washed out to sea?

Chapter VII

Mehmet

On 25 December 1960, bundled up in "the" fur coat, I barely made it to the Ottawa airport for the grand meeting. It had snowed all night and I was afraid the plane would be unable to land. I got there early and began to wait.

As soon as he got off the plane, I recognised him immediately. He wore a grey Canadian style coat but no boots, exactly like all the Europeans who travel to Canada in the winter. After completing the customs formalities he came towards me holding his baggage check and bluntly asked: "Where are my suitcases?" His first words lacked even a touch of romanticism, but there was so much emotion in the air, he could not have uttered anything else. I looked at his huge green eyes looking at me, his curly dark hair, his lovely straight nose and had the impression that a God from Olympus was in front of me. Despite the thousand questions in our heads and the fear and anxiety that everything could crumble, our first meeting went well and within a few hours, we knew we had been friends for a long time. We found his luggage, two suitcases covered with hand-painted fish. It was a rather unusual sight and I understood at once that Mehmet was surely not the kind of person you meet every day. We left the airport and went to my apartment where we were alone, or almost alone, for of course Mrs Myner was there. Bonnie had left to visit her family for the holidays. Since it was Christmas Day, we had decorated the house and the meal was almost ready when we arrived. Mehmet was fascinated with our electric stove and studied how it worked with great interest. Outside it was snowing heavily. Our life together had begun.

Because I was on duty at the hospital, we had to stay in Ottawa for a few more days before taking the bus to Malartic so my family could meet Mehmet and we could celebrate the New Year all together. After many hours of travelling through the snow-covered forests in the huge reserve of the La Verendry National Park, Mehmet began to wonder if the driver had lost the road. He could not believe his eyes when he saw Indians climbing into the bus in the middle of the forest and getting off a few hours later, again in the middle of nowhere. Finally, the sight of a small village in the middle of the park made him feel better and more secure.

Arriving in Malartic, we saw Father and Claudette waiting for us at the bus stop. We drove home in great silence. I was very happy, but I felt my Father did not share this joy. The other members of the family were waiting for us at home with great curiosity and Mother did all she could to maintain some harmony despite the tense atmosphere. To begin with, my sister, proud to show her knowledge and calling her history book to witness as irrefutable proof, took advantage of this occasion to inform us that Turks were barbarians. These "great truths" which we are taught at school, in addition to giving rise to false ideas, surely do not favour deep understanding between individuals of different cultures or countries. To many, Turkey remains an unknown country of which they have a rather bad opinion. The fact that Turkey is a Moslem country and then the long saga of the Crusades has surely influenced everyone's way of thinking. Seeing Mehmet dressed like us, something she had not expected, my sister asked him where he had left his national costume.

The first serious crisis arose when the time came to decide where Mehmet would sleep during his stay with us. Father wanted him to go to the hotel whereas I, knowing perfectly well that he did not have the means to indulge in the luxury of a hotel, wanted him to stay at our house. After some discussion it was decided to give him my father's famous sleeping bag and let him use the second floor of the house. Mehmet never complained about this "warm reception" but later, my experience with Turkish hospitality convinced me that he must have taken the members of my family for savages and thought *we* were the barbarians...

The only relaxed period we had was during dinner when Mehmet ate with great appetite the spaghetti sauce Father had prepared. This was the only dish Father could cook. At dessert time, Claudette and Jacques went absolutely wild when Mehmet looked at his plate of Jell-O with some curiosity and asked why the substance started moving the moment you tried to take a spoonful of it. The atmosphere in the house was such that I had the feeling of going from one crisis to the next. Then one night, Mehmet and Father shut themselves in Father's office and began conversing for what seemed like hours. Of course, Father was curious to learn what our plans were and was especially anxious to learn how Mehmet thought he would provide for his daughter if we did get married. Following this conversation, even though Father was not convinced of our common sense, peace seemed to have been established between us and–thank God!–the time had come for us to leave. Light hearted, we took the road back to Ottawa aware that we were leaving "grey clouds" behind us.

My landlord was from Serbia and felt no sympathy towards "the Turk". The roots of this great animosity reached back several centuries to when Serbia was defeated by the Ottoman Empire in the very famous Kosova battles. This deep, long-lasting hatred may seem difficult for us to understand, but having witnessed the horrors of the Bosnian war, we have all seen how events that occurred centuries ago can still affect people today. The landlord would watch our comings and goings with great interest, probably wondering whether Mehmet spent the nights in my apartment or not. Mehmet never got used to wearing overshoes and always forgot them on our doorstep, irrefutable proof of his presence in our house. One day the landlord even insisted on inspecting our house thinking he would find "the Turk". To his great surprise, Mehmet was nowhere to be found in the house!

After Mehmet found a room to rent near my apartment, he began attending the English courses organized by the Canadian government for new immigrants. Before leaving Paris, besides his plane ticket and two hundred dollars in cash, his father had given him a few paintings, which he had immediately left for sale at an art gallery. We spent a few weeks peacefully getting to know one another better and enjoying the experiences couples usually have: our first cinema, our first dinner out, our first party and our first photos together. Mehmet was no longer a ghost, but was now well anchored in my life. The fairy story-like period of our life was over and we were now very much travelling down the usual paths all lovers take.

In the meantime, we learned that a fire had caused some damage to the gallery where he had left Bedri Rahmi's paintings. This most unexpected news upset us at first because we had totally forgotten the existence of fire insurance. Mehmet went to the gallery convinced he was ruined, never thinking he would come back richer then before. Of course the gallery and the paintings were covered by fire insurance and so to his great surprise, when he showed his receipt, he was handed a check for the exact amount of the value of his paintings. To celebrate he went out and bought himself a suit, his first ready-made suit.

In February, Father's first check-up did not reveal any abnormalities but a short period later, he was stricken by a slight paralysis caused, as we learned later on, by brain metastasis. He returned to Québec City and had a delicate operation that did not improve his general status, but instead most likely accelerated the course of the disease. Mehmet and I went to Québec City to be with him and offer comfort during the process of this second intervention. Despite our efforts, at the time of our departure, we left behind us a very sick man, unable to walk. A few weeks later, Mother asked the son of one of Father's best friends, a doctor in private practice in our city, Dr Richard Authier, to bring Father back to Malartic, since his condition seem desperate. In May she sent the car to Ottawa to bring us back to Malartic. I left my job and the apartment where I was living with Bonnie. Leaving all our friends behind, we left the capital city where we were to return only twenty-five years later in 1991.

A sad period began. Father was hospitalised in Val d'Or, some eighteen miles from Malartic, painfully awaiting an end he knew was near. Had he resigned himself to our marriage? Maybe, but he chose to show his disapproval by deliberately omitting to mention my name in his will. During the short period of time he had left, he managed to sell his insurance office and the house we had always lived in. He died on 9 June 1961. A few days before his death, mother insisted we go shopping for black dresses, a must when in mourning. This move, before the actual death of Father, seemed to me an awful and most unbearable thing to do.

In a few weeks, we managed to empty the house in which I had grown up and then move into an apartment we owned. In the meantime, we wanted to visit Mehmet's parents who were then in the United States and spend some time in New Jersey. We had decided to get married and Mehmet wanted to introduce me to his family before we told them about our plans. We first took a bus to Montreal, then a second one to New York. Despite great moments spent visiting that spectacular city, it was overall a very difficult trip, and the atmosphere was not much better than the one we had experienced with my family during the New Year holiday. All the important conversations were held in Turkish and Mehmet did not translate everything. I will never really know what was said, but the atmosphere was far from being joyful, especially on his mother's side.

During my in-law's stay in New Jersey, an international symposium on painting organized by a Turkish painter, Tosun Bayrak, was held at Fairleigh Dickenson University. While we were there, Mehmet was offered a foreign student scholarship, a welcome offer indeed for, to tell the truth, at the time we had no definite plans for the future. We saw it as a good opportunity for Mehmet and an ideal solution for both of us.

Back in Canada, we completed all the necessary intricate formalities and finally got married in Malartic, on 5 August 1961. We were married in the sacristy of the church because only Catholics couples can be married at the altar. It was a simple ceremony and only a few members of Mother's family attended, with Grandfather Omer and Uncle Hervé acting as our witnesses. Grandmother Rose, Aunt Thérèse and her daughter Chantale, Aunt Lucette and her second husband, Mother, my sister Claudette and my brother Jacques were present. I wore the white dress I had worn on Mehmet's arrival, adding a short veil and carrying a bouquet of roses. After a brief reception in Mother's new home, we left for our forest cottage to spend our honeymoon. I have never discussed this event with anyone from my hometown and never asked anyone, but I am sure that the whole family and all the people we knew must have literally thought we were crazy. We were at the very beginning of our lives and had nothing but each other and a great confidence in our love and our future. Mehmet had exactly twenty-five cents in his pocket and a telegram from his family with wishes that we, "grow old on the same pillow"!*

Our wedding in the sacristy of the church on 5 August 1961

I must confess that one of the greatest problems of my life was to find a way to get married. I have great respect for civilised countries that do not mix their civil code and their religious beliefs. During this period in the Province of Québec, one could only get married in a church. Mehmet was a Moslem and I a Catholic, but neither of us were practising. I was ready to elope to Ontario so we could have a civil ceremony. The Church wanted Mehmet to convert; we were subjected to all sorts of pressure, a very unpleasant situation that only served one purpose: to keep us away from any type of religious practice. Thankfully, our Province later finally accepted civil ceremonies, but most couples were by then opting for co-habitation, void of any formality whatsoever.

When we returned from our honeymoon, we had two massive wooden boxes built to contain all of our possessions. By the end of August, we had sold Mehmet's return ticket to Istanbul and so with two hundred dollars in our pockets, we left by bus for the United States en route to the small town of Madison, New Jersey.

---

* An expression used when offering congratulations to newlyweds after the wedding ceremony.

Chapter VIII

Eren and Bedri Rahmi Eyuboğlu, My In-Laws

My first meeting with my in-laws took place in July 1961 in Madison, New Jersey, where they were participating in an international seminar on painting organized by Fairleigh Dickenson University. Mehmet's father, Bedri Rahmi, had received grants from both the Ford and the Rockefeller Foundations and had also been invited for a year's stay as a guest professor at the Berkeley campus of the University of California. I found myself somewhat frightened in the presence of a man in his fifties who, in addition to being a painter and poet famous in his country, was also a Professor of Art at the Academy of Fine Arts in Istanbul. As for Mehmet's mother, Eren, I had to blindly rely on what her son, describing her in most flattering terms, had told me. In those days I certainly was not able to fully understand, let alone appreciate, my future in-laws. To me they were primarily Mehmet's parents, people I had to meet, to get to know and, if possible, to love.

Upon our arrival, we were first met by Bedri Rahmi because his wife had fallen ill, indisposed by the very humid New Jersey weather. From the very first moment I felt strong vibrations and a sense of intense human warmth that seemed to emanate from my father-in-law. He had abundant curly, black hair that floated freely around his face, paying absolutely no heed to a sense of style. His nose was long and wide, identifying its owner as a proud citizen of the Black Sea region. His brilliant black eyes were almost overwhelming and reflected the full scale of

My in-laws, Bedri Rahmi and Eren Eyuboğlu

his emotions. They were the eyes of Lucifer that would pierce you as if deciphering your soul. At once caught under the spell of this look, virtually paralysed by the inensity of it, I suddenly saw such a disarming smile on his illuminated soft face that all my fears were dispelled. No harm could possibly come from such a person. In the flash of a moment, his eyes softened and warmed. I could read a message of friendship. In time, I rapidly learned that his eyes were the mirror of his state of mind and thus were the key to understanding him.

The sound of his voice was not exactly what you expected to hear from a poet, but his language was so colourful, so passionate, it was impossible not to pay attention to what he was saying. He was the type of person who would enter a room gradually projecting his energy and swiftly capturing the attention of everyone. Within no time, he would become the centre of attention. His attitude had nothing of a star trying to overshadow others, crushing them under the weight of his fame. No, he would enliven the conversation with his zest and let everyone actively participate, giving them the feeling that they were important and had something to contribute. He knew how to bring out the best in everyone. He loved to share his experiences and the striking events he had lived with others, thereby managing to energize everyone present.

He was of average height and, since he hated shirts and ties, rarely dressed with care. He never looked too comfortable in his clothes, all of which harboured traces of his art–spots of acrylic paint. He would even work in his best clothes, to the profound despair of his wife. His worst enemies were the buttons of his shirts and his well-ironed clothes! Needless to say, he looked as if he couldn't find what he was looking for when he got dressed.

He simply adored drinking coffee and was never far from his coffee cup. His, however, was not just any cup, but an Ottoman cup that was virtually an extension of his hand itself. After a certain hour, the coffee was replaced by a glass of raki, the traditional alcoholic drink of his country. When he wasn't painting, he was writing. He was a prolific writer who used the Turkish language in a most vivid way, a master in the art of using words. When he painted he would sit in the most unusual, contorted positions, on the floor most of the time, scrunched on one leg. I never understood how he could actually get up so easily after many hours of work without feeling numb in the limbs. He looked more like someone in a Yoga position than one painting.

Although he was as nervous and unpredictable as most Mediterraneans, he was as patient as a saint with students and children. A famous painter, he would show great enthusiasm for the paintings of children or folk art, let it be a rug, a kilim, a block print, a piece of copper, a simple wooden box or a primitive tile. He always showed great respect towards anonymous craftsmen, masters in their own right who moved him deeply. He was enraptured with folk music and often cried while listening to melodies he loved.

It was impossible for anyone who had the good fortune to come in contact with Bedri Rahmi, for whatever reason, to remain indifferent to the energy and enthusiasm that emanated from this extraordinary man.

I never really experienced serious difficulties in my relationship with him. A teacher in heart and soul, he was one of those who helped me to understand and love Turkey. Since I was his daughter-in-law, he asked me a lot of questions, obviously to get to know me better. Our relationship was not always an easy one of course, but once in his homeland, I became more and more indebted to him as he helped me to discover Turkey in all its different aspects. Two proverbs he taught me at the very beginning have helped me to interpret behaviour that I otherwise couldn't possibly have comprehended.

Bok'tan terrazi tezekden olur dirhemmi.
If a balance is of shit, the weights are of manure.

Cihalletin bu kadarı ancak tedris ile mümkündür.
Such ignorance is only possible with instruction.

Establishing a relationship with my mother-in-law proved to be a very delicate task for both of us. A few explanations can be offered to explain our difficulties: first of all, my mother-in-law was excessively attached to her only child, her son, and secondly, she had a strong depressive temperament. Having to share her son with another woman appeared to be very threatening to her. The idea of a marriage taking place in such a precarious financial situation seemed to be an insurmountable obstacle; this was a most surprising attitude for a woman who had married under similar conditions, as they say, moving mountains to be able to marry Bedri Rahmi.

Eren Eyuboğlu, named Ernestine at birth, was born in Iaşi, Romania. She met the love of her life in Paris in 1933 while they were both students at the studio of the French painter André Lhote. After many hardships, long separations and numerous sacrifices, including battles led against both families, they finally succeeded in getting married in 1936 in Istanbul. This was followed by World War II and, a few years later, the fall of the Iron Curtain that was to separate her from her family for more than thirty years. We learned all the details of this great love story when, in 1999, Mehmet undertook the reading and translation into Turkish of the many letters[*] his parents had exchanged between Paris, Istanbul and Bucharest.

Even though she was endowed with huge talent, she deliberately stood aside all her life and worked diligently towards a successful career until her death in 1988. Living alongside a man filled with charm, a

---

[*] Three books were published in Turkish from the translation of these letters.

man so utterly fascinating as her husband, she managed to safeguard her independent character and perfected her art without letting it be the least bit disturbed by the litany of painful events she endured through the years.

A woman of great beauty, with green eyes and curly red hair, she dressed marvellously and had an inclination for all that was eccentric and flashy. Her two weaknesses were a love of furs and extraordinary hats. Even at the age of eighty and despite being overweight, she remained a striking woman who knew very well that she could attract attention. Her disarming smile was very like that of an ingenuous young lady. She was very good-natured and I don't think she ever harboured a bad thought towards anyone. She was very generous and always ready to lend a helping hand or a listening ear to those who confided in her. She also made an effort.to comfort those in need.

The great love that bound her to her husband was rapidly transformed into a tumultuous life beside a man caught up in numerous love affairs that left her deeply hurt. Isolated from her country and her family, she was left to face a loneliness that only her art could help appease. The attachment that she felt towards her son can thus easily be understood.

Needless to say, Mehmet and I were children of very different worlds. One thing is for sure; both of us had very understanding and patient parents.

Having reached a certain age, I can analyse our situation in those days. I now understand that being in love and young is almost synonymous with being illogical and touched by madness. With what passion and courage we faced our parents in our defense of a most illogical story, devoid of any plausible argument, but instead using the eternal grand declaration: "We love each other, so everything will be fine." This is what love must be! To realise the impossible, totally opposed to all common sense. I sometimes wonder if I would be able to show the same understanding towards a couple approaching *me* with such an improbable story.

Chapter IX

Years Spent in the
United States of America

We lived in the United States from September 1961 until July 1966. Never in my life had I dreamed of living in that interesting country, and my first great surprise was to observe how different that neighbour country could be from Canada or, to be more specific, from the Province of Québec. Young, in love and bursting with energy, the idea of moving, of having to begin a new life in another country did not stir up any apprehension. Applying for a visa so I could reside on a permanent basis and be able to work, also, had not seemed to even enter my mind! With very little money in our pockets, we set off on the road to New York, without feeling even the slightest bit of worry about what lay ahead.

By the time we arrived, my in-laws had left New Jersey and were in New York living temporarily at the private residence of the Turkish Ambassador to the United Nations, his Excellency Mr Turgut Menemencioğlu. Together with two other Turkish painters, Bedri Rahmi was preparing an exhibition, sponsored by the Turkish government, to be held in one of New York City's best galleries, the Angeleski Gallery. We were generously offered lodging with them in a very pompous atmosphere with strict protocol. It was quite a different environment for us but, frankly, rather pleasant. Our hosts and their numerous guests were most interesting; the conversation was brilliant and a very refined cuisine was served.

As is the case with all parents, we, the young couple, quickly became

Mehmet and I in Morristown (1962)

the one and only topic of conversation. Everyone was preoccupied with Mehmet's studies and whatever we said, the subject always came back to his choice of school and the field in which he should continue his studies... His dream had been political science, but with a foreign mother and a foreign wife, a status the Turkish Foreign Office* found incompatible with the profession, it was concluded that there was no possible future for him in that field. After many debates, it was finally decided that marketing, a new concept in Turkey, and advertising would be better choices.

After many lovely pleasant days, the time had come to leave New York and begin our down-to-earth life. We left for Madison, New Jersey.

After quite a search, we finally found a very suitable furnished apartment in Morristown, a town right next to Madison and close to Fairleigh Dickenson University. For a few weeks we split our time between the very exciting life of my in-laws in New York and our simple student world in New Jersey. The opening of the painting exhibi-

---

* A law forbade diplomats to have foreign spouses. This was modified by Minister Ismael Cem in 2001.

tion was followed by the celebration of the Turkish Republic Day on 29 October. That evening, the Ambassador held a huge reception at his home, an evening of sumptuous display and refinement for selected guests. The entire diplomatic corps was present along with a large number of politicians. That was how we got the opportunity to chat with one of the most remarkable political personalities of that time, Mr Adlai Stevenson. I must confess that during the course of the conversation, we had no idea who the gentleman was because he looked quite different from the pictures in the newspapers. Just imagine our astonishment when, following his departure, we were questioned about what we had talked about so seriously with "Mr Stevenson".

Finally, after all this excitement, our student life began. Our new home was situated on the top floor of an old white colonial house. It was a comfortable house with a large garden to which we had access. The large window of our living room faced a huge magnolia tree that bloomed in profusion every spring, a magnificent view that never ceased to dazzle us. The owner of the lovely big house was an American of Italian descent. His wife was from Milan. They were a nice couple, but Sylvanna was somewhat too refined for the surroundings she lived in and could never really adapt to the United States. This lovely residence was later sold to a Catholic priest, an immigrant from Sicily. We finally came to suspect that this jolly fellow was in close contact with the Mafia of Jersey City, where he had a parish. The great number of Cadillacs regularly parked in front of our house and the flow of visitors looking as if they had stepped directly out of an Al Capone film just increased our suspicions. We lived in this lovely home for four years and left it one year before our departure from the United States.

In 1995, with my son and his small family at my side, I returned to Morristown and to 268 South Street where we used to live. Rahmi wanted to visit the town where he had been born and see the places where he had spent his first years. We found the house transformed into an office building. It was no longer white but a pale grey colour. The garden had disappeared, leaving in its stead a parking lot.

Once set up in our home, I looked for and found a job in one of the hospitals of the city, Morristown Memorial Hospital. Not having the necessary papers, the famous Green Card, which would allow me to reside and work in the United States, I had to return to Montreal to apply. Living on a tight budget, all this had to be done with the least possible expense. Once my papers were in order, I began to work on the night shift in the laboratories of the hospital. I was on call two days a week from five o'clock to seven o'clock p.m. and three days a week from five o'clock to ten o'clock p.m. Both my diploma and my Canadian credentials were accepted by the American authorities, thus giving me the right to the salary scale set by the local association. This amount of money was sufficient to provide for our small family.

During those few weeks between our arrival in New Jersey and my first pay check, money was scarce indeed. Some work Mehmet found at the cafeteria of the university was the source of our livelihood for that span of time. Nothing could discourage us or weaken our determination and our confidence in our future.

Mehmet was now a student of marketing and advertising at Fairleigh Dickenson University. This institution had three campuses in three cities: Teaneck, Rutherford and Madison. Mehmet was in Madison, also known as the "city of roses". This campus was on beautiful grounds with buildings partially hidden by huge trees in impeccably well-kept gardens. The main building, a superb colonial style mansion, was the pride of everyone. Its famous rose garden was usually the centrepiece of all activities and important receptions. It was the site where Mehmet received his diploma in June of 1966.

Mehmet was also a member of the soccer team made up of foreign students from different African countries and one Greek Cypriot who later became a good friend. His studies were progressing fairly well, but since Mehmet was not very fluent in English, we bought a small tape recorder so he could tape his courses. I would type the notes and translate the most difficult passages into French. His only problems at school were an English teacher of Greek descent and his adviser who was of Armenian origin. Both teachers did not harbour great sympathy towards Turks in general, although they were careful not to express it openly.

We did not have a car, so getting to the campus proved difficult, especially since we lived in Morristown, a few kilometres away. At first, Mehmet used a bicycle, a gift from Ambassador Mememencioğlu who had wanted to get rid of his now grown son's bicycle. However, riding

Both of us with Mr Sammartino at a Fairleigh Dickinson University meeting

the bike.became impossible during the winter time and so finally, with Mother's financial help, we managed to buy a second-hand car, a 1956 Dodge, a purchase which made our life much easier.

Since we were both foreigners, living in the United States did require some adaptation. I was astonished to discover that, despite a similar lifestyle and the use of similar products, differences between the States and Canada abounded.

One of the most striking and surprising features of the country was the profound religious feelings of the American people. The beginning of our stay coincided with United Nations Day in October. During this particular month, several American families invited us to dinner. They usually chose Sunday at noon, and the meal was preceded by a visit to a church, usually of Protestant denomination. Used to living under the Catholic monopoly of the Province of Québec, we were introduced to a wide range of Protestant sects unknown to us. We also had to withstand the all but discreet attempts to convert Mehmet to Christianity. He is Moslem but not practising and religion is not a vital part of either of our lives. Following these experiences, Mehmet concluded that in order to be left in peace he had to assert himself as a Moslem. We soon learned that one had to conform to certain criteria in order to live in that society; one was to choose a place to go on Sundays. A group, whose name I cannot recall, but which sounded like a church without being one, offered us what we were looking for. The members would gather in a hall and listen to a music recital with a different program every week, varying from harpsichord to opera arias. Usually coming from New York, the performers were talented artists, and their performance was followed not by a sermon, but by a brunch.

Our most interesting religious adventure allowed us to meet a very nice family that we are still in touch with to this day. A charming woman phoned us one day and asked to talk with Mehmet. She then invited him to dinner, but Mehmet–by then a bit leery after so many conversion assaults–asked her quite frankly if she was trying to convert him. After a few seconds of silence, she burst into laughter, adding she was herself a member of the marginal Quaker group and that she had no such intentions. All she was wanted to do was to give an example of American hospitality to a foreign student. Mehmet accepted her invitation with pleasure and we rapidly became good friends. Penelope Pullock was a radiant woman, cultivated and lively. She was also the author of several children's books and the mother of five children. Good hearted, she became like a mother to me and her help during the first difficult months with our young baby was most precious. Since she had a daughter slightly older then Rahmi, she really was a helping hand when she offered to lend me her baby bed and all the other baby furniture she had.

After some time, invitations of a religious nature ceased and thus did an interesting chapter of our life in the United States come to an end. It is intriguing to observe that even now at the beginning of the twenty-first century, one can go from one society to the other and, while the religions may change names, the religious aspirations of their followers remain virtually the same.

Another aspect of American life that surprised us was the great reserve and the deep hesitation Americans showed in making friends. Quite contrary to the images projected in Hollywood movies, I can affirm that Americans are afraid of establishing ties and will think twice before opening their houses up to strangers. The case is very different in Québec and even more so in Turkey. The United States is not a country where you can arrive unexpectedly somewhere without having called first. One risks knocking at a closed door or just being left to stand there before it, for no one is in a hurry to say, "Come in, please." They may live on the same floor of the apartment building, meet you in the stairway or empty their garbage at the same time as you without as much as uttering a single word. This behaviour I cannot understand and would even qualify it as rude for us who come from societies where contacts are mandatory and where certain rules of courtesy exist. I do not believe that it is because they are shy or because they respect the private life of others. In reality, they like to keep a wide empty space around themselves that they tend to safeguard. It is a very unpleasant thing for those who are not used to this practice.

On the other hand, for those who prefer an organized life where everything is anticipated and where one can find a solution to all problems, the USA is the ideal country to live in. If you enjoy working and being surrounded by highly qualified people, if you are dreaming of employees to whom you do not have to repeat twenty times what to do and how to do it, and whom you have to check on constantly, this country will suit your desires. Working in the United States is a charm; it's marvellous. Everything works well. You are offered all the facilities modern technology can put at your disposal and everything is done to improve your output and suck your honey till the last drop. If you are an expert in some field and want to enter this ballet for high-qualified dancers, go ahead, for you will enjoy every moment of the dance!

There are plenty of qualified individuals in the United States. You could die on the job and be replaced within the hour without the least hesitation, a fact not very flattering to the ego. If you are not made of the necessary stuff to withstand such competition, such performance, you risk feeling like a spare part amongst the the millions of others around you. This ballet, always performed on your toes, may exhaust you or even kill you for there is the strong chance that this feat will drag the last breath out of you and leave you completely exhausted. The price to pay is high, for living in such a way requires that you lead a lonely life among people who have no place for emotions, human relations and even less time for strong friendships: it's a battle for giants.

Another aspect of the American way of living: this society does not

From the Steeple to the Minaret

like marginal peoples. The current of their way of life flows in a well-defined direction and you, as a member of this consuming society, must behave as the average does. The notions of great liberty and American democracy should be more closely analysed and accepted with certain reserve. You are absolutely free–free to do what they want and what they have decided and planned. During this period, with a multitude of radio stations on the air twenty-four hours a day, I had the feeling they were trying to prevent people from thinking. That assault directed by the media seemed to choke the small voice in our brains. Their only aim is to have people consuming. Although this behaviour has in the meantime become universal, I can confidently assert that this tendency definitely originated in the U.S.

The few years we spent in that country coincided with one of the most distressing periods of its history. We lived through painful events: the civil rights movement and the assassination of President John F. Kennedy. Having lived through these, I always feel stunned when I hear the American government preach about great principles such as human rights or–even more so–when it passes judgement on the behaviour of other countries or on events unfolding abroad. The attitudes and the interventions of the Americans do not always coincide with the great principles they preach all over the world. Their style of racial inequality was surely not more humane or moral then some of the attitudes they allow themselves to criticize in other parts of the world.

Nevertheless, living in the States was an interesting experience and there was a lot to gain from these people, especially their great sense of initiative and their spirit of responsibility at work. But after a stay of three or four years, just not to lose the little that makes us different, one should leave that country to avoid being swept away by the main current of events and to not become a statistic among the many others.

Their lack of interest in anything not in their immediate surroundings and, of course, the rest of the world, shows itself in often bewildering ways. On Turkish Republic Day, Mehmet came to pick me up from the hospital when I finished working. He had proudly fastened a Turkish flag to the front of the car for the occasion. A group of people at the front door suddenly cried out, "Ah! The Russian flag!" I could understand that the Turkish flag was unknown to them, but not knowing the

Russian flag, the flag of their then so-called worst enemy... Dear Lord!

In 1962, the most important event of the year was without a doubt our trip to the West Coast followed by the long drive back to New York. We were going to visit Mehmet's parents who had been living in Berkeley for the past year, as Bedri Rahmi was at the time teaching as a guest professor at the University of California at Berkley. The first stretch of the trip was by plane to San Francisco, a magnificent city where we stayed for a few weeks. His parents had already planned their return trip to New York and Turkey. Since their departure from Istanbul, they had crossed a good part of Europe and all of the United States in their blue 1957 Volkswagen. The car still had the original license plates issued in Istanbul. Since the word Istanbul was very visible, it caused amusing reactions along our path across the States. We often heard people singing the song "Istanbul was Constantinople now it's Istanbul not Constantinople..." as we went by. This was the car we would travel with on our way back to New York, allowing us to get a better idea of the country.

The few weeks we spent in their company in one of the nicest American states were among the best we experienced in the country. California is a splendid area with a gorgeous climate. We visited the San Francisco area and its magnificent surroundings, such as the Yosemite National Park with its huge sequoia trees. We then spent a week in the absolutely charming city of Carmel, where my father-in-law held a symposium on painting. Because of his very limited knowledge of the English language, he spoke in French and it fell upon me to translate. This small city is absolutely the loveliest American city I have had the luck to visit. The architecture, the vegetation, the boutiques, all are in good taste and perfect harmony with one another. After so many years, I often wonder if all these aspects still exist. Venice is the only other city that has impressed me as much as Carmel.

What's more, this charming spot just happened to be located on the seaside near a large beach. However, this is where we learned that swimming in the Pacific Ocean is neither easy nor recommended. The powerful waves would surely break your legs if you just tried to walk in more than ten inches of water. What fury! You can hardly maintain your equilibrium and the surf could surely drag you out towards infinity... Of course, signs all over warn you to beware of sharks. How can this corner of paradise be so infested with this voracious predator?

During the course of the symposium, we had the chance to swim at the private or semi-private beach of the famous Kelloggs, the well-known cereal family. Lovers of art, they immediately got news of Bedri Rahmi's symposium and managed to invite us to their mansion, which housed an imposing collection of paintings. This home had access to a lovely cove filled with giant seaweed, reminding you of the huge trees in the magic forest of Sleeping Beauty. The seaweed was in constant motion, a strange ballet in the deep blue and luminous green sea. Bedri Rahmi was in an exuberant mood that day. Dragging seaweed torn from the sea, on the fine white sand he proceeded to draw a picture that seemed to come to life before our very eyes. Adding a stroke here and there, he managed to draw necklaces that appeared filled with magic, born directly from a fairytale. You had the sensation of being a part of "A Thousand and One Nights". But then suddenly a strong wave rushed onto the shore and erased the creation we had taken such delight in watching during the last hour. It had truly been an unforgettable day in marvellous surroundings.

Taking the road to Monterrey, we left our wonderland for Los Angeles to visit a friend of my in-laws. As all adult tourists who still maintain their childlike souls, we discovered Marineland and Disneyland where we managed to spend two enchanting days. Our return trip began with a stop in Las Vegas in the Nevada desert. This is the city where everything is super, bigger, larger and more extravagant—a city where mediocrity reigns, a sad and depressing city where nothing is produced, which is arid and sterile, totally in harmony with its desert-like surroundings. The state of the human condition is very sad to witness in that land of make-believe.

We crossed several states: Arizona, New Mexico, a small corner of Texas, Oklahoma and Missouri, before arriving in Chicago, Illinois. My memory is a bit weak, but I do recall a desert-like, boundless area, followed by greener places that took days to cross. I remember a motel in Arizona, in the desert, where we stopped to take advantage of the swimming pool to cool off and drink a beer. For miles and miles in that torrid heat, huge billboards advertised the charms of the place. It turned out that the swimming pool was more like a hot tub and the cold beer was a glass of root beer, a strange tasting beverage quite different from the classical beer we expected. Once having crossed the Great Plains of the midwest, it was with great excitement that we reached the shores of the Mississippi, near the city of St-Louis. We had been talking about this river for hours. Our dreams of this river had been fed for years by American literature and the movie industry... We were a bit deceived, but the scenery still did bring to mind the famous "Old Man River", a song from the movie *Showboat*.

Finally we arrived in Chicago, the Windy City, where I left the VW and ended my trip so I could fly back to work, only a few days late. A bit confused by the gigantic airport, I caught my flight to New York.

Heeding the call of the sea and sea shells, we several times visited towns on the New Jersey shore, towards Atlantic City and Cape May. Unfortunately, the Atlantic Ocean is not always very calm. We also would often go to Pennsylvania either to ski or to admire the gorgeous autumn scenery.

Chapter X

First Contact with Turkey

I n the spring of 1963, Mehmet, Mother and I made an important decision: we decided to take a trip to Turkey at the end of August. I was becoming more and more curious to see the place where I would spend the rest of my life. I also wanted to get a better idea of how I should prepare myself to move from one country to the other. We took advantage of a reduced fare offered by The Turkish-American Friendship Society. Mehmet was not overly excited at the prospect of this trip and I could not figure out why. I didn't realize the problems he would face because he hadn't yet done his military service. I had absolutely no idea about the difficulties encountered when dealing with Turkish bureaucracy; I could not possibly imagine the terror that overcame a student at the thought of all the procedures he would have to complete. The possibility of being asked by a customs officer to produce a special form no one knew of and therefore could not show terrified Turkish students studying abroad at that time. This is but one illustration of why a citizen may lack confidence in the system of his country and also serves as an example of the poor state of information exchange existing between various government agencies in Turkey. In Canada, we don't know what travel restrictions are; we can't comprehend poor communication and we also don't have any idea what it is for a young man to leave his country without having done his military service! The notion of serving others is not an inborn quality that the offspring of the Ottomans possess and we often face serious problems with bureaucrats who see themselves as being way above the "ignorant" citizen who comes to ask for help. Quite to the contrary, the Canadian consulates exist to help their citizens. It seems, however, that the staff of most consulates of other countries in the world prefer impressing their own fellow citizens with their own importance.

Mehmet, who had not yet done his military service, asked his consulate what formalities were required in order to go to Turkey for a holiday and then come back to the United States to continue his studies. He went to the Turkish consulate in New York where a very good friend of his family, Miss Nedret Uzunbekir, worked. She prepared all the required documents, forms of all colours that would allow him an easy entry into and exit from Turkey. Although still not completely reassured, he did his best not to show his apprehension.

A few months before our departure, I learned I was pregnant. Unfortunately, this happy event also included morning sickness, which made my life miserable everyday for several hours. I had to be hospitalised for a time and everyone was hoping the condition would improve in a few weeks time, before we left for the trip. Nothing of the sort occurred and I suffered from morning sickness until the morning of my delivery! Despite this problem, I wanted to go to Turkey and so after much preparation and a lot of shopping for all the friends and family members, we were ready to leave New York at the end of August.

For those of you readers who have never travelled with Turks, let me tell you, they are great shoppers and they travel with a large quantity of heavy, cumbersome baggage. The notion of overweight baggage does not exist with them. I had never seen so many suitcases, such a mass comprised of conventional and unconventional bags alike. In these bags, there is always food and something to nibble on. This is a habit acquired through the centuries, when big networks of restaurants or food service did not exist or were not easy to access. This behaviour, which I was then witnessing for the first time, later on became an intrinsic part of all my future travels with Turks. Whatever the means of transportation or destination, they eat and nibble constantly.

Being hours late, following battles and arguments, the desperate pilot most likely gave up on the idea of having the baggage load reduced and just left the American continent and flew via

Newfoundland and Ireland to land in Istanbul eighteen hours later.

Landing in Istanbul was accompanied by applause from all the passengers. Immediately, they all stood up and at once rushed to the exit doors. We, the great disciplined ones, got in line and waited patiently for our turn to come. All the non-Turks on this plane suffered their first culture shock on the spot: Turks hate waiting in lines and each and every one has a special urgent reason to pass in front of everybody else. This behaviour can be observed everywhere when standing in line is required for whatever reason, either for taking the ferryboat, at the post office, at the bank, at the bus stop, in short, anywhere and everywhere. Through the years, I have had ample time to observe and experiment with this special behaviour, especially considering the large number of queues one has to put up with in this country. Even today, long queues persist in the entire public service sector. Could this be taken as an indication of how well things are (or are not) organized here?

We walked to passport control and Mehmet was the first one to go through. To his great surprise, he encountered no problems whatsoever. I followed showing my Canadian passport and after several minutes of reflection, of going over the different pages of my passport at length, the customs officer wrote a note on one of the pages while telling me a lot of things in Turkish, which of course I, not knowing the language, was incapable of understanding. He gave me back my documents and so I, too, seemed to have made it through without any difficulties, followed by my mother, who likewise passed through with no trouble at all. Welcome to Turkey! Mehmet had a quick look at the note written by the officer, and gave me the news that was to transform our trip into a nightmare and be a source of many an inconvenience for the whole Eyuboğlu clan. Tired, wide-eyed, unable to comprehend what was happening, I could not evaluate at once the significance of the problem. The officer had simply written that I could not leave Turkey without a Turkish passport!

The heat was suffocating. We also had to open our suitcases at customs, a first for me and a most uncomfortable formality to meet in front of everybody. Having to open a suitcase filled with personal effects and this under the eyes of everyone made me uncomfortable. Add the fact that I was also witnessing the ordeal of many exasperated folks who just could not manage to open or close their suitcases. All the travellers were gathered in a provisional hall–because of construction work at the airport–and facilities were rudimentary. What a strange destiny this airport has had; despite endless planning and numerous modifications through the years, it is always in the process of being renovated and rearranged every time I travel. Despite the confusion, we managed to get out of the customs area and find our way through the crowd. Many members of the family were waiting for us. There were screams, kisses, hugs and a great uproar! The news about the note in my passport quickly reached the ears of all present and, despite their welcoming smiles, I could read the uneasiness in everyone's face. The spectre of this problem followed us everywhere we went and, although I did not understand Turkish, I felt that a great part of the conversation was devoted to this intricate question and to the possible ways of solving it.

My first contact with Istanbul was surprising. It's a beautiful city with a long history and has remains, many of which are many hundreds of years old. The presence of several bodies of water such as the Golden Horn, the Bosphorus, the Sea of Marmara and the Black Sea in its immediate surroundings lends the city a seductive character. The charming sight of mosques on each hill turns the city into one of the most bewitching silhouettes you may ever see in your travels. I knew at once that I would feel a passion for its past, for its history, even for its archaeology, a science difficult to master in our young countries. Despite my tiredness, I was all attention as we passed between the Old Walls and the Sea of Marmara on our way to the car ferry. The bridges now found on the Bosphorus uniting Europe and Asia did not exist at that time. A ferry shuttling between both shores was to take us to the "other side", to Asia, where Mehmet's parents lived.

We arrived at a great square filled with cars merging into long lines comprising a massive queue. This area was filled with sellers of all kinds. Their shouts distracted me from the ongoing conversation, and I began to observe the parade of vendors of sandwiches that looked more like American hot-dogs, of lahmacun or Turkish pizza and, of course, the tea vendor who was to be, from then on, part of the scenery, even in the most unusual of places. Offered by the peddlers were cigarettes and lighters, balloons and toys; there was even a mobile supermarket squeezing itself between the cars. If you don't take into account the multitude of beggars asking for charity in the name of Allah, the finishing touch was added with the arrival of a gypsy in her colourful clothes, completely in rags, who insisted on telling our fortunes.

It was while waiting in one of those queues on the Asian side that for the first time I heard the call to prayer, that strong symbol of Islam. Several lovely mosques are close to the wharf in Üsküdar, a very old section of Istanbul, a part of the city made world famous by a popular folksong.* At certain hours of the day, an almost synchronized call to prayer is heard from the different minarets in the area; it is a sound that fills you with an indescribable feeling that carries you and lets you float in an atmosphere, till then unknown to you. This spell is something I always feel despite the passing years and in spite of my lack of interest in religion.

This chaotic passage was experienced whenever we travelled to the centre of the city by car... Patience! It is a country where time does not have the same value as it does in Canada. Vendors can be found everywhere in Turkey. It is the paradise of private enterprise and services to the home. Every hour of the day one can hear the yoghurt vendor, the milk or drinking water vendor, the fruit and vegetable vendor, the shoe shiner, the strolling plumber, the wood cutter, the second hand man, the fish vendor, the simit (a kind of large, ring-shaped pretzel) vendor, the boza or salep vendor (both drinks are very popular in the winter) and this process goes on endlessly. From morning till night, there is a continuous movement in the streets as bargains of all types are offered to the inhabitants of the neighbourhood. The coming of each vendor is usually announced with a traditional and picturesque cry to let the residents know what he is selling. You may not understand the words of the sales pitch, but after some time you will begin to distinguish and recognise the sound and the object sold. My first reaction upon hearing these shouts in the street was to presume there had been an accident. Compared to my uneasiness, the cold-blooded attitude of Mehmet and other members of the family surprised me.

---

* "Üsküdar" became popular in the west when recorded and sung by Eartha Kitt in the 1950's.

It was difficult to get oriented in the city of Istanbul. At first distinguishing between the European side and the Asian side seemed very difficult, learning where the Asian side began and where the European side ended was confusing. Some foreigners confuse the Golden Horn with the Bosphorus, and even with the Dardanelles. One thing is sure; Istanbul is a crowded and noisy city leading you to believe that a good part of its population lives in the streets! On this, my first visit, it was impossible not to notice the dirt prevailing everywhere, for the streets, the sidewalks and the seashores were absolutely littered with trash. Corncobs, watermelon rinds, paper of all type were scattered here and there with hundreds of cats wandering about. Istanbul is a city swarming with cats. I desperately tried to look at this dirt with a poetic eye labelling it as picturesque! But... I was shocked and it certainly didn't help my morning sickness.

Turks, while being very warm, are also extremely curious, so unending questions were asked all the way home. As we set foot in the house, our arrival was punctuated by screams of joy from the neighbours and the few members of the family who could not make it to the airport. We were finally in the famous house Mehmet had talked about so much: a huge house of several stories, modern and spacious, quite original in aspect, situated in the middle of a large garden. It served a double function: besides being a studio for two painters, it was also the home of their family. Only one room with a door could be found and that was the small room that used to be Mehmet's bedroom. The remainder of the house area was an open plan, three-story structure–a remarkable house abounding in paintings and objects of art of all kinds. At first it was impossible for me to comprehend anything because there was so much to see. This was at once both a living place as well as a great museum. During the course of the coming month, I realized that this house was the centre of intense activity, all of which appeared to be the usual pace of living. Countless people would come and go, with many staying for different meals; the amount of food prepared took on extraordinary proportions in my eyes. Some thirty-seven years later and despite the loss of my in-laws, nothing has changed; it is still the same lifestyle. It has no relation to the isolated, lonely life we led in the U.S... Now I can understand why Mehmet found the American people distant. This word, in this sense, probably does not exist in Turkish.

The most important phase of this trip was my meeting the different members of the family. Since our marriage, Mehmet often talked about his relatives and I had sufficient basic knowledge to be able to recognise each member. This family could easily be the subject of a great saga, for it is not an ordinary family. Almost every member is a personality in his or her own right in a particular field, a respected authority of some importance in Turkish society. I was reliving much the same emotions I had felt when I first met my in-laws, as I found myself once again meeting quite a few intimidating characters.

My first encounter was with Mehmet's eighty five year old grandmother. She was a surprising woman from the Black Sea area who at that time still–I was told–had the characteristic accent of the area. A lot of time had gone by since she and her husband had so strongly reacted to the marriage of her son Bedri to a foreigner. Without mercy, life then brought her a German son-in-law, a Swiss daughter-in-law and now, her grandson was bringing her his Canadian wife. Our conversation was rather brief since she did not know any foreign languages and my Turkish was nil. Her face was very expressive and her eyes, just like those of her son, reflected her thoughts. Her peaceful face emanated great warmth. Only God could have understood the tempests that must have shaken her soul each time a foreigner entered the family. She surely must have questioned the destiny of hers that was forcing her to live through such turmoil. At regular intervals she would disappear to pray, fulfilling her duty to Islam. She seemed to appreciate the intense guest traffic in her son's home, where she herself was a visitor.

Ever since his childhood, Mehmet had had a very close attachment to his grandmother. He had never forgotten the marvellous stories she told him when he was a child. When I first saw her she had been a widow for ten years. Bal Nene, or "Honey Grandmother", as her poet son would call her, had not received a formal education, for in her childhood girls usually did not attend school. Coming from a family with means, she had had private tutors as was the custom then. Her profound knowledge of popular Turkish literature and of epic stories surely must have influenced her children who, to the credit of their mother, all showed a great attachment to the culture of their country. She knew the great Turkish poets and she would often recite their work at family get-togethers. She had of course received a good religious upbringing and would often sing hymns and psalms that all her children and grandchildren learned and still sing when remembering her. Following the reform of the alphabet by the founder of the Turkish Republic, Mustafa Kemal Atatürk, when the whole country had to abandon the old Arabic script and adopt the Latin alphabet, she and all the members of the family had to re-learn how to read and write.

Grandfather Rahmi Bey, who died in 1952, had also originally been from the Black Sea region. Climbing through the different levels in the hierarchy of the civil service, he had been Governor of Kühtaya before becoming the Governor of the Province of Trabzon. He was elected as a Member of Parliament from the Province of Trabzon during the time of Atatürk. He ended his career as the Director of the Turkish State Monopoly. A cultured gentleman, he knew French and taught French poetry to his two elder sons. Strongly bound to both immediate members of the family and distant relatives, he discreetly helped those in need, a virtue his family learned of after his death. He oversaw with great care the education of his children and also that of nieces and nephews living away from Istanbul. His house was a centre where everyone found lodging and a family atmosphere during the course of their studies. He had five children, three boys and two girls, Sabahattin, Bedri, Nezahat, Mualla and Mustafa.

The oldest of the family, Sabahattin, was successively a Professor of French literature and art history, a writer, a translator, a producer of documentary films, a photographer and a great humanist. Besides being held in high esteem by the literary circles of the country, he assumed an important place in the family. Once his university studies in French literature had been completed, he spent two years in France on a scholarship from the Turkish Government, an advantage he chose to share with his young brother Bedri, who was a graduate of the Academy of Fine Arts in Istanbul. While Uncle Sabahattin was teaching at the University of Istanbul, the Ministry of Education asked him to work at the Translation Office. This was a newly founded department charged with the mission of introducing classic literature masterpieces to the Turkish public. *The Essays of Montaigne*, *The Fables of Lafontaine*, *Utopia* by Thomas Moore, Shakespeare's *Macbeth* and *A Day in the Life* *of Oblomov* by Goncharov were among his numerous translations. Between 1940 and 1944 he actively participated in the great mobilization movement of the Turkish government that aimed to give Turkish villagers access to the education system. Sans financial aid of any sort, thanks to the hard work and ingenuity of numerous idealists, the Ministry of Education was able to establish village institutes* in twenty-one districts of Turkey. These institutes assumed the responsibility of training teachers who would afterwards work in village schools. Only one of these institutes, Hasanoğlan in the town of the same name, was at college level and this is where Uncle Sabahattin played an important role. The rather revolutionary program was unique in style. The program consisted of both theoretical and applied courses during which the students would build their own school with the means available in their regions. Afterwards, they would cultivate fruits, vegetables or greens according to the climate. In a very short time, an extraordinary network of education was established in the country. Students were taught to read, to write, to build and to cultivate. The principles of hygiene, the knowledge of first aid, foreign languages, music, literature and theatre arts were also taught. The art of thinking was taught, students were learning, learning... These institutes accepted students of both sexes without distinction, an act that was to attract the attention of both politicians and religious authorities who did not quite appreciate the possible increase of an aware population, perhaps becoming difficult to control. They were quick to view them as a threat to their authority and they did not lose time in using the most venomous labels of that time. Besides being accused of being immoral, they were also labelled as being "communists"! In rapid order, first modifications were introduced, then the Village Institutes were closed and so in a short time, this network was transformed into a more classic and less dangerous system of training of teachers. Following the dismemberment of these institutes, Uncle Sabahattin returned to his post at the university.

Several years later, following the military coup in 1960, his name was placed on the list of 147 professors labelled as "dangerous" by the

---

* Fay Kirby, the second wife of sociologist Niyazi Berkes, wrote a comprehensive doctoral thesis on the subject at the Teachers College of Columbia University. It was later published in Turkish by Imece Yayınları.

government. All were forced to leave their positions, but, later on, despite the insult, they were asked to return to their teaching duties as if nothing had happened. The only one to refuse this demand was Uncle Sabahattin. During our visit we were informed that he had once again been accused of communist propaganda and was being tried in court because of his translation of a book by Graccus Babeuf, a French writer who lived between 1760-1797! Courageously, he pursued his translation work and continued his literary work, writing essays. He was a pioneer in the field of documentary films. His film "The Hittite Sun" about Boğazköy, the ancient capital of the Hittite empire, earned him the Silver Bear, the highest award at the Berlin Film Festival, in 1956.

A great admirer of the innumerable cultural treasures of Anatolia, he multiplied his efforts both in his writing and films to raise awareness and bring about acceptance and preservation of the ancient Anatolian cultures. Knowing that the general tendency was to reject these elements as foreign to Turkish culture, he considered them a precious inheritance belonging to every citizen. At a time when travelling in Anatolia was difficult, he was one of the first to visit and photograph the then unknown, but now very popular, archaeological sites such as Mount Nemrut as well as the very unusual landscape of Cappadocia.

Every Monday, Sabahattin would open his home to everyone and usually personalities of the literary world would come. Guests would bring some food to contribute to the meal and some rakı, the national drink... Although alcohol did flow abundantly, the conversation was nevertheless stimulating and often there would be a slide projection of magnificent sites of the country.

Just the opposite of his younger brother Bedri, Sabahattin did not talk much, but when he did, what he said usually made a strong impression. He also had the great talent of knowing how to get everyone to contribute his or her best. A very patient educator with an untiring, inquiring mind, he knew how to encourage research on various subjects. He was a very modest person with no pretensions whatsoever; a prima donna he certainly was not. He lived very simply in the heart of the city in a humble garden flat. He liked teamwork, "imece" in Turkish, a style of working he pursued all his life with a group of writers. He even started a literary revue entitled "Imece" with former students of the Village Institutes. He was the second in the family to choose a foreign spouse, Magdalena Rüfer, a professional pianist of German-Swiss origin. Magdi, as she is called in the family, maintained a polite but distant and reserved relationship with the family. She was known to have a weakness for alcohol. Their marriage was never formalized because at that time Turkish nationality was given automatically to foreign wives and, once a Turkish citizen, these foreign spouses were then submitted to the same severe travelling restrictions as the Turks themselves. Since she was a concert pianist with a musical career requiring constant travelling, she refused the marriage. They did not have any children.

Following studies in philosophy the elder daughter, Nezahat, spent her life teaching Turkish and literature. She spent most of her life in Ankara. Her husband, also originally from the Black Sea area, was in politics but disagreed entirely with the Eyuboğlu brothers as he himself held considerably more conservative views. This resulted in poor relations with the family in general. An active member of the right-leaning Democrat Party at the time of the military coup of 1960, he was imprisoned for one year, then exonerated and set free. Having a passion for writing, he began a career in history and wrote a series of books about the beginnings of the Turkish Republic. Aunt Nezahat, like her brother Sabahattin, was poised by nature and never displayed the emotional outbursts or eccentric behaviour of her sister Mualla or her brother Bedri. Well-educated, she was deeply attached to the Turkish language and to its literature. Her knowledge of French was limited due to a lack of practice. In the family, she was known to be somewhat miserly. She has had a history of long periods of depression that have made her life miserable. Her two daughters were students at the time of that first visit; Ayşe was in medical school and Zehra was studying psychology. Since then they have both left Turkey and are now living in the United States and Canada respectively.

I found the younger sister, Mualla, to be exuberant, brilliant and sensitive with a strong temper, much like her brother Bedri. A woman of great talent and inexhaustible energy, she has devoted her life to the restoration of ancient national monuments. Her great masterpiece is without a doubt the Harem, an important section of Topkapi Palace, now an important museum. As a young architect, she also worked in the Village Institutes. The prototype home she designed was considered the ideal model of architecture in the building courses she taught in those institutes. She visited most of the institutes in Anatolia, but was forced to return to Istanbul when stricken by malaria. The day we went to the Tokapi Museum to visit her, we found her bravely perched on one of the staggering domes from whence she directed the workers. Through the years, most likely influenced by her work in the Harem, she seemed to have acquired the character of a sultan's mother, the Valide Sultan, a detail reflected in her somewhat commanding and unique behaviour. Her style of dress still remains out of the ordinary. She and my mother-in-law both shared this feature; it seemed as though they both belonged to an ancient palace of former days. Without a doubt, they certainly knew how to draw attention! Aunt Mualla could speak only German as a foreign language, so our first contacts were with the help of translators!

Her house was, and continues to be, a small museum with display cabinets filled with hundreds of objects that have come from all corners of Anatolia. Added to these is a large collection of objects from the Far East that belonged to her husband. A woman of exquisite taste, she succeeded in gathering the best examples of folk art in the country and she displays them with great talent and extreme care. Her great love for a German Turcologist caused some uproar in the family. He had originally abandoned his own country to save his Jewish wife, a woman whom he divorced some time later. Robert Anhegger was a colourful but blunt person and was the cause of many conflicts. Despite his often revolting behaviour, he loved his mother-in-law. Extremely devoted to her, he took great care of her, in fact spoiling her terribly. A very competent man, he was then the Director of the Goethe Institute in Istanbul, a position he held for many years. Having an excellent knowledge of the Turkish, Persian and Arabic languages, Anhegger was a great researcher known for his many publications and contributions to the scientific world. His rather tempestuous union with Aunt Mualla remained childless.

Mustafa, the youngest member of the family, was the only one who couldn't speak a foreign language. Compared to the personalities of the family, he is a simpler person and leads an ordinary life. Like his father, he is strongly bound to his family and has a warm character. An agronomist, he was also drawn to the Village Institutes and even wed one of his young students, much younger then himself, to the great dismay of his family. When the institutes were dismembered, he witnessed how the tractors razed the fruit trees his students had planted. That destruction extinguished the flame in his eyes and destroyed his joy for living. Afterwards, he worked in the loan department of a large Turkish bank. His wife, Sevim, a very efficient housewife, has always been, despite her efforts, a source of contention in the family. Lively and extremely avid, she keeps her eyes on the greener grass of the neighbours and has always wanted more than she can afford. Their daughter Şirin is seven years younger than my husband. She had a difficult adolescence and never showed great interest in studies. Since her parents resided in Izmit, some ninety kilometres from Istanbul, my in-laws, in an effort to have her complete high school, took her into their home.

Our first stay in Istanbul was punctuated with visits to the most well-known touristic sites of the city. Following the Topkapi Palace Museum where we spent unforgettable hours under the direction of Aunt Mualla, we visited the St-Sophia, or "Hagia Sophia", Museum, the Sultan Ahmet Mosque, better known as the Blue Mosque, the Covered Bazaar, the great palaces of Dolmabahçe and Beylerbey and took a cruise on the Bosphorus. Everyone seemed to be charged with keeping us busy, and we met a great number of very interesting people.

This is the period when I met the painter Arif Kaptan and his family who used to come and spend their summers in Istanbul. Thanks to my father-in-law, their son, Hasan, a prodigal child, had won a scholarship to study art in Paris. Our neighbour, the composer Yalçın Tura, was often at our house diligently working with everyone to prepare a volleyball court in the garden. Since everyone spoke French, Mother and I had no problems understanding what was going on! One day, we were invited to dinner at the home of a well-known architect, Utarit İzgi, a colleague of my father-in-law at the Academy of Fine Arts. They lived on the Asian side of the city in a splendid old wooden house with a huge garden. It was a very elegant and fancy dinner and everyone was on his best behaviour. In its best style, the Turkish meal began with a countless variety of "meze" (appetizers), followed by meat, desserts and fruit; nothing was missing. Everyone spoke French, so we could follow the conversation and the evening was progressing most pleasantly. Everyone was talking about a new fantastic dessert that no one knew. We were most curious to see this marvel. When the time came and the dessert was placed on the table, Mother and I witnessed in sheer delight the unveiling of a mould of green Jell-O, shaking on its plate! Mehmet could not help smiling as he remembered his first meal at my family home in Canada... One has to belong to the paradise of baklavas to try new desserts.

Most of our time was spent sailing to the shores of the Prince's Islands, a most popular summer spot, where we went swimming. The population of the islands was mostly Greek, Armenian and Jewish along with some wealthy Turkish families. Beautiful wooden houses painted white with magnificent carved wooden trim can still be seen there in the middle of lovely gardens, partly hidden by a great variety of flowers and fruit trees. As we walked along the streets where cars are strictly forbidden, the sound of horse-drawn carriages seemed to recall the islands' former glory days. That quiet corner sheltered Trotsky between 1929 and 1933 after his escape from Stalin and Russia.

Mother, on her first long trip outside Canada, took advantage of the proximity of Greece to take a short trip to Athens and its surroundings. The Greeks, excellent organizers, helped her complete the trip of her dreams filled with historical facts and ruins as well as meals often accompanied by improvised folk dancing. They surely knew how to charm everyone. She came back radiant and impatient to relate all she had seen and done. Years later, while looking at the pictures of that trip, often recounted in different versions, my sister and I finally understood that Mother had had a short love affair in Greece! We discovered what she had never told us about her journey... As a matter of fact, the trip to the Middle East turned out to be quite romantic for Mother, who also almost found herself a Turkish husband. Always elegant and well dressed, she attracted attention, especially the looks of one of my father-in-law's friends. He was a lawyer, a deeply devoted Marxist, a skirt-chaser... He openly courted Mother, who fortunately was able to resist the approaches of that old wolf. The visits of the great Don Giovanni became more and more amusing as our visit progressed.

Everyone was so nice and showed such hospitality to me–the "gelin" (daughter-in-law)–and to my mother that it was impossible not to fall under the charm of the inhabitants of this city. Among the people I met, there was a well-known gynaecologist working in one of the big hospitals on the Asian side, the Zeynep-Kamil Hospital. Her late husband had been the anatomy teacher at the Academy of Fine Arts. My great curiosity pushed me to ask her if I could visit her at work in order to see what a Turkish hospital looked like, since one day I was bound to work in a similar place. Also, she was convinced that she could find a remedy for my long-lasting morning sickness! The visit proved to be a shock. I could not establish a comparison between the great comfort and luxury found in our institutions in North America and what appeared to me to be the epitome of shabbiness, over-crowding and lack of hygiene. As a hospital, it was a deception. How can I ever forget the lack of serum bottles for perfusions and the poor quality of the equipment in use? Disposable material had yet to come to this corner of the world. The problem of sterilisation was acute and everything just deteriorated rapidly because technology was not available. This first contact shook me a bit, but my missionary soul feared nothing and took it as a challenge. In return I felt most powerless in the face of this injustice and the flagrant unfairness among the human beings of this planet. I reflected upon how nice it would be if we could sometimes send our most difficult patients to this hospital on a flying carpet. They might learn to be less capricious, more patient and less demanding.

Despite very good intentions and good will, our gynaecologist never succeeded in eliminating my morning sickness. The invasion of the market by American drugs had not yet occurred and the only drug available on the market did not meet my needs. I was near the fourth month of my pregnancy, but mornings continued to be very unpleasant as did the numerous long meals at night, held usually in my honour. There was such a variety of food one could hardly survive until the end of the meal. Turkish cuisine is rich and refined and the Turks love to eat while drinking rakı. Meals can last three or four hours or more. As is generally the case, at the time the conversation would become animated under the influence of alcohol, with all subjects covered and all the problems of the country at the very least touched upon–except for mine! Usually they would sing in my honour, a song about the "gelin". I could not help thinking that this abundance of songs about daughters-in-law could only mean that in this country, the "gelin" must often find herself in difficult situations!

In many instances, the language problem restricted conversation... I often wondered if the improvised translators really translated all that was said. Generally the Turks are very nationalist and strongly bound to their country; they do not appreciate critics. I often remember conversations we had with some of Mehmet's friends during which some of them would express a total lack of hope in their future. At times they also expressed serious doubts about the possibility of attaining a satisfying lifestyle in their own country. They had dreams of working and living in a foreign country. They would ask me, "What are you doing or looking for in Turkey? We are trying to go to your country while you choose to come and live here". Little did I know then that I would hear these comments for all the thirty-seven years I have spent so far in this country! This surprised me for I belonged to the generation that still believed in the magic formula: complete your studies successfully, work hard and the road to success will open in front of you. They, however, were young and still studying, yet they had already abandoned their dreams and despair filled their souls.

Despite the holiday atmosphere everywhere, I could still see some unease in Mehmet's look, wondering how I would leave the country. Since I couldn't contribute to the solution, I didn't ask too many questions. Finally, everyone came to the conclusion that a trip to Ankara was necessary. This problem could only be solved by the Fourth Branch of the National Security Office, a place no Turk seems to like. My father-in-law had to show extreme caution and deploy all his resources to find high-placed bureaucrats who could help to solve the problem. Once again the network of friends was activated and finally someone knew somebody working in the Ministry of Internal Affairs. That person introduced us to the director of the department involved in solving such problems.

What was the problem exactly? It took me some thirty years to understand thoroughly the exact nature of the problem and its complexity. Many years later, as the President of the Network of Foreign

Spouses, I had to learn about the laws governing the residency of foreigners in Turkey. At that earlier time, the law decreed that any foreign woman married to a Turkish national was to automatically be given Turkish citizenship whether she wanted it or not, and whether her country allowed it or not. The application of this law lasted until 1964, after which the foreign women were allowed to decide for themselves whether they wanted to assume Turkish nationality or not. Nevertheless, foreign spouses have continued to encounter "still partially unsolved" problems even after the modification of this law. According to that earlier law, I could not enter or leave Turkey with a non-Turkish passport. But the passport officer did not know all the details of our life. Technically, when a Turkish citizen marries abroad, the marriage should promptly be registered at the nearest Turkish consulate, which then transfers the information to the register in Turkey. Once these formalities have been completed, the marriage is declared valid by the Turkish authorities. At that time, however, our marriage had not yet been registered because of the problems associated with military service. Therefore, according to the Turkish authorities our marriage was not valid, and I was not a Turkish citizen and thus could enter and leave Turkey using my Canadian passport.

While in the middle of summer the people of Ankara dreamt of coming to Istanbul, going the opposite direction was certainly not popular with the people of Istanbul. Everyone was doing his best to give this trip the appearance of a pleasant touristic journey across Anatolia. We travelled in two cars. We rode in my father-in-law's Volkswagen while the second car, belonging to a famous Turkish historian, Şevket Sürreya Aydemir, carried Uncle Mustafa's family. We stopped at many lovely places during our trip, the first being Sapanca Lake where Uncle Mustafa had a summerhouse. After a pleasant picnic, we drove a few hours more and stopped near the forest around Lake Abant. The closer to Ankara, the more evident the character of the Anatolian plateau became. Herds of goats and sheep were eating up every single piece of grass they could find, leaving behind large dried up surfaces scorched by the heat of the summer combined with the lack of rain in that region during the summer season. We became aware of the deep contrasts at all levels in this country, between regions, cities, towns and villages.

Once in Ankara, we settled down in Mehmet's cousin's house, made a program for our visit to the city and discussed the tactics we should use in the bureaucratic offices. Ankara is not a city with much to see. The most important site is the mausoleum built for Atatürk, the founder of the Turkish Republic, and the very important Anatolian Civilisations Museum. Rapidly the hour we had all been waiting for arrived, and we began our circuit of visits to high placed bureaucrats.

Led by my father-in-law, Mehmet and I went from one office to the other, all of which were dominated by a huge framed photograph of Atatürk, a fascinating sight. Each of these visits was accompanied by many phone calls to various high-level personalities and by the traditional drinking of a cup of Turkish coffee. At one of our stops, we learned that the director of the section dealing with foreigners, Mr Nevzat Ayaz, later to become governor of Istanbul, was ready to receive us. The atmosphere was extremely tense and only the calm attitude and charm of Bedri Rahmi could melt the ice in the room as we sat waiting under the huge picture of the Father of the Turks. Finally admitted into the presence of Mr Ayaz and following the usual litany of polite sentences, he took hold of my passport, had a look at what had been written by the passport officer and then wrote a long paragraph explaining why I could leave the country with my Canadian passport. This was followed by his signature and the almighty seal of his authority. He then asked for our discretion and kindly requested us not to inform the Canadian authorities of this incident, because the passport officer should not have written such a thing in my passport! We were so happy to get rid of this major problem that such an idea never entered our mind. But in fact, the correct procedure would have been to contact the Canadian Consulate in the first place! This was a small detail I was to learn many years later from an ambassador friend. We left the office feeling as light as birds, thanking everyone we met. Despite our success, we were still apprehensive. Mehmet, who had been so afraid he might have problems at passport control, could not get over the fact that I had been the one to have the problem. But we still wondered if all would go well when we actually tried to exit from Turkey.

In the meantime, I took care to note various items that would be good to bring from the United States when we moved to Turkey. There were then great differences between the lifestyle of the United States and that of Turkey. Turkish refrigerators were new on the market and in most houses a place of honour was chosen to display them in the living room, covered with their own special, very fancy handmade lace cloth doilies. Useful small electrical appliances were few, ugly and expensive. One could notice a great difference between European and American appliances, the latter being almost indestructible... No furniture was available on the market. One had to find a good carpenter, show him a picture of the piece of eagerly wanted furniture... then pay the price. Fashion wise, the concept of ready-to-wear had not yet reached this country; Turkey was still in the glorious period of seamstresses and fabrics, of dress patterns found in German magazines. Very practical children's underwear was nowhere to be seen and the gorgeous pyjamas for kids of all ages did not exist. With so many items on my list, I was bound to suffer from lack of this and that, but one simply cannot buy and bring everything from America.

The days went by very quickly and we noticed that my birthday was just on the eve of our departure. My father-in-law organized a huge garden party and gathered all the close friends and members of the family. After a day of intense work in the kitchen and with the help of many women, a huge table covered with an extraordinary variety of food was prepared for the evening. A grille was lit in one corner of the garden and all types of meat were readied for cooking. The general atmosphere was absolutely full with the sounds of a gypsy orchestra and the talents of a very ugly belly dancer who incited the guests to dance. At the wildest moment of the evening, a cousin of my father-in-law, a respectable lawyer, appeared on the balcony in a flowery pink dress and a green scarf and began a most successful belly dance. He was so good and gave such a performance that he completely overshadowed our gypsy... I have often seen similar performances by men who manage to imitate women in a most extraordinary manner. When we learned that it was also his birthday, the party turned into a delirious evening. Every once and a while, everyone would join in to sing a song where the word "gelin" would be emphatically stressed. They have so many songs about daughters-in-law, I could not possibly have learned so many songs in one evening. Such was our magnificent evening just a few hours before our departure!

And so the hour of our departure arrived. Mehmet and I had only one desire, to get through passport control without any difficulties. I was the first to pass the checkpoint and had no problem. Then Mehmet and Mother followed and crossed as easily as I had. On that day mother was not feeling well at all, having eaten a lot of unusual food, in particular kokoreç, a very special preparation of stuffed intestines usually eaten by heavy rakı drinkers!

Light-hearted, we walked to the plane. All our fears and apprehensions had proven unfounded and we were leaving enriched with memories and much to reflect on. It was a rapid and silent return. The shock of our return to American soil was such that we spent our first hours back in deep silence. I cannot find the right words to express all my feelings. Suddenly and brutally, I became aware of the great differences between the two countries and any comments I might have made would have been unkind. Very conscious of the fact that our pathway had already been chosen, I made a silent decision to never again travel non-stop between America and Turkey. A stopover somewhere in Europe would help lessen the feeling of surprise and the great shock that arises when facing the differences.

I now saw New York through another eye. The organisation, the abundance found here made me question whether we really should go and live permanently in such a poor and deprived country. Fortunately, time soothes everything and my doubts about our future gradually began to taper off.

Autumn arrived. I returned to my job and was slowly preparing for the birth of our child. A few months had gone by when we were confronted with the news of the assassination of President John F. Kennedy in Dallas, Texas. Several days of agony were spent in front of the television in an effort to give meaning to this drama. For the country, a dream had crumbled: an era straight out of a fairytale in which a fragile, elegant, distinguished lady reigned, a patron of the arts. At her side, a handsome and rich president of Irish descent, the first Roman Catholic leader to rule in the White House, the White Knight... Americans were filled with sorrow. The funeral was followed by the enquiring commissions, the so-called guilty assassin's arrest and his murder live on television. This was a climate of madness. Then slowly all was forgotten and the routine of everyday life returned.

In early February of 1964, my maternity leave began and I completed my preparations for delivery. The female doctor I had chosen to deliver my baby informed me that she would be taking a leave of absence for a weeklong cruise in the Caribbean. In an effort to calm me down, she told me that I didn't yet seem to be anywhere close to delivery. I felt a bit disturbed by this news, because I had taken great care to find a female gynaecologist and I didn't want to deal with the male doctors I worked with at the hospital.

No man can possibly imagine how unpleasant it is for a woman to go through these gynaecological examinations every month and deliver in their presence. I considered myself a broad-minded person, but since in this world we must deliver in pain, why do we have to bear the presence of a man at that time, even if he is a doctor and capable of saving our lives? Why are there so few female gynaecologists?

Two days after the departure of my doctor, in the evening around six o'clock as Mehmet was getting ready to go to his night classes, I felt some pain I could not identify, but I paid little attention to it. When Mehmet returned later on that night, having freshly completed his prenatal education, he interpreted my symptoms more clearly and assured me that my delivery had begun. I immediately got in touch with the resident on call. He gave me a few instructions and advised me to go to the hospital when my contractions increased to every five minutes. The night was so long; I felt tired and my irregular contractions never reached the level described by the doctor. I felt absolutely helpless.

Around seven o'clock in the morning I was told to come to the hospital. After the night I had experienced, I felt like the hospital was a kind of paradise, the oasis where everything would be perfect and painless. A few more hours went by, but nothing seemed to be happening. Impatience and exhaustion were hand-in-hand. The traffic seemed to increase around my bed and I was finally told that things were not going as they should: it seemed we were experiencing foetal distress. I was quickly carried to a delivery room and while being tied to the delivery chair I felt a sudden atrocious pain as if my back were being torn apart. After several efforts it became evident that I would be unable to have a normal delivery. They therefore had to proceed to an urgent Caesarean section.

From that moment on, the events acquired a hectic pace. My bed was pushed into the corridor towards the elevator reserved strictly for patients, but to no avail, for it was out of order. The bed was then pushed into the already full visitors' elevator. In the meantime, everyone was busy doing something, an intravenous drip was started, the doctor was examining and checking the heart beat of the baby. Modesty had suddenly disappeared and shyness didn't exist. Unwilling witnesses could not decide how to behave or where to look, while I lay there helplessly undergoing a process out of my control. The doors of the elevator opened, the ceilings and the lights went by and finally my bed was brought to the doors of the operating room. Everyone was busy doing something, but not busy with me, as if I were merely part of the scenery. From then on I was an emergency; the actions of the personnel had become automatic, as if they were only efficient robots. I had become an abstract case requiring a lot of necessary routine acts. I had to sign the required papers for the surgery because Mehmet had been sent home by the doctor to shave, change and freshen up. I dared to ask if they would finally put me to sleep because I was tired of suffering. Then, the sequence of events reached that stage and finally there was darkness, emptiness; I no longer felt anything...

I woke up to see the soft paternal face of our pathologist, Dr Hugh Luddecke, informing me that I had delivered a boy. Happy and relaxed, I felt like sleeping when suddenly, I began shivering like a leaf in the wind, most likely the secondary effects of the anaesthesia. A nurse covered me with a warm blanket she had taken from an incubator. The soft warmth calmed me but soon the shivers returned and I felt like I was at the North Pole lying on an ice floe! Slowly I slid into a soft sleep and when I woke up, I was in my room. Mehmet was next to me and I could feel every stitch in my incision. In the evening around nine o'clock my son was brought in for the first time. He was a small but well-formed ball of life to whom I sang a lullaby. What a miracle!

My one-week stay at the hospital was punctuated by a series of unforgettable experiences. To begin with I discovered that my morning sickness had disappeared. I hesitated when breakfast was brought and, remembering the nine months of nausea, cautisouly took my first bite. What a pleasure it was to be able to eat normally! The elation of this discovery, however, was soon followed by astonishment as what should have been a most ordinary matter turned out to be a nightmare! I was asked to complete a birth registration form so that we could obtain a birth certificate. "What is wrong with that?", you may ask. Well, if your husband is Turkish, your child will be given a Turkish name, but since Mehmet was not there, it was left up to me to write the name without making a spelling mistake. My God! I will never forget the look of the person waiting for the forms to be filled in while I was writing all possible variations of the name: Sabahattin Rahmi, Sabahittin or Sabahiddin or Sabahaddin! We had agreed that our son, as custom required, would be named after both Mehmet's uncle, who had no children himself, and his paternal grandfather. I was desperate; I couldn't bear being caught in such a ridiculous situation. Tears I couldn't control burst forth and spoiled this most promising day. Fortunately, an angel must have helped, for I finally managed to write the name correctly.

Another event stirred up quite a commotion in the department as well: my decision to breastfeed my son, something that was not, then, very common in the United States. Following the directions given by the nurse at first all went very well, but my breasts became so sensitive that every feeding caused pain. The nurse was informed, but it was only several hours later, when the night shift arrived, that something was brought, without any explanations, in a small paper cup. Unable to establish a connection between my complaint of several hours before and the brownish substance, I very heroically swallowed, with great effort, the thick horrible medication.

The next morning, I naively asked the doctor about that strange substance he had prescribed. With nothing written in my chart, a frantic activity began on the floor and finally the night nurse was asked what I had been given on her shift. We then learned that I had been given something called Balsam of Peru, an ointment used to soothe sensitive skin and which should have been applied to my nipples. Once again I was rapidly taken out of my room and I found myself in the emergency room having my stomach pumped. The ointment I had swallowed could have been harmful to the baby since it might have contained injurious substances that could have passed in my milk. Several hours had gone by since the incident, but as a precaution, I was nevertheless submitted to this drastic treatment.

How could I ever forgive myself for having behaved so stupidly! Second crying episode! Mehmet could not believe his eyes when he saw me crying again that evening. During the course of my life, at those moments when all is going fine and I succumb to a tendency to think flattering thoughts about myself, recalling such incidents rapidly puts things back into a more realistic perspective!

At the end of the week, all three of us returned home and so the work of parenthood began, a job that never seemed to end. We had the paediatrician's prescription in our hands, Dr Spock's famous book and unlimited good will. Happily, most parents survive this phase and even in periods of despair, when no solution comes to mind, somewhere there is a guardian angel connecting us to the knowledgeable person we need to help us in our distress, especially if grandmothers are very far away. There are intangible and formal principles, transmitted from generation to generation, according to which maternity and the job of motherhood are instinctive and natural functions for women. Despite widespread belief in this traditional vision concerning the joys of motherhood, I must be honest and confess that, as far as I'm concerned, this does not seem to be the truth. To begin with, no phase of our education prepares us for this most demanding function and for the important role we must play in the education of a child. This is only learned painfully, step by step, and from crisis to crisis as the years go by. There is not a more difficult, a more ungrateful task than the job of parenting. The young couples who imagine that the arrival of a baby in their family will usher in a great period of joy to their lives, that their child will be the cement that binds husband and wife forever, do not realise the ordeal they will be submitted to. To the mothers dreaming that the new arrival will guarantee them eternal love, I recommend some reflection and I think they should seriously rethink their conception of maternity. Any marriage built upon weak foundations, that is, foundations that do not include a profound friendship, cannot possibly last!

Rahmi was never a difficult child and, after having acquired habits based on what he could expect from us and what we wanted from him, all went relatively well. The summer after his birth, Mother, Claudette and Jacques came to visit for a few days to get to know the new addition to our family. Life went on, for me it was the routine of work and for Mehmet the completion of his studies. My well-organized American neighbours had created a baby-sitting club in the compound where we lived. One accumulated hours while helping others, in return for which one was entitled to the same number of hours of help. I am most grateful to them because I often required their help and when we left, they overlooked my debt of many hours that I owed to the club. Without this precious assistance, it would have been impossible for me to work at night while Mehmet had to attend some of his classes.

Our life was concentrated entirely upon two objectives: bringing up our child in the best possible manner and having the father complete his studies. Mehmet was a patient and devoted father and he took his role very seriously. Since my work started at five o'clock, he had to prepare Rahmi's supper and give him his bath before putting him to sleep. To my great surprise, Mehmet knew the taste of all the varieties of the food we bought for our baby. He knew which fruit was tastier and which meat preparation was the best because his feeding was based on, "One spoon for the child and one spoon for the father". Aware of the great quantities Mehmet usually consumed, it must have been interesting to observe the evening meal every night as my son swallowed his feast. The evening bath must have also been most amusing considering the tremendous amount of baby powder used every week. Rahmi must have been literally white from head to toe before getting into his pyjamas. With such a talented father at his disposal, I very rarely had to come to the rescue. I vividly recall an evening when I came home to find a blanket fastened between two ropes attached somewhere in the room near the ceiling. Rahmi was sleeping inside the blanket having been rocked by his father in this makeshift cradle. I had never seen such an unusual sight in my life. I asked myself what was going on, what that thing in motion in front of me could possibly be. Mehmet looked at me and proudly declared: "For centuries Turkish children have been put to sleep in this fashion and my son will also be put to sleep in the same way." However, he never did it again.

Slowly but surely Rahmi was growing and gaining more weight and becoming a very heavy baby, difficult for me to carry around. Ever since my delivery, my back had been fragile and lifting heavy objects caused sharp pains. It was suggested that I should wear a brace and undergo physiotherapy. Finally, I had to be admitted to the hospital for a good ten days. Rahmi was fourteen months old, not walking but rapidly crawling everywhere. It was decided that he would go to Canada to spend the summer with my mother. We took a flight from New York to Montreal where Mother came by car from Malartic to meet us. My dear son took his first steps during this flight, in the aisle of the plane as we cruised between the two countries. Could this be an indication of a very animated life? I think so, because he has travelled a lot by plane ever since.

When I went to Malartic to pick him up a month later, he had already forgotten who I was and seemed very happy to be with his grandmother, Aunt Claudette and Uncle Jacques. The night before my arrival he had managed to knock over a nice lamp in Mother's living room and cut himself deeply over the eyebrow, a wound that required three stitches.

At home, the preparations for our return were in full swing. We had decided to buy most of our electrical appliances from the United States, such as a refrigerator, a music set, a hair dryer, an iron, a blender, a sewing machine, whatever our budget allowed. Having learned on our trip to Turkey what was missing clothes-wise, we tried to buy those we would not be able to find there, such as the lovely one-piece pyjamas for children, size ten shoes for me, sewing patterns for children and women, and spare parts for certain appliances, some of which are still in our cupboard waiting in case they are needed. The list appeared never-ending: the number of suitcases increased as time went by, while we were simultaneously also selling all our furniture.

During the month of February of our last year on the American continent, we planned a trip to Québec City to participate one last time in the Winter Carnival. We left Rahmi with our good friends Jacqueline and Clement Joris of Morris Plains and headed towards Canada. We were accompanied by two American couples as courageous as our ourselves, willing to drive this distance in the worst month of winter. As always, Québec City was literately engulfed by snow, but the atmosphere was such that it was impossible not to feel the joy of living in the air. Terrified of the cold weather, Mehmet was wearing several sweaters, a woollen hat and a hood and mittens over a pair of gloves. He could hardly move and we had to stop often to warm up and have a coffee break. Our days were filled with activities, visits and some skiing. The nights were wild: how could we have ever forgotten the Friars Inn, where the only things served were wine and bread and where drinking was the prime activity, the purpose of course being to keep you warm while you danced until morning!

Just as I had during my years at Laval University, I once again experienced the parade of the carnival, filmed with great care by Mehmet who could not prevent freezing his fingers in the process. That evening to warm up we had to use "caribou", a strong alcoholic beverage not tolerated by everyone. It was one of the rare occasions when Mehmet could not remember afterward how the evening had ended. The outdoor dances and the tremendous energy spent fascinated our American neighbours. The day of our return coincided with a stupendous snowstorm that reduced the traffic towards Montreal to one lane, the bumper-to-bumper cars keeping the road open for the time being. This calamity, almost routine for us, scared the non-Canadians who, not realising that it was now or never, hesitated to begin their return journey. A slight hesitation and delay would have kept us in Québec City for several more days. We did finally reach the American border, but we were met by a cold shower once we got there! Because he had just completed his studies, Mehmet no longer had student status and therefore was denied entry to the U.S. With great difficulty–and in return for eight hundred dollars given as a guaruntee–he was allowed in and given permission to stay until our departure scheduled for July. This money was refunded to us upon our departure.

From the very moment of our return, days passed in a blur of activity. Our plans were to travel by ship, to experience the illusion and the luxury of the days of comfort once offered by cruises. We were due to arrive at Cherbourg, pick up a new Volkswagen and begin a small tour of Europe. Two lovely teachers, Dawn and Patricia, neighbours in the apartment where we lived, were thrilled by our plans and offered to join us, paying their own expenses. Planning every aspect of the trip using the then famous book, *Europe on Five Dollars a Day*, we made our reservations in various recommended hotels and pensions. We planned to visit Holland, Belgium, part of Germany, France, Spain, Italy, Yugoslavia and Bulgaria en route to our final destination, Turkey. The whole trip went as planned, except for a labour strike on the Cunard line... With no settlement in view, our plans had to be modified. We had to leave New York by plane and pick up our car at the airport in Holland.

In June came commencement day with a ceremony taking place in the rose garden of the university. Following the event, we had planned a champagne breakfast with our closest friends. But on that very day, Rahmi woke up burning with a fever. How could I leave him in such a state to go to the ceremony? Even the prospect of receiving guests frightened me when I saw him that ill. Thanks to a marvellous neighbour and the cooperation of my very good son, the problem was solved and everything went as scheduled.

During our last months in New Jersey, we bought an old 1951 Ford for twenty-five dollars. It wasn't an automatic, but the old stick style, so I could learn to drive the conventional way and use a Volkswagen in Europe. Those last few weeks I could be seen driving up and down the hilly streets of the town, trying not to slip backwards while waiting for the green lights. Those days prepared me for driving in Istanbul, a city of many hills, just like Québec City.

All our baggage was sent to a Turkish cargo ship en route to Istanbul. Our possessions had been stuffed into our two big wooden Canadian boxes and five trunks. I left the hospital and the laboratory where I had worked some five years. Morristown will remain engraved in my memory as the city of my first car, first home, first child and the first chapters of our married life.

Our five-year stay in the U.S. came to an end on 2 July 1966. We were taken to the airport in the old Ford that we then sold for ten dollars. As we boarded the plane, we learned that there was to be a general strike paralysing all airports the next day. Such was the prelude to the second adventure of our life.

An Ocean Apart:

A Canadian Wife in Turkey

ours–our European tour could begin. For the previous six months, we had been dreaming of this trip and now, here we were! Mehmet was a veteran driver of a similar trip made with his parents five years previously and, although very preoccupied with his military service problem, for my sake, did not show any signs of weariness.

With the itinerary carefully drawn up and the reservations made and paid for, I was convinced we would have no problems whatsoever. What a preposterous idea to assume one could stick to such a strict itinerary without running into any problems! My lack of experience and my great enthusiasm caused me to dismiss the mishaps that might possibly occur while travelling. So numerous were the places we had planned to visit that anyone could see that what lay before us was not a trip, but a veritable race through the continent! Thank God Mehmet, who faced a very difficult driving task, enjoyed driving so much!

Accompanied by our neighbour Patricia, we threw ourselves onto the roads of Europe as we ventured to conquest a series of capitals, museums and restaurants. The concept of distances in Europe is different from ours; in a single day, you can cross quite a few borders. Holland, a lovely country, peaceful and clean, was crossed without any problems. The inhabitants were welcoming, the number of bicycles surprising, and one was not the least bit disappointed by the scenery and the sight of windmills. The museums were rich and one could never forget Van Gogh after a stroll through the Van Gogh Museum. Rahmi was thrilled with the good food. Never again would he find such good milk on the continent.

Belgium, as always, was buried in grey, and rapidly crossed with a pleasant interlude in Brussels in honour of the "Place Royale" with its laces and chocolates. We also had a look at the site of the famous 1957 International World Fair where Mehmet's father had prepared a 225 square meter mosaic panel for the Turkish pavilion. He had been awarded a gold medal for this huge work that he had prepared in the garden of his home in Kalamış. Afterwards it was transported to Brussels and set in place by Turkish workers. Among the trees of the magnificent huge park, only the symbol of the exposition, The Atomium, remains to remind visitors of the past event. At the close of the exhibition, the Turkish Pavilion building, its entire contents and the mosaic panel were all sent back to Istanbul by train. That was the last that was seen of the entire building. The panel itself, except for one wooden box that had suffered damage during the trip or the transfer, was sent to Cyprus for an exhibition that took place during "Turkish Week". The story then becomes fuzzy. Later during our investigations, we managed to find a few fragments in the Military Officers Club in Nicosia. Apparently the panel, more or less reassembled in the restaurant of a similar building, changed hands a few times during the war until it was finally transported by the soldiers from one side to the other. Many pieces were damaged or disappeared. It is said that some of these panels were "saved" and can be found in various lovely homes of the island, but who knows. A few fragments were found during a thorough cleaning of a city bus garage in Istanbul. Those panels are now in the garden of our residence in Istanbul. So much for art and gold medals!

We slowly left Belgium for Germany and the well-known spa city of Bad Kissingen, a few hours from the East German border. Patricia wanted to visit a good friend whose husband was stationed at an American base near this city. We eventually went to visit this border with its barbed wire patrolled by well-armed soldiers accompanied by specially trained dogs. This sight awoke feelings of deep sorrow and a certain amount of dismay. Compared to the United States, the sobriety of the German villages was surprising and left us with vague reminders of the paintings of Bruegel. Scenes observed in the restaurants were quite surprising and unusual for us: nobody was talking or making any gestures; the clatter of utensils was the only noise to be heard. One had the impression that the people did not come to the restaurant for their pleasure or for diversion, but only to eat, and that they did with great discipline.

Our entrance into Strasbourg marked our arrival onto French soil and this time we were astonished to witness the shabby state of the villages of my "Mother Country". We slowly found our way towards Paris singing the famous song of Yves Montand:

A Paris quand un amour fleurit
Ca fait pendant des semaines
Deux coeurs qui sourient
Et tout ca parce qu'ils s'aiment
A Paris...

This song conveys exactly what happened to our two friends in this magical city. We found our second passenger, Dawn, transformed into a bewildered girl-in-love. In this legendary city she managed, within a week, to meet the man of her dreams and informed us that she would no longer take part in our long-planned trip. As for Patricia, she found her parents, also in town for a visit, and, filled with dreams of love, decided to leave us and try her own luck. So much for the plans and the shared trip... We left them without bitterness to continue our own adventures. We never heard from them again.

Mehmet knew Paris very well and took his guide role very seriously. Patiently, with Rahmi on his shoulders, he visited the museums once again. Of course, to know and appreciate Paris requires many visits, each one based on one particular theme. After five years of life near New York City in the land of skyscrapers, our first glimpse of Paris was rather disappointing. The city appeared chaotic; the stores were filled with disorderly piles of merchandise and the personnel were not at all helpful. Only the sunset in Montmartre at the foot of the Sacré-Coeur Church left us with some pleasant memories. I have had to return to this city several times to enjoy and appreciate it in a better way. Our itinerary led us to Chartres, then towards the imposing castles along the River Loire. Both their age and their great beauty charmed us, the swans and the ponds, the rich tapestries, all were breathtaking... Thus we drove through the region, visiting the castles in the cities of Blois, Amboise and Tours along the way. The French have learned how to preserve their heritage and know the art of keeping lovely gardens. In Tours, we had to consult a doctor for Rahmi who did not feel too well. I could not believe my ears as I listened to the paediatrician restricting food such as brain, bone marrow and kidney for our son. Until then, Rahmi had never eaten such food. Since then, I have always wondered if French children are fed such delicacies during their childhood.

It was a long road to Bordeaux after which we headed for the Spanish City of San Sebastian. As we approached Spain, we were caught in a line of cars the likes of which I had never before seen in my life; all of them were waiting to cross the border. There were so many people waiting that the officers hardly even looked at our passports. Those were the golden years of tourism in Spain; the country was offering good service at cheap prices. Huge hotels with high ceilings and faded rugs reminded us of the great days of bygone times. They offered a magnificent view of the sea. A few days of rest and the race towards Madrid began. The weather was hot, the land was arid and the villages revealed their poverty; there were times when I felt as if I were in Turkey. Madrid is proud of its gardens, but after visiting France, one can no longer be impressed by any other gardens. The Spaniards were rather distant with tourists and very few could speak English or French. The unforgettable sights of the Prado Museum compensated for the inconvenience of the siesta, a lapse of time during which nothing can be done and no food can be found. Of course, like all tourists, we did not think of leaving the city without a black lace mantilla and a fan!

Driving between Madrid and Barcelona was a feat. The road was bad, narrow and clogged with trucks you could not pass. That stretch of our trip seemed unending and we arrived at our destination on the Costa Brava during the night, totally exhausted. The last kilometres were particularly tiresome, but, thanks to Mehmet's driving skills, we reached the coast safe and sound. Dreaming of sun, sea and wonderful days of rest, we had the surprise of waking up the next morning to the sound of pouring rain that lasted the whole day. The following day, wrapped in a warm sweater and lying on my sun chair next to the Mediterranean Sea, the same way the hundreds of English tourists hunting the sun did, I tried to enjoy my holiday! At night, Flamenco dances gave the illusion that we were enjoying the atmosphere of the country. It lacked some spontaneity, I must admit. Since the sun was in no hurry to come back out, we cut our Spanish vacation short and left for France and the "Côte d'Azure".

To our surprise, we found wonderful weather in Saint Tropez and Saint Raphael, so we stopped for a few days. For both of us, lovers of the sea, the French Rivera was a pure delight, a corner of Paradise. Mehmet began looking for good diving material so that at last he could realise his long-time dream. He bought diving fins that he used for the next twenty years, good goggles and a powerful underwater spear gun with different harpoons. As for me, I made, for a woman of the North American continent, a rather heroic decision: I decided to buy a bikini. American bathing suits at that time were quite modest and it took a lot of courage to go around almost naked! Slowly we progressed on to Cannes and Nice and spent a wonderfully magical day in Monaco and Monte Carlo before crossing into Italy.

Welcome to Italy, and to the long lines of cars waiting to be searched and checked by the customs officers! They were looking for cigarettes. Finally, all our documents were stamped and we were ready to conquer that great country. This was the part of my journey I enjoyed the most and felt absolutely enchanted by. Why Italy? It's a beautiful country, as a matter of fact, a very beautiful country. The Italians are filled with a joy of living that they express without inhibition at every opportunity. Quite the opposite of the French, they even appear to enjoy tourists. They sing, express their admiration of beautiful women with zest and serve their delicious food in great surroundings. The pleasure I took in experiencing this country was probably due to a gradual fading away of the American way of life that I had been a part of, a way of life that was for me now in the past, and I was most likely feeling ready to enjoy the atmosphere. I felt good in that country. I was on holiday and happy. Finally, I understood why I enjoyed Italian films so much; Fellini, the great Fellini, what a genius of the cinema, Scola, the Taviani brothers, Visconti... It is also the country of opera, Verdi, Puccini, the country of great voices. The sight of the great Scala Opera House sent me daydreaming! Unfortunately, it was July and the theatre was closed. Again, we were driving through a torrential rainfall, quite unusual for July. We finally reached Venice, a city as spectacular as its reputation, a city that can soften even the hardest of hearts. The greatness of the buildings, the abundance of art objects, the refinement found everywhere... How can one resist such charm? How can you not feel sorry as you leave this magic city? We promised we would return one day, but have never done so.

The general holiday feeling ended as we set foot in Trieste where we began the last part of our trip, the long road leading to Turkey. We had decided to bypass Split and Dubrovnik, opting instead for the road to Bulgaria. The general landscape was beginning to change, and greater poverty could be observed. Most striking were the discoveries we made about the many different characteristics of the communist regimes as they began to unfold. In Yugoslavia, we saw that the glories of the founder, Marshall Tito, were emphasized every-where. When we arrived in Bulgaria, we observed that partisan praising was more accentuated with statues of Lenin and other political leaders all over the place. The country was destitute and sad; there was a limited amount of goods in the stores and the inhabitants avoided contact with us. The villages were hidden and far from the main roads,

With Rahmi in Venice (Summer 1966)

as if to avoid contact with anything foreign. The general atmosphere was such that our only desire was to leave the country as soon as possible. Very early in the morning, before sunrise, we saw many buses transporting workers, while others were carrying small children to nursery school. Road directions in the whole country were only in the Cyrillic alphabet. It became impossible to understand if we were on the right road or not. Without the help of previous Turkish drivers who had written a Turkish translation on almost every road sign, Istanbul would have been difficult to find. The Bulgarian customs officers were very rude and tried every way they could to keep travellers inside the country so that they would spend foreign currency. They were particularly threatening towards carriers of Turkish passports. Addressing them in Turkish, they called them "neighbours", but made them wait hours before returning their documents. Once near the Turkish border, the officers decided to thoroughly search the Jeep just in front of us, using the tools Mehmet had in the car and leaving the Jeep almost in pieces; although we in the meantime grew more and more impatient to get to the other side, we did not dare to complain! After a few hours of this stupid game, we were allowed to leave the country–with our tools!

After years of planning and talking, the awaited moment finally became reality; we had finally made it, finally arrived in Turkey, at the entry point near the city of Edirne. We were tired and our nerves were shattered after the unpleasant hours spent at the Bulgarian border. Mehmet, filled with emotion, swore never to return to Bulgaria again, got out of the car and kissed the ground of his country. As I looked at him, my eyes filled with tears and Rahmi, somewhat frightened, looked around not conscious of the great changes occurring in his life.

The Turkish police ran to us to learn what had happened on the other side of the border. They offered us tea and from there on I could no longer understand what was happening. It was the beginning of a phase where I would feel like a mute, knowing it would take some time for me to learn how to express myself in an intelligent manner. We were given information on how to proceed to complete the customs formalities for our car.

Rahmi with his grandfather, Ömer (Summer 1965)

Then, finally, we were on the road to Istanbul. Thousands of thoughts ran through my mind. I was quite aware that some difficult times were ahead. We had to face Mehmet's military service, a period of two years he was required to complete. Thank God we trusted so much in our future and ourselves that nothing could cast a shadow on our horizons. Driving through the heat of summer, we passed by such magnificent fields of sunflowers that even Van Gogh would have been jealous. Silently, I compared the new landscape with that left behind in North America and in Europe. Ever since Yugoslavia, the sights had become very different, and I felt I was in another part of the world, on very dry land. We had left behind the rains of Spain and Italy; it was hot and the road was in poor condition even though it was the gate to Europe, to the West. I felt euphoria, though, at all the new things to see and discover.

After many hours of driving, we finally reached Istanbul. The crowds, the ferryboats, the street vendors; this was the Istanbul that I had discovered in 1963. As Mehmet drove towards Kalamış, we saw that the neighbourhood had changed a lot during the last three years. Many lovely summerhouses had been replaced by apartment buildings and the beautiful gardens had been destroyed. We could hardly find the house! Finally, we stopped in front of Manolya Street No: 8. The front door opened and my in-laws greeted us with cries of surprise and joy. In the garden where two pine trees had been planted at his birth, Rahmi, for the first time, slowly walked toward his grandparents.

Chapter XII

Turkey, My New Home

Knowing a country is one thing, but discovering its profound meaning is something else. The longest part of my life so far–thirty-seven years–has been spent in my adopted country. Of the remaining years, twenty-one were spent in Canada and five in the United States.

As I write these words, I have no other intention but to try to describe as correctly as possible my personal experiences during the course of the many years I have spent in this interesting country. Of course, others may relate a similar experience very differently, giving a totally different account and interpretation of what they have seen and how they have lived it.

Turkey is not a country that is known well and it is therefore often depicted in an extremely unfair way. This ignorance tends to be valid for all aspects of life, especially the political and the cultural. The foreign media are often unfair and interpret events incorrectly. Many countries may have a similar complaint, but I think that none has suffered from the repercussions of such a negative approach as much as Turkey has.

People conceive of Turkey in various ways, many of which, interestingly enough, tend to be conflictual. In some individuals, the colourful universe of the sultans is evoked, filling the mind with harems and the four or more wives supposedly allowed by the Koran. Of course, the "fez" is part of the scenery as well. To others, it is a country of barbarians, descendants of the well-known Atilla the Hun, who have nothing else to do but dedicate themselves to the persecution of the Greeks, the Armenians and more recently the Kurds. To the people of my native province, the word rug is always related to the word Turkey.

Europeans are usually more informed about Turkey. They know the country, mostly by hearsay, as a sunny coast and an ideal vacation spot. A lot of information has of course been gained these last forty years from the numerous Turkish workers who have migrated to various European countries. Directly or indirectly, they have helped to improve Europeans' knowledge of many aspects of Turkish culture. But on the political level, myths persist. It would be more correct to say, most likely, that either Turkey doesn't know how to market its image or has simply neglected to do so through the years. One must recognise that very few people possess the required knowledge of history to understand the complex problems of the great Ottoman Empire, now a secular republic. I would go even further and say that most are not committed to facing the problems of this country as they really are because of the deep conflicts of interest between the Super Powers involved. The historical background of previous rivalries remains the basic argument behind the interpretation of any event.

To North Americans, Turkey is one of those countries no one can locate on a map, despite the fact that it is a NATO country, a small detail few seem to be aware of. Such was the situation in the sixties, when we were in the United States, and so it was twenty years later, when my son was in Montreal for his studies. During the course of the few trips I have taken to my native country, I have been asked many times if I had come by train to visit my mother! There has been very little improvement in the knowledge of people during the last thirty years. Despite the interest shown to the so-called persecutions of the Armenian and Kurdish peoples, geographical knowledge of Turkey has remained a blur for the great majority of people. Following the dramatic earthquakes of 1999, or the Iraq questions of 2003, thanks to CNN, the curiosity of some Americans may have been awakened and they may now be better informed. Each trip I take to Canada is a revelation. It allows me to witness the ignorance of people in general, but especially to evaluate the wrong done to a country by the spreading of spiteful information. The dreadful images of the film *Midnight Express* will not easily be erased from the memories of moviegoers and the damage caused by this film is impossible to estimate. It may be of interest to mention here that, by a great coincidence, the ghostwriter of the book *Midnight Express*, William Hoffer, later collaborated with Betty Mahmoody on her book, *Not Without My Daughter*.

Turkey is classically described as an important, strategically located bridge between two continents. We find very little mention of its being the cradle of many Anatolian civilisations almost totally unknown to the world. To the Westerner, civilisation began with ancient Greece, and so most tour organizers support this thesis when designing their "package tour" of Turkey, thereby reinforcing a false notion about the country in the minds of travellers. The accent is on Greek Asia Minor, with the focus being placed on the city of Ephesus. The Cappadocian region, with its unbelievable panoramic fairytale-like scenery, is of course very popular because it shows the hidden dwellings of the persecuted seventh century Christians. The nearby ancient Hittite city of Hattusha is usually neglected to the point of being completely overlooked. Why aren't tourists encouraged to discover Anatolian civilisations? Why are we ignoring those sites? Is it the lack of four-star hotels? Unfortunately, the Turks themselves are a bit responsible for this negligence. They have failed to recognise these cultures as their own and have neglected to include them in their own heritage. They have preferred to consider them as foreign cultures and for a long period chose to merely tolerate their existence on Turkish soil. Only now have they slowly begun to recognise their influence upon the culture of the country. No one bothers to assert that the great Apollo, the merry Dionysos, the lovely Artemis–the later version of the Anatolian Kibele–are all gods and goddesses of Anatolian origin. We prefer to ignore the fact that before Olympus, deities with different names like Enlil, Enki, Nanna, Sun, Innana and Dommuzi lived on the shores of the Tigris and the Euphrates, displaying the same whims and performing the same feats as their Greek successors.

Visiting Turkey means visiting the ruins of ancient cities such as Troy and Alacahöyük, getting to know the kingdoms of the Hatti, Hittites, Hurri-Mittani, Urartu, Phrygia, Lydia, Caria, Lycia, tarrying in the Hellenistic regions such as Ionia, Eolia, which later belonged to the Romans, the city of Konya, capital of the Seljuk kings, the sites of the Commagenes, not forgetting glorious Byzantium and its treasures and finally coming to the 600 year Empire of the Ottomans.

Through the ages, numerous illustrious citizens have left their marks at the crossroads of these many civilizations: Homer, citizen of Izmir and the great author of the Odyssey and the Iliad; Herodotus, the historian from Halicarnassos (Bodrum); Croesus, the king of Lydia and minter of the first coins; Midas, the Phrygian whose touch turned everything to gold; Mausoleus, satrap of Halicarnassos for whom one of the marvels of the ancient world–the first mausoleum–was built; St-Paul, citizen of Tarsus and St-Nicholas, the bishop of Myra who was later transformed into the famous Santa Claus or Father Christmas. Mystics rush to Israel, the Holy Land, to find a religious environment, forgetting Anatolia, a land filled with cities where religions met. How can one overlook Antioch, where the first church of St-Peter was built; Urfa, the ancient Edessa, land of Abraham and his family, refuge of Job and his misfortunes; the charming city of Iznik, close to Istanbul, once called Nicea, the cradle of the famous Nicean Creed, "I believe in God". Some will search for the path of St-Paul, the great traveller. God knows how he travelled all the trails of the country! Others may attempt to follow the road of the Crusades. What a past!

Head of a Moslem empire with a Sunni majority, the Ottoman Sultans, following their conquest of the sacred cities of Islam, were endowed with the title of Caliph and became spiritual leaders of the entire Moslem world. This title was retained until 1924, when it was abolished by the secular state of the Turkish Republic. This reform left the Moslems without a spiritual leader and many religious authorities of the Islamic world have never forgiven Atatürk for this bold reform.

The Alevis, a very interesting Shiite minority that is different from the Iranian Shiites, can also be found in Turkey. They are described as a sect that has adopted religious concepts from Shamanism, Manicheism and Nestorianism with a varnish of Islam. Through the centuries this minority contributed to safeguarding traditional Turkish culture while the elite, living in palaces, were slowly being absorbed into Arabic and Persian culture. Persecuted for a long period of time, they had to hide their real identity, but their survival bequests to the country a treasure of music and literature, saved mostly through the oral tradition. It was only in the last decades of the twentieth century that this minority was able to come out in the open and reveal its cultural identity. Some have unfortunately tried to provoke dissension between the Sunni and the Alevi groups in an effort to divide Turkey, but their efforts have been in vain.

The Ottoman Empire, a mosaic of many nations and various cultures, always showed tolerance towards the practice of other religions. The Greek and Armenian minorities lived without knowing persecution, and even today the Patriarch, the head of the Orthodox Greek Church, is still found in Istanbul. This tolerance and close contact with various religions has influenced the approach to the practice of Islam in Turkey. Believers practice their religion discreetly without any fanaticism. To realize this, all you have to do is observe the amount of alcohol drunk in the country and the large majority of unveiled women in the streets. As a matter of fact, some women are lobbying and protesting the fact that they are not allowed to go about veiled! The code on how to dress, accepted in 1925, stipulates that when women enter a government building, be it a school or university, a hospital, the parliament, a court or the official residence of the President of the Republic, their heads must be uncovered.

At the time of the Spanish Inquisition, the Ottoman Empire was the only state to welcome the persecuted Jews, to accept them and to offer them the possibility of a new life. That praiseworthy attitude was strongly emphasised in 1999 during the celebrations in Istanbul commemorating the 500th anniversary of this exodus. While many history books still like to identify the Turks as the barbarian descendants of Atilla the Hun, one should not forget that it was the young Turkish Republic which also welcomed numerous Jewish professors from Europe as they fled from Nazi persecutions. Those scholars enabled many of the schools of Istanbul University to attain their high reputations. One can only wonder what grounds are used to determine the criteria allowing you to label the inhabitants of a nation as barbarians.

In this land filled with the imprints of many cultures, wide intellectual horizons allowed great thinkers to flourish and enrich world literature. The great mystic, Celalettin Rumi (1207-1273), better known as Mevlana, was considered a symbol of tolerance despite the problems encountered in Anatolia during the era in which he lived. The great poet Yunus Emre (1240-1320) also produced an exceptionally tolerant body of work filled with love towards all human beings, whatever their religion. A great humanist, he did not write in Arabic or Persian, as would the elite of that era, but rather in the vernacular of the people, the Turkish language.

It was on the ruins of a divided and Allied occupied empire that the Turkish Republic was founded in 1923 by the great Mustafa Kemal Atatürk. This military personality and remarkable statesman became the soul of the War of Liberation. Later, he also became the initiator of several reforms; he introduced a new civil code that included the enfranchisement of women and the garment code forbidding the veil at public functions and in schools. During four long years, 1919-1923, in a country in which there remained but tiny cells of the former army, he succeeded in inspiring the common people to bear the sacrifices of war, while he conducted successful military campaigns against the French and the Italians as well as the English and their associates, the Greeks. It was a dramatic struggle between life and death. The country survived and is now bordered by Greece, the Aegean Sea and Bulgaria to the west, the Black Sea to the north, Iran, Iraq and Syria to the east and southeast and the Mediterranean to the south.

After centuries of the Ottoman occupation of Greece, the occupation of the Aegean coast by the Greek army upon the instigation of England became a source of political animosity and turmoil between the two countries. At the close of World War I, the Greek army invaded more than half of Turkey but, following tragic battles, was pushed back at Izmir. In the beginning, despite the excellent relations that existed between Venizélos and Atatürk, the situation deteriorated progressively with increasing antagonism felt on the part of both sides until the severe earthquakes that hit both countries in 1999. Following these catastrophes, mutual assistance emphasised the wishes of both countries, which have so much in common, to pursue their way not as adversaries, but rather as allies. The Greeks no longer oppose Turkey's efforts to enter the European Community.

This political hostility between the Greeks and the Turks reminds me of an experience I had in Montreal in 1980. I was there on a research trip at the University of Montreal. The head of the department, Dr Marc Cantin, a serious researcher and a charming colleague, was kind enough to hold a dinner in my honour at the end of my stay. A few members of the staff, those I had worked with, were invited with their partners. One of those partners was of Greek origin and held an observer post at the United Nations. The evening was progressing in a delightful way when this gentleman asked me if I were conscious of the persecution of Greek citizens in Turkey. I almost choked on my food when I heard those words, for Turkey was then in chaos after many years of anarchy. During this period at least twenty-five people were being assassinated daily. Bombs exploded in the universities where students of rival factions confronted each other with violence. The general population was in despair and feared that peace would never be re-established. All this had abruptly ceased with the sudden military coup on 12 September that year. Persecuting the Greek minority was most likely the last thing on the minds of the Turkish authorities! The country was simply trying to survive these painful events. Despite my explanations, my interlocutor, who had never visited Turkey, held such strong convictions on the accuracy of his words that nothing I said could possible persuade him otherwise. The daily death toll of twenty-five Turks did not seem to bother him in the least.

I have no training that allows me to understand the art of politics and its multiple hues, therefore these questions are beyond the scope of this book. I would simply like to relate certain facts that I feel are important. Turkey, the State, arose from the ruins of the Ottoman Empire, an ally of Germany during the World War I. When a peace agreement was finally signed, the Allies did not foresee that a strong and independent Republic would emerge from the ashes of this dying empire. The sudden apparition of a nation capable of becoming powerful in the Middle East worried the great nations of Europe and various tactics to create disturbances were applied at one point in the 1970s, but in vain: the dismemberment of Turkey never occurred.

In the 1970s, the Armenian question acquired unprecedented momentum and many Turkish diplomats and innocent bystanders were assassinated or wounded by international Armenian terrorist groups. The killings ceased abruptly and the cause disappeared in the same fashion it had appeared, no one knowing how and where it went. But then another problem rapidly succeeded it–the Kurdish question. I wish here to relate a few interesting facts and then leave to the readers the task of drawing their own conclusions. In addition to Ismet Inonü, the right hand of Atatürk and his most devoted collaborator, during the last fifteen years alone Turkey has elected of Kurdish descent a President of the Republic, several leaders of the National Assembly, a Minister of Foreign Affairs and a large number of Parliament Members. The poor economic state of the eastern part of the country is a general one not limited to the Kurdish villages. Primary education is barely accessible to children in the Turkish language. How can we even pretend to establish a Kurdish system of education or say that it is refused to the Kurds? France, our most severe critic on this matter, defends with great ardour the rights of various ethnic groups, but seems to forget that she has never established, in any of her former colonies, an education system in any other language but French. Economically, it is true that the Republic almost deliberately neglected the eastern provinces, failing to promote investment in those regions while encouraging it in those more privileged parts of the country. Such a great contrast between regions can only bring agitation and division. Those who sow dissension do not have a more generous soul towards the minority they dream of exploiting one day. Many of the countries that are our neighbours are current victims of the policies of division favoured by certain great powers.

The greatest problem of the country is the education system. The government has only recently adopted measures to extend compulsory schooling to eight years. This law, unfortunately, remains to be applied in many of the more remote regions of eastern and southeastern Turkey where girls, according to tradition, are generally not sent to school at all. Very often, many of these girls do not have official birth certificates because the marriages of their parents are not in conformance with the laws of the country. According to statistics, eighty-five per cent of the total population knows how to read and write, while in the group over twenty-five years old, the percentage is seventy. Thirty percent of women are illiterate. Although we cannot consider Turkey to be an illiterate country, we must understand that the mean level of schooling for the whole population is three years of primary school. This is an insufficient level of education to establish and maintain a real democracy, to elect conscientious Members of Parliament who will work for the benefit of the country rather than their own profit. Far from fulfilling these aspirations, the current system instead faces serious problems of corruption and has exhibited a dubious performance in the arena of human rights.

Fortunately, there are always exceptional people, leaders who work with tenacity on the path carved by Atatürk to maintain the country at the level it deserves. Had the mobilization movement for education, developed during the forties with the Village Institutes and not been wilfully disrupted, many more areas of the country would today be in much better condition. The architects of this exceptional movement worked miracles at that time and the seventeen institutes founded and constructed by the students themselves, with their meagre means, trained teachers who carried the torch of education to Anatolia. However, the success of these institutes in such a short period caused an almost immediate violent reaction at the legislative level. The Members of Parliament became aware of the fact that an educated population was a menace to their privileged life and could bring an end to their feudal reign. The closing of these institutes dealt a fatal blow to the education movement throughout the country and caused it to lose much of its momentum from that point on. A very high birth rate brought a second crisis to the field of education, because there were not enough schools to accommodate the growing population. In the seventies, the schools were organized in such a manner as to handle two groups of students every day: one group in the morning, a second in the afternoon. This method is still applied. This difficult situation has, however, led to an alternative, very expensive but reassuring private sector for parents who prefer knowing their children are in school all day, and not in the street half of the day! A third problem arose in the nineties as the schools of the eastern part of the country were paralysed when Kurdish guerrillas began targeting teachers whom they massacred without mercy. The government could no longer authorize personnel to be sent to these regions, which had already been suffering from backwardness at every level as it were.

The Turkish Republic, despite great efforts, has also not succeeded in establishing a health system from which all its citizens can benefit. Only civil servants and some, not all, employees in the private sector are covered by a retirement and health insurance program. The self-employed sector is covered by an optional but mediocre program that offers little protection. Such arrangements leave a large portion of the population, some forty percent, including most of the people of the rural area in Anatolia and the unskilled workers, without any protection. A large section of the population lives on the threshold of poverty without any social protection while a large part of the manual labour force is unemployed.

A deep wound in the Turkish economic system is brought about by the coexistence of two parallel economies of which only one is official. This peculiarity leads to an important loss of revenues for the state in income and other taxes. The last few decades have witnessed a series of devaluations of the Turkish lira together with a high inflation rate, for many years a mean rate of over sixty-five percent. The loss in value of the Turkish lira can be best understood by a simple example: on my arrival in Turkey the US dollar was worth nine Turkish liras (TL); it is now worth about 1,500,000TL. During an economic crisis two years ago, the value of the dollar jumped from 600,000TL to 1,280,000TL within a few days. Any Turkish citizen who has a few extra liras will immediately change them into dollars or Euros. The price of rent, paintings, imported furniture and many others is all expressed in dollars, a strange system to say the least. Up to twenty years ago, the possession of foreign currency was strictly forbidden. At that time finding such currency for the few trips I took abroad was difficult and limited to a ridiculous amount. These are examples of just how shattering the recent changes brought about by our adherence to the liberal economical system have been!

Turkey is a country of contrasts. Amongst these strong opposites, a trained eye can perceive a deep economic problem, acknowledge social unrest and observe rich cultural diversity. On a simple cruise along the Bosphorus, you can see sumptuous residences filled with valuable hand woven rugs, tile work, precious porcelains, copper work, furniture inlaid with mother of pearl, decorated ceilings, exotic woodwork and

Ottoman objects saved from one generation to the other standing side by side with the miserable one room dwellings built overnight and in which a whole family tries to fit in with nothing else but poverty to account for. Suddenly, you will see a beautiful looking girl, dressed to kill in the latest fashion emerge from this home unworthy of the word, making you wonder if what you are seeing is real or not.

In the traffic of Istanbul where Mercedes, Grand Cherokees, over-crowded city buses and acrobatic mini-buses come and go you may be puzzled at the sight of shabby-looking gypsies in a horse-drawn carriage making their rounds of the garbage cans. This is Turkish style recycling at its best. As you stroll through the city you will be astonished by the elegant ladies dressed in the latest Paris and New York fashions, side by side with women covered from head to toe in the black of Islam. You will be even more surprised by the modern Moslem women in long colourful skirts almost touching the ground, their heads draped in over-sized designer scarves. Your head filled with these images, you may then see a village woman, beautiful in her simplicity and so far from political conventions in the way she dresses. How can you not wonder if the abyss that separates these women from each other will ever disappear? Who dares to think they can understand this country at first sight?

The abundance of fruit and vegetables in the open-air markets is astonishing. The huge variety of flowers sold on every street corner will enchant you, while their cheap price explains their presence in most homes. Comfortably seated in a restaurant at the seaside, enjoying some of those excellent mezes you most likely knew before with an Armenian or Greek nametag, but which in reality are part of the excellent Turkish cuisine, you may notice a few meters from you a man on the street eating his bread and fish and drinking his tea, the national drink found everywhere in the country. In his own way, he is also enjoying the scenery. Despite their often very limited means, the Turks know how to enjoy life and its good moments.

The opulence and abundance found in the large cities can easily mis-lead you to think that this situation is representative of the overall state of the country. The destitution, poverty and desolation of many Anatolian villages, especially in the east, will shock you to a point where you may ask yourself: During the seventy-eight years of its existence, has the Turkish Republic ever set foot in the surroundings of these iso-lated places? The style of life and its rhythm, the rapid pace characteris-tic to Istanbul have nothing in common with the slowness and the non-chalance of the people in Anatolia. To them, time has no monetary value, and hospitality is a way of life.

The important role played by the Turkish Armed Forces in the safe-keeping of the country's democracy is a peculiarity often misinterpret-ed, for the two concepts, military and democracy, seem opposed to each other. Remembering the numerous revolutionary junta takeovers in Latin America, it is normal to automatically associate all military coups with such previous models, without knowing the history or under-standing the origin and the value of these symbols in certain countries. In the Occidental world, the separation of civil and military institutions is a rule. In contrast to the societies of the Western world that have developed along a horizontal functional line with socio-economic class-es sharing common identities, Ottoman society grew on a vertical line. It was built into a hierarchy and included the elite and the periphery. The civil and military bureaucracy played an intermediary role between the two classes. The new Turkish Republic also assumed the same struc-ture. In the event that the elite weakened, the gap between the classes could potentially threaten the stability of the Republic, and this is where the military intervenes. This intermediate role of the military continues in the Republic and concedes a primary function to the Armed Forces to not only defend the Republic, but also to be the guardian of the secular state and of the principles of Atatürk.*

The modern Turkish Armed Forces were established by Atatürk and supported and assisted by the elite officers of the Ottoman Army. With the help of this military institution, Atatürk established the basis of the Turkish Republic and then entrusted to the army the duty of defending the Republic and safeguarding its principles. From the ashes of an empire, almost without any financial means, but inspired by a firm determination and a great ideal, this great commander and his staff of officers succeeded in creating an army which, in desperate conditions, succeeded in saving the country from what seemed to be imminent dis-

---

* Nilüfer Narlı, *Turkish Studies*, Vol 1 (Sping 2000), page 107-127.

memberment. He mobilized the people, also impoverished, to share what little they possessed with the soldiers. The women, to ensure supplies to the army, transported the necessary ammunition hidden in straw in their carts over long, almost impassable roads. During the course of this drawn-out and painful struggle for survival, a great degree of confidence grew between the army and the people and, through the years, the course of events has proven that the military establishment is worthy of this confidence. Today, research shows that the army still enjoys the confidence of the great majority of the population.

The Turkish army is most likely the best functioning institution in the country. Its high level of excellence, its fidelity and attachment to the principles of Atatürk, its important role held in the formation of young men who often arrive to do their military service almost illiterate and its coherent behaviour through the years are all elements contributing to its reputation and explain why it is the source of such confidence. On three occasions, in 1960, at the beginning of the 1970s and in 1980, the army had to intervene in order to redirect the politicians back onto the road to democracy. In 1960, Adnan Menderes, democratically elected, but slowly sliding towards the road to dictatorship, was the cause of the first military coup. Some ten years later, on 12 March 1971, the army had to exert its pressure and give an ultimatum to the government which was at the time distancing itself from the principles of the Republic and driving the country towards chaos. In September of 1980, at a time when the country was daily witnessing bloody battles between certain rightist and leftist factions, a second military takeover became necessary to rescue democracy. Obviously, in a country where the civilians are unable to govern, the army, for whom governing is not a profession, might show some clumsiness and make some mistakes; however, in the case of Turkey, the army has ultimately succeeded in establishing peace and order in the country and in preparing a return to democracy. Still today, it continues to maintain its role as guardian of the secular state, a role that we all highly appreciate during this period when many of our neighbours are battling retrograde Islamic fundamentalism.

If you come from a country that is in a state of perfect bliss because the political system is well-established and there is absolutely no possible threat against the existing democratic system, it is certainly most difficult to understand a country like Turkey and even less possible to understand the role of its army.

Turkey is currently faced with a serious identity crisis. The country is trapped between the legitimate desire of a large part of the population wishing to join the Occidental world, to follow the developments of a secular contemporary society according to the teachings of Atatürk on the one side and the strong desire of a minority wishing to entrench itself in the past, opting for the rules of life closely related to Islam, on the other. I cannot really believe that these women wrapped in their lovely Dior scarves really wish for a regime where they, according to strict principles of the shari'a (Islamic law), one day might be stoned for adultery. History books are filled with examples of countries where religion wanted to rule the state but never achieved the results they had dreamed of. Is it necessary to rediscover these facts over and over again?

I love Turkey, its sun, its natural beauties, its long history and its miseries. In the beginning, however, it was a challenge I had to face. I spent a lot of energy unraveling this heterogeneous mosaic of cultures and civilisations, striving to visit its numerous and varied regions until I finally came to appreciate the country so much that I realized I sincerely loved it. It is not a country easily accessible, nor does it yield its secrets freely. One should persevere and investigate. One day you will solve what you thought were enigmas and begin to understand the country. The results are extremely enriching. Turkey has taught me different values and ways of thinking and reasoning quite different from those of my native country and it has also helped me to develop the virtue of tolerance. Thanks to this country, I have discovered the joys of archaeology, the pleasures of the sea and the world of underwater diving. I still suffer from the country's general lack of organisation at all levels, a gap contributing to keep it in what seems like a perpetual state of chaos. I cannot help but have a broken heart observing and enduring the everlasting political apathy that never seems to improve.

My life through the years has helped me to appreciate many values we often take for granted in other countries, values such as: the respect we have for human rights and for individuals in general, the well-functioning social security system, the order and the strong democracy found in our political system. To be a citizen of two countries is a great advantage if one succeeds in achieving the synthesis of these two cultures and applying it to everyday life. The most important lesson is to learn to love and respect others.

But, back to my story: The first weeks following our arrival went by peacefully in the carefree summer life of Istanbul. A pleasant life mostly made up of boat excursions on the Marmara Sea or to the Prince's Islands, or of swimming on the shores of the Bosphorus or the Marmara Sea. The whole family flocked to see Rahmi, the one and only grandson. Friends, meals and evenings at the open-air cinema were the main events of that uncomplicated life. Unfortunately, that life could not last much longer and economic needs rapidly brought us back to reality.

For many years, our objective had been to return to and establish ourselves in Turkey. Up until then, we had concentrated all of our energy on that very concrete aim. However, once we had arrived, we had to establish a new order and launch elaborate new projects and life began to look like a complex algebra problem with many unknowns. For example, where would we live? What were the chances that Mehmet and I would find jobs? If I worked, who would take care of Rahmi? What would we do during Mehmet's military service?

We lived with my in-laws for the first eight months, in that famous house not at all suitable to accommodate us. There are no separate rooms in the house and we found ourselves sleeping on the first floor where the living room and the dining room were located. With people circulating constantly, we were virtually "living in public". Almost immediately, I realised that cooking the Turkish way is a real science and that preparing Mehmet's favourite dishes here would require some knowledge and skill! The long and frustrating period of living "without this and without that" had begun.

Rahmi, until then a child with a normal appetite, stopped eating and only agreed to drink "Tang". Where could you find Tang? That brand was not available then and has only appeared on the market recently, some thirty years later! Rahmi rejected milk after we left Holland because obviously the taste did not suit him. I couldn't blame him too much, because milk in Turkey at that time was neither homogenised nor pasteurised. Since it had to be boiled, the texture and the taste were modified, which made it not very pleasant to drink. Not understanding any Turkish at all, Rahmi and I no longer took part in any conversations. Rahmi, who had barely begun to speak the last few weeks we were in the United States, entered a second period of silence. We had always spoken French to him, but he had begun using a few English words with the neighbourhood children in New Jersey. Now he was probably wondering exactly what it was we actually wanted from him in Istanbul. I was unable to cook a decent meal, and even the local steaks seemed united against me, as if they had come from an anatomically different animal than the ones in North America.

During that period, I also had the strange and unpleasant sensation of suffering from overall clumsiness and total incapacity. Every action required an adjustment, gave rise to comments or raised a problem. The capable, independent and intelligent woman I had been found herself transformed into a strange specimen unable to function without her husband's help. The daily electricity cuts and the water shortages we suffered several hours each day made me wonder if I were slowly spiralling towards a state nothing short of madness. Making any kind of decision, solving any kind of problem inevitably brought me face to face with yet more constraints. Without realizing it, I found myself slowly being engulfed in the quicksand of a strange foreign culture. A night out with my husband provoked a sharp remark because we came back home a bit late. Was that any of their business? Such was my reaction, but I had to suffer it in silence!

One of our first tasks was to clear out of customs the things that we had shipped from New Jersey, personal effects and electrical appliances. With all the required papers in hand, Mehmet went to the pier where our shipment had arrived. Accompanied by a customs agent, the formality progressed until the final "expensive" signature! The idea of having to pay a bribe to get my own effects out of customs revolted and shocked me deeply. What an insult! Yes, it was an insult but without "the" signature, it appeared we would not see our things very soon. Bitter and deceived, we had to follow the requirements of the corrupted system. With a feeling of disgust, I witnessed our hard-earned dollars being neatly disposed of in an envelope and given to the official. To my horror, I learned that the officer in question was a woman! That was to be my first lesson in bureaucracy: when dealing with the public services, one not only learns the art of preparing "envelopes", but especially the art of distributing them with dexterity. I have made great efforts through the years so that I would never have to practice such an unpleasant task and I must admit that I have not had to submit myself to this procedure very often. As soon as the bribe was paid, our belongings came out of the warehouse at an unbelievable speed.

We had reached the stage where Mehmet's military service had become a pressing and vital matter. In this country, so I learned, life is divided into two main periods: before and after your military service. Once your studies are completed, it is no longer possible to avoid this duty, but everyone nevertheless does their utmost to bypass it. Since the army calls you when they need you rather than you going when you are ready, we had to live with the uncertainty of not knowing when Mehmet would be called for duty. While waiting we were faced with the question of finding work, which was also a problem since no one wants to hire anyone who has not yet done his military service.

Thus I learned a very Turkish thing: the syndrome of military service. This is a very normal reaction since one cannot travel abroad or find a job without having crossed that barrier. During the sixties, the military service was a period of three years for the regular soldiers and two years for the officers, a category that included university graduates. Such a long period was mostly perceived as a loss of precious time while trying to establish a career or as an obstacle to marriage. This often leads men to have neither the means, the time nor the occasion to marry before reaching the age of thirty. For Turks living abroad, military service is a duty to get out of the way as soon as possible. To all, it is a task that cannot be bypassed, but is often deferred and postponed up till the last possible moment. Many men have spoiled their lives trying to avoid it.

Several years later, while working on the archives of my father-in-law and reading the letters he wrote during this period of his life, I realised that he, too, had faced this problem of military service when he returned from Paris in 1934 and had tried to postpone the duty until later. This problem has haunted the Turks for a long time and will continue to haunt them for a long time to come. Many solutions have been attempted through the years, among which are allowing military candidates to purchase costly exemptions, or allowing university graduates to complete their service in four months as regular soldiers. Such solutions are often suggested when the waiting list is very long. Currently military service for university graduates is twelve months for officers with a six-month option as a regular soldier; this is true as long as you don't have a profession that the army has great need of. Those without university degrees must complete fifteen months as regular soldiers.

Next, we had to face the question of what I could or should do myself. Luckily, since our marriage had finally been registered, I had been given Turkish citizenship, so I could work and reside in the country without any problems. This is a stage in the life of many foreigners in which men and women who are married to Turkish nationals find themselves faced with the many restrictions of Turkish laws. Generally, the Turkish consulates abroad are not very helpful in informing you about these problems. They choose rather to answer only the questions asked, and usually no one asks such specific questions because no one suspects the existence of such problems. One is usually ill-prepared for intercontinental love affairs and we take it for granted that all laws must more or less function in the same coherent way all over the world. Besides, it is a known fact that love is blind and paralyses its victims to a point where they cannot think. Who could help us and where could we find answers to our questions? Again, luck was on my side, this time in the person of a close friend of my in-laws, a lawyer at the New York Turkish Consulate, Miss Nedret Uzunbekir. She prepared my documents with such care and competence that I was completely freed from all these problems.

All women marrying Turkish nationals before 1964 were automatically endowed with Turkish citizenship, without exception. In 1964, this law was modified and only those accepting Turkish nationality became Turkish citizens. In instances where the ceremony was held in Turkey, this consent was given during the ceremony. If the marriage took place outside Turkey, the request for citizenship and the registration of the marriage at the Turkish Consulate had to be done within

forty days of the ceremony. Those who did not fulfill these requirements and those whose own countries do not accept dual citizenship
had then to overcome the constant hurdles of the residence permit; the
foreigner in question would initially be granted one year and then, perhaps, in later years, a series of three year permits. This time period has
now been raised to five years, if–and only if–the non-citizen continues
to be married to a Turk. This residence permit does not automatically
give the spouse the right to work. Annual work permits, which are often
difficult to obtain, had to be applied for separately. Citizenship laws for
foreigners changed, however, in 2003. Turkish citizenship can no
longer be automatically obtained upon marriage. Now newlyweds must
be married for three years in order to be eligible to apply for Turkish
citizenship.

The right to automatic Turkish citizenship was never available to
foreign men who married Turkish women. This difficult situation has
been the source of so many problems that such couples often choose to
live abroad to ensure the survival of their marriage. Had I not obtained
Turkish nationality, I could not have financially survived in Turkey during Mehmet's military service!

But who would hire me in this country since I had absolutely no
knowledge of the Turkish language! I had to work, but I also knew that
my mother-in-law was not in a position to take care of my son on a permanent basis. All these questions had to be answered and, needless to
say, every problem appeared to give rise to a second!

Mehmet, actively working to be accepted by the military authorities,
learned what we already knew: having married a foreigner, he could not
be an officer, but would have to do his military service as a regular soldier and for a period of three years. That was the reason why we had
not registered our marriage in the first place, hoping for a modification
of the law by the Turkish authorities in the near future. However, with
the arrival of Rahmi, we had to consider a revision of our plans and had
both our marriage and child registered. We also were aware that without these procedures it would be impossible for me to practise my profession in Turkey. Certain advantages often counterbalance other dis-
advantages! Like many other couples in the same situation, we therefore had to face the possibility of a divorce, thus shortening Mehmet's

military service by allowing him to become an officer. The Turks are more accustomed than we are to similar types of acrobatics performed in the face of bureaucracy, but for us it was a painful and difficult procedure to accomplish, and for me it was most difficult to accept. All was conducted calmly and with the greatest discretion: in January 1967, our divorce was decreed. Needless to say, I did not even try to explain this to my mother! In March, Mehmet had to leave us to go register at the Polatlı Artillery Officer School near Ankara.

From September 1966 to February 1967 Mehmet had a part-time job in a firm specializing in market research. Since we had not returned from the States with anything resembling a small fortune, I also had to consider working. There was no point in reading the newspaper ads or in sending my resume to hospitals in the area. This was not the way to proceed in this country, especially if you were a woman! With Mehmet at my side, I visited a hospital on the Asian side of the city to meet the head of the biochemistry department and see if any work was available. Dr Kemal spoke French and his eyes expressed genuine surprise to see that a person of my "standing" was looking for work in such a place. He did not recommend my working in a state hospital where my profession did not even exist at that

The three of us in 1966

time... However, he had with two associates opened a private laboratory on the other side of the city where he invited us, adding that that establishment would accept a person with my qualifications and competence.

During our conversation, I discreetly observed the activities of the laboratory, the comings and goings, and I felt a bit disturbed by some of the practices I saw, practices that would have been judged unacceptable in any laboratory worthy of its name. That, however, was but the beginning of my surprises. Following a visit to the private laboratory in Şişli, on the European side, I decided to accept the position offered despite the fact that it was a bit far from where we lived. In October, I began to work in that laboratory with the half-English-half-Turkish name of "Check-up Sağlık Kontrol Laboratuvarı".

Living in Asia and working in Europe required good timing because, like thousands of residents of the city, I had to go to the boat landing every morning, take a ferryboat across the Bosphorus and then find a shared taxi to the part of the city where I worked. The one-way trip took over an hour. On my first day of going to work by myself, I learned many things. My great discovery was the shared taxi, the dolmuş, a car leaving only when all the seats are filled. These cars follow a predetermined route, which can be understood from the sign hung in the front window. Each passenger must indicate where he wants to get off. Mehmet had written out for me the shortest sentence I could use to have the car stop near the lab. Repeating this sentence along the whole course of my trip, I was proud of myself as I realized I could indeed function in Turkish. Recognising the corner where I should get off, I realised that the magic sentence had flown out of my mind. A few streets later, in despair, I screamed, "Stop"! It may not have been Turkish, but it worked... Living in Asia and working in Europe would be the daily routine of my life for the next twenty-five years. In time, the Bosphorus Bridge became an alternative to the ferryboat and enabled me to drive to work. I have tried all possible means to beat the heavy traffic of the city. Getting around in this city requires a lot of time, skill and patience and unfortunately the problem has only increased with the years. That proved to be the main reason why I retired from active work: two hours of travelling every morning and again every evening was just too much!

Rahmi had to be placed in a nursery school and he was just two and half years old the first day I had to leave him. I felt an extreme sadness I can still today recall with the same intensity despite the many years that have passed. Nobody can tell me if there is a more acceptable way to face this daily drama affecting all women trying to do their best in their double role of mother and career woman. Although we hide and bury these feelings deep inside, the wound always remains in our hearts. Nothing can dispel the feeling of guilt you feel seeing your child leave home early every morning while other children are still sleeping or playing at home... This feeling is accentuated at times when the child is ill. How many children in this world have been carried just like parcels, from home to nursery school, or from their home to the home of a grandmother? The feeling of guilt consumes you and at the smallest problem in school, you feel absolutely inadequate in your role of mother. Now that I have reached the age of retirement, I often ask myself what the ideal solution is that could prevent women from being torn apart–is there a solution?

Thus I began to work in the small "Check-up" laboratory. Despite its simple appearance, the laboratory material was of good quality and the personnel charming and careful. I felt a great emptiness around me because I couldn't understand most of the conversation or follow what was going on. I felt like a student attending an intensive course on all subjects touching upon life in a foreign country. It was a task of survival!

After a few weeks of work, my assistant, a young chemistry student originally from Maraş, a region in southeastern Turkey, invited me to a local restaurant so I could taste the spicy food of his region. The main dish, lahmacun, can be described as a local type of pizza. The next morning, I found myself suffering from a severe attack of diarrhoea, the first episode of a problem I would often have to deal with for the next two years until my body adjusted itself to the different types of oils and the great variety of food... Weakened and shaking like a leaf, I couldn't travel on my own and Mehmet had to come to fetch me by car so I could get home that day. A week later, having lost fifteen pounds, I was still not feeling well. In order to find a good doctor, my father-in-law, by then most frightened by my condition, sent an alert out to all his friends. A close friend of the family, the writer and translator Vedat Günyol, referred the problem to his brother-in-law, a specialist in gynaecology. That same evening, a specialist in internal medicine, speaking impeccable French, came to examine me. Despite my weakened condition, I found sufficient energy to ask him if I could find a job more suitable to my qualifications. As I described my profession and my preference for haematology, I could see his dark eyes open wide as he informed me that he also specialized in haematology. I had the feeling that I might be on the right track. Within a few days, I was feeling much better until, cured at last, I had completely regained my former strength. Mehmet and I next paid a visit to Dr Bülent Berkarda at the University of Istanbul, in the well-known clinic he worked in.

At that time I had no idea that a woman in Turkey could not work without the consent of her husband! That was why Mehmet accompanied me every time I went somewhere looking for a job. Of course, he also had to see if the place was suitable for his wife. Again, I was told what I already knew, that I could not find work at the university because there were no posts available for a professional with my qualifications. My profession was still unknown in Turkey. Doctor Berkarda suggested a very popular clinic in the private sector. It was in Laleli, a district in the old section of Istanbul, very close to the Grand Bazaar. The owner of the clinic had expressed a desire to meet me and discuss employment.

A few days later I visited the clinic and its laboratories, a very busy place with a large staff, made up mostly of people trained on the job. I found myself hired at once and given the title of "head of the laboratory chief". My first day of work coincided with Mehmet's departure for his military service. My Turkish vocabulary was extensive, approximately fifty words. That period was surely the most difficult time our little family went through: Mehmet had to readapt to the country and Rahmi and I had to live alone together for the next two years. We could not follow Mehmet, who was then a divorced man. Thank God he was able to come home almost every weekend during the three months of his training as a reserve officer, driving the old Volkswagen his father had given us. After those three months, he was commissioned to another unit for the next twenty-one months. Knowing two foreign lan-

guages, Mehmet took an exam to be selected as a translator. He had
hopes of obtaining a good post either in Ankara or Izmir. He was
accepted as a translator, but, from the four available positions, he was
assigned to the NATO base in Erzurum, a city situated in the eastern
part of Turkey near the Iranian border. We were devastated when we
got that news. Of course he would be in a comfortable place in that
cold province, but it was so far away that there would be no chance of
seeing each other except during his very few leaves. I seriously considered making a trip to the region to pay him a visit, but Mehmet was
opposed to my travelling alone by train. He claimed that we foreigners
are always very friendly and readily smile at everyone and that could easily be misinterpreted by the male travellers on the train. Mehmet told
me I might be kidnapped by someone who thought I was being friendly with him and it would be impossible to ever find any trace of me in
Anatolia(!). I found those explanations rather strange and concluded
that Mehmet must have been somewhat jealous. I listened and quietly
remained in Istanbul for the duration of our separation. How could we
possibly have been aware of the great dangers Mehmet was going to
face as the bachelor son of a well-known family, going to an isolated
part of the country where many high-ranking officers had their families
and lovely young daughters who were looking for a proper husband?
The news of his arrival rapidly spread and from the very beginning he
was asked to give foreign language lessons to those lovely maidens! As
time went by, circumstances required that he come to Istanbul to consult with his family. They suggested that we should get engaged, otherwise the situation would become unbearable. Mehmet returned to his
base with a ring on his finger, thereby losing all his students, but feeling much better himself, while I remained in Istanbul, worried to
death...

Chapter XIII

The Laleli Clinic

Mehmet left Istanbul for the Artillery Officer Training School in Polatlı on the same day I began to work as the head of the laboratory at the Laleli Clinic. With my very limited vocabulary, I was terrified by the idea of having to communicate with the fifteen members of the laboratory staff. How was I going to manage that? With quite a few years of experience behind me, nothing else bothered me because I knew my job so well.

The reason I have devoted a whole chapter to the Laleli Clinic is to stress the important role it played in my new life. It became a second home to Rahmi and me, alone in Istanbul at the time. It became a second school to me since it was where I learned Turkish and the art of getting along and living with the Turks. It was where I would be able to observe their behaviour, their customs and learn the dozens of small details that contributed to and helped me achieve my integration in the country.

The owner of the clinic was Dr Salih Osmanoğlu, a specialist in internal medicine, but first of all an excellent businessman with inexhaustible energy. His right hand at the clinic was Dr Kemal Atay, a white-haired Anatolian with a golden heart, a very pleasant radiologist whom I can best describe as the ideal father figure. In time, I learned to appreciate this man and enjoyed having tea in his company every late afternoon, despite the fact that I only understood about fifty percent of what he told me, mostly colourful stories about his experiences as a doctor, always accompanied by abundant demonstrative gestures.

My first days at work were quite hectic and filled with terrifying observations and experiences. Every step of the work done was a series of procedures unthinkable or impossible to imagine in our profession. From the first day on, I realized that one of the greatest problems of my career would be the problem of sterilisation, a topic that haunted me until the sudden appearance of AIDS, after which disposable injectors were imported and later manufactured. Everywhere I worked in Turkey, this very important procedure would be one of the main problems I would constantly have to deal with. In the sixties, due to the lack of autoclaves, injectors had to be sterilised using dry heat. How many times I witnessed the metal part of these injectors melt during the process, ruining the material and making it unusable. Such working conditions surely do not favour the teaching of sterilisation techniques! I often asked myself if the marketing firms were not buying rejects from somewhere or if the material were labelled "Good for the Middle East".

A second problem was that the sterilisation process was often entrusted to the hands of non-qualified personnel. I witnessed some rather surprising scenes. One day, I asked the helper in the nephrology department just how he did the sterilisation of his material. He answered that he would heat the oven until a smell developed! Astonished and perplexed, I tried to understand and then I realised that the paper used to wrap the material gave off a burning smell when it reached a certain temperature. To his mind, that was the time when the process was completed. Many were the times at conferences or courses when the nurses and mid-wives must have hated me because of my remarks and criticism of their famous sterilization method of "a few minutes of boiling in left-over water which was used again and again", a procedure long abandoned by medical centres with any sense of self-respect. In short, from A to Z, I had to observe, modify, rectify and teach again each and every method used in the laboratory. I found myself facing a Herculean task.

Once settled in my new surroundings, I was first of all surprised to observe the great confidence shown to me in matters of work. This boundless admiration towards a foreigner astounded me and was also a source of uneasiness for me with my Turkish counterparts. All of my comments and suggestions were taken very seriously. The behaviour or the methods I criticized were modified with great earnestness, while identical comments made by my Turkish co-workers did not seem to have the same impact. Dr Osmanoğlu was very careful of all I said and fulfilled all my wishes and material requirements. I never quite understood why he had not earlier supplied his own laboratory with the required material his storeroom was filled with. In any case, nothing was refused me. The devoted staff worked the best that they could, if you take into account their lack of training. They accomplished marvels under extremely difficult conditions. They were a marvellous team of workers, eager to learn, with a genuine desire to improve themselves and a great curiosity towards new techniques. They worked with utmost enthusiasm and were always careful with their new material. The kindness, the understanding and the devotion they expressed towards me were more than touching. Very rapidly, I felt as if I had a new family and was working in an ideal atmosphere.

From the very first hour of my job, we were faced with a severe communication problem due to my–then–very poor knowledge of the Turkish language and their total lack of knowledge of any foreign languages. No one in that establishment, not even the doctors, knew a word of French or English. Only the weekly visit and consultation of Dr Berkarda reminded me of the existence of such languages! One may wonder why the director of a clinic would have the brilliant idea of hiring someone like me, or what great idea pushed me to accept such a post! Most likely, the lack of qualified personnel justified the choice of Dr Osmanoğlu at that time. Despite the difficulties, we managed to communicate and succeeded in modifying the state of the laboratory. Most of the time, I made myself understood by giving an example and doing the required technique myself. The first months, I was more a laboratory technician and a teacher than a laboratory head. In a short time, and with the good will of everyone involved, the laboratory was transformed into a first-class establishment coping with a heavy workload and everyone hurrying and working to the best of his or her capacities. We managed to have an hour of teaching every day and once a week we held discussions with a consulting biochemist, haematologist and bacteriologist on the choice of techniques to be used and on their difficulties. The general atmosphere was very dynamic and everyone had the feeling of participating actively in the work and was aware of his or her contribution to the proper functioning of the establishment.

Profits increased; the staff received a bonus, and the atmosphere was excellent. My statistics on the workload pleasantly surprised the clinic director for the curves were rising in terms of performance and we were raking in record profits.

During this period, I am sure I must have given everyone around me, including my boss, a solid dose of what was to them undoubtedly a shocking performance, without even realising my social faux-pas. We had a few heated discussions because I considered the doctor was poking his nose into many matters that were not really his business. I was still very much Hughette, the Westerner, who had not yet really learned the art of tact. However, I made a great effort to be more diplomatic and less abrupt towards the man who, after all, was my boss. The Turks were not yet and–to a certain extent–are still not totally imbued with the democratic concept of equality between human beings, especially between men and women. I highly respected Dr Osmanoğlu and he tolerated and most likely endured my very colourful ways of addressing him in my very primitive Turkish. Whether in a state of immersion or submersion, this language is not easily learned. Turkish is a difficult language with a completely different sentence structure. Many foreigners never quite manage to master this tongue even after many years of life and practice in the country.

The clinic director was also a born philanthropist and with his deeply generous heart acted as a father to his personnel. How very many young students he helped by providing them with a place to live, food and some pocket money in return for a few hours of work in his clinic! Conscious of the huge improvement shown by the personnel, we organized a monthly social evening at the clinic. That was a rare event in a country where the social life of young girls was, and to a certain extent still is, quite restricted. Those evenings usually included an evening meal followed by an entertainment program we usually prepared ourselves. I had to make a great effort and work hard to memorize the words of the popular songs we would sing all together. Once, we managed to get the great minstrel Aşık Veysel to come for such an evening. It was quite an unforgettable event. Some thirty years later, Dr Osmanoğlu tried to revive the Laleli evenings in the new hospital he now heads.

I wish to spare the readers who are not members of the medical profession the very specific details of my job. It is undeniable that during my first days of work, I had one shock after another and the surprises I faced were major. Many difficulties especially arose when patients wanted to explain their particular case to me. Many did without even noticing that I did not understand a single word of what they were saying. Happily, the staff was extraordinary and they usually managed to rescue me from these delicate situations, where all I could do was keep smiling sweetly. You cannot imagine how difficult and frustrating it was to stand like a statue, without understanding anything or, once I began to understand, not being able to give an intelligent reply, or if and when I dared to answer, most likely sounding like a small child.

A second very big problem in a laboratory was the proper identification of urine and blood specimens. What battles we had to fight to solve this problem! Blood would arrive at the laboratory already clotted in injectors or in non-identified tubes carried by a helper who could not read or write. How could you trust such a specimen and who could you rely on? At that time, an adequate labelling system was not in existence since glass-marking pens were not yet on the market. In later years when I went to Canada, those were the objects I was to fill my suitcases with on my way back to Turkey.

My salary was 1,500 Turkish liras per month. This allowed me to pay the rent, the expenses of my car and Rahmi's daycare fees. I had decided to rent an apartment on the European side of the city because I was seeing so little of Rahmi due to my long working hours and commuting time, not to mention that living with my in-laws on the Asian side limited my free time drastically. My new apartment was comfortable and well heated. The flat was situated in a very Turkish area of the city and soon everyone in the building learned who I was and that my husband was doing his military service. Everyone was helpful and protective toward us, a very touching aspect of Turkish behaviour in general. Unfortunately, I proved myself several times to be a bad neighbour because I forgot to turn off the faucets when the water was off

Halloween in Istanbul with the laboratory workers of the Laleli Clinic

during the day. That caused serious floods when, during my absence, the water came back on. One should have seen the joy when they saw me coming back from work! In time, Rahmi and I learned to check the faucets before leaving the house.

My first experience as a hostess might have been catastrophic had it not been for the kind help of Dr Osmanoğlu, who so graciously saved the evening. On Halloween, I decided to organize for the laboratory personnel a party to which, needless to say, everyone had to wear a costume. Among the many new innovations that would come to my mind through the years, this brilliant idea taught me a lot about the art of entertaining in this country. Since my tableware was limited, I could only invite a restricted number of guests. That was my first mistake, since Turks, without telling you, will often show up accompanied by a sister or a visiting friend. We were twenty-six instead of the planned fifteen. Most of the guests, in a variety of costumes, arrived in the clinic ambulance with the driver dressed as an American Indian, feathers and all. Imagine the reaction of the neighbours as they saw the ambulance stopping in front of the house and the Indian getting out! The evening progressed more or less successfully, but everyone looked a bit tired. My father-in-law, who was present for the event, finally asked me if there was any food because everyone was starving as they had come without eating. I had planned to serve a snack at the end of the evening, like in Canada. The second lesson to be learned: in Turkey, everything begins with food; the fun only starts once the food has been served. I rapidly set the table, while my boss sent the Indian and the ambulance to fetch more knives, forks, plates and glasses. Once fed, the guests began to enjoy themeselves. It was a most unlikely party that progressed into an unforgettable evening.

Several of the people trained in our laboratory became first-class technicians and continued their careers with great success. Selva and Emine, two lovely girls who bloomed into excellent workers, are still working with Dr Osmanoğlu in his new Osmanoğlu hospital. Mr Ünal, a quiet and brilliant young man, was to become and remain for several years the pillar of the Laleli laboratory along with his wife, Gülderen. A young part-time biochemist of Italian origin named Gabriella was to become one of my best friends and we wound up working together later at the university while she was doing her degree in pharmacology. Her Levantine family had been established in Turkey many years before, during the Ottoman period when they enjoyed certain commercial privileges in accordance with the capitulations[*].

Following a year of full-time work, Dr Berkarda finally found me a position at Istanbul University. I decided to accept the position while continuing part-time at the Laleli Clinic. My boss was furious and could not understand how I could possibly prefer the university. Nevertheless, I left the clinic to begin a new career at the university.

---

[*] Capitulations: dating from the sixteenth century, these priviledges gained a new status in 1839 and then in 1856. They were abolished in 1923 when the New Republic was founded.

preoccupation they have for the welfare of others. Conversations never begin without the classical elaborate formulas aimed at gaining insight on the well being of the interlocutor and his next of kin. Special expressions exist to express good wishes and they are adjusted to different events of life: disease, separation of the members of the family for any reason, trips, military service, etc. Various expressions exist to express best wishes when one buys a new car, a new apartment or begins a new job. One must show great prowess in the conversation to relay the correct interest and use the correct formula. After such an inquiry you can finally get on with talking about whatever you originally intended to discuss. It may give you the impression of living in a series of clichés and you cannot but wonder whether the people really and sincerely feel so interested in you or your family. But after a certain time, it grows on you and you will take notice at once if anyone fails to use one of those refined expressions!

Turks are very curious and love to ask a lot of questions, and consider it normal to do so, even at the first meeting! They are also very helpful, ready to stop whatever they are doing to help you find your way, find the store or the address you are looking for. They are more than eager to help you if you are moving or to cook food if you are ill. Time is of little value to them and they do not hesitate for one moment to leave what they are doing to look after you or to help you solve your problems.

Men are generally very polite to women but, unfortunately, seem to have a fondness for foreign women whom they consider easy to seduce. This is because the usual reaction of foreign women is to treat Turkish men as they would treat men in their own country, using our own cultural signals. Without realising it, many of us are unaware that, by simply politely smiling at these men, we unfortunately encourage their advances. Your most innocent smile will only encourage these daring males who immediately imagine you are responding to their irresistible charms. Just observe the impassive expressions on the faces of the Turkish women you see on the street to understand the mistake of your own more open demeanour. If you wish to avoid this type of harassment, you must learn to go about with a serious expression. Our cultural mishaps often lead us to suffer from sexual harassment.

The members of this society, interestingly enough, abhor male misbehaviour of this kind and when it is brought out into the open, can respond with very harsh repressive measures. Why, then, do males behave in such a way with us, while they would not hesitate for a moment to beat to death anyone who would behave in such a manner towards their sisters or wives? Before giving ear to the question, I recommend to everyone that they take advantage of this strong reaction in order to bring such acts to an end by being loudly vocal in the effort to to dispel such unwanted behaviour!

As for the origins of the matter, they should most likely be sought in the strict restrictions governing the relationships between the two sexes in traditional Turkish society. Young couples can hardly ever be on their own before getting engaged and, even then, they are always under the strict surveillance of the girl's family.

A second, very characteristic feature of the Turks is their generosity. Without any hesitation, they can share all their possessions with others even if they possess very little. A Turk will never eat in front of you without offering you part of his food. If, when visiting an Anatolian village, you show admiration for an object, it will be offered to you on the spot. When a friend is in need, there are no limits to the profuse help offered to him. Without any hesitation, they will lend their cars or even large amounts of money. They will never abandon a friend in need, even when they are themselves in a precarious situation.

Hospitality is a deeply embedded concept and a Turkish hostess will do everything to make her guests happy. The more you respect and regard a person, the more you do your best to please them when they are in your home. A great variety of food is prepared, requiring a lot of time and competence, and of course tea, coffee, chocolate, nuts, a variety of fruit and then desserts are also offered. All these will be served to you continuously until you almost feel uncomfortable! When I first entertained guests in my home in Turkey, I had the feeling I had spent days and days cooking continuously in an endless effort to prepare the required amount of things to offer my guests. As the guests were departing, I heard my husband apologise for our having prepared so little food. I thought I would faint. What an inconsiderate remark! It took quite some time for Mehmet to explain to me and convince me that those words were the usual expression used in such circumstances!

One of the most remarkable qualities of women in this country is the unflagging smile they can show their guests on every occasion, even if the guests arrive without notice at unseemly hours. This national habit of making impromptu visits is probably, for the foreigner, one of the most difficult customs to cope with. "While in the neighbourhood, we decided to drop in!" is the usual explanation you will get. In a very short time, Turkish women magically know how to prepare an excellent meal at any time of the day, whatever the number of guests. There is always a surprise in the refrigerator ready to save the day! However, I must stress that the Turks are usually very polite and not at all demanding. They will eat whatever they find, although they like eating and do enjoy good food! But here, friendship is important! While travelling, they always have something to eat in their bag: nuts, cookies, cake or fruit... They like to say it is a precaution they take in case no facilities are found while travelling. Well aware of the problems of cleanliness in certain public places, they also never travel without toilet paper and wet wipes.

While not sanctioned by their religion, the Turks love to drink, especially rakı, their national drink. This strong anise-flavoured drink must be drunk slowly accompanied by a few "mezes", usually prepared with olive oil. Their pleasant drinking sessions usually last the whole evening with intermittent eating while all the political and financial problems of the country are discussed and usually solved. Once that delicate task is performed, the guests will join in singing either Turkish classical music or if a saz, a Turkish stringed instrument, is available, they will sing folk music, songs from an old repertoire that has been transmitted by minstrels through many generations. Most of these songs are touching, delicate and lovely poems that inevitably touch you in some way. Many a tear will be shed during the evening.

Bıçak yarası geçer,
Dil yarası geçmez.

A wound caused by a knife heals,
But one caused by a tongue doesn't.

Being very sensitive, they very easily feel offended and can pout for long periods after a disagreement. Sometimes, they will not reconcile and will only do so after the intervention of several friends. Moslem religious holidays often present an opportunity for such reconciliations. The Turks are also very proud and strongly nationalist. Amongst each other, they allow themselves to criticize their country, to swear at the political establishment in very strong terms, but cannot tolerate it if a foreigner utters the smallest criticism, because then it becomes a matter of honour.

Another peculiar characteristic shared by the people of this country, who exhibit a great love for music in general, is their boundless admiration for singers of all types of music: popular, Turkish classical, folk music and arabesque music. These performers are the focus of interest to such an extent that they become heroes, with their deeds, their lives and their dramas holding a larger place in the news than the fundamental problems of the country.

While the moral values of the country are usually quite conservative, it is interesting to note that an impressive number of male performers are homosexuals, and that these figures are nevertheless idolized. One particular star, now legally a woman, dresses in an extravagant fashion that very few women would be able to carry off. She still uses a male first name and sings in a very masculine voice. On the other hand, male stars who are perfect machos and who openly exhibit violent behaviour towards their women companions still manage to maintain a high degree of popularity with the public, amongst both men and women alike. How can such a paradox be understood?

If you ever travel by bus, do not be too surprised if you see passengers handing music cassettes to the bus driver who then very diligently plays them, thereby forcing all the passengers to listen along. Thanks to this practice, during a two-hour bus trip between Selçuk and Bodrum, my sister, who can't speak a word of Turkish, managed to learn all the words of a popular Turkish song.

Hekimden sorma,
Çekenden sor.

Don't ask the doctor,
Ask the one who suffers.

One example of the most astonishing behaviour of the citizens of this country is their relationship with the health system and their general attitude toward illness. Working in the health system for long years, I had many occasions to observe this. Turks, with good enough reason, hate hospitals and all that has to do with the medical world. To them, the smallest allusion to the word "disease" is virtually synonymous with the word "death". Living in a country with a moderate climate, the two main sources of disease are referred to as "getting chilled" and "getting caught in a draft". At the first sign of an illness, it becomes immediately evident that they have caught a chill somewhere, usually in their stomach or in their lungs. Perspiring and then staying in damp undershirts, even during the summer, is a guarantee of certain death for children. How many devoted mothers have I seen in the middle of the street, patiently exchanging the sweaty undershirts of their kids for the dry ones they always carry with them no matter where they go! On the other hand, the terms "preventive medicine, family doctor, and yearly check-up" are concepts they have never heard of.

God forbid! When Turks fall ill, they will panic and at once mobilize a huge network of friends and family members. Within a few hours, all the accessible knowledge on the presumed disease, its course, the name of the medication to be taken, etc. is gathered. Very concerned about their health, they consider it a duty to apply consciously and as rapidly as possible the "directives" they receive.

After several days, when it becomes evident that a doctor should be consulted, the same network is activated and this time the name of the "famed" professional to be consulted is found. They particularly avoid getting such information from a member of the medical profession and even on the rare occasion when they actually do so, the advice is rarely taken! Once a name has been obtained, the most rapid way to approach the famous doctor is investigated since the disease seems to have reached a critical stage. Again, the network moves in and designs a way to obtain from his secretary or better yet from the doctor himself, and if possible, on that same day, the greatly desired "appointment". Absolutely terrified and usually drowning in anxiety, the patient is finally in front of the doctor, but now appears unable to describe his symptoms or the early phases of his illness. Thank God, there is always a next of kin capable of the task.

Once the consultation is completed, prescription in hand, the unfortunate patient leaves the doctor's office to be again assaulted by the network of friends, eager to learn what has happened. The prescription is scrutinized and in many instances opinions are given, objections are formulated against the treatment proposed, especially if injections are recommended, and the health worker giving the injection may even add a comment or two. Thus does our dear patient, who has just spent a fortune, come to an impasse. Many cannot cope with so much stress: they lose their courage and let themselves be taken to another doctor, or accept a different treatment. Often, seriously ill patients, unaware of what is happening around them, may see their fate compromised simply because their sister maintains that she has a better idea for the treatment of the disease. The patient may even fall into the hands of faith healers or quacks.

The special custom requiring that people extend their best wishes for a prompt recovery to anyone they know who is ill contributes to the perpetuation of the bad habit of giving unwanted advice in profusion, all in the so called "best interest" of the patient. This most uncalled for type of behaviour unfortunately occurs all the time and one cannot but admie the doctors and family members who have to put up with it. What else can be done when one is faced with a whole population blessed with an inborn knowledge of pharmacology and internal medicine?

I worked many years with cancer patients and experienced some unbelievable moments with the families of those patients. Tradition seems to demand that you do not inform the patient of his condition, especially if the disease he is suffering from is serious. At once, the members of the family and the patients are transformed into very keen foxes, each trying to fool the other, with the medical team caught in the middle. Some families asked us not to give any original medical report to the patient, but instead to prepare fake reports with normal values. The general idea is to keep the patient in good spirits. Sometimes we had to degrade ourselves with a series of acrobatics, to hide or mask medication by changing the boxes or any number of stratagems you can possibly think of.

Except for very few drugs, Turkey is the paradise of medication without prescription[*]. This practise is especially dangerous when you consider the enormous quantity of antibiotics consumed by a very daring population. It is most difficult to understand this practice, but in Turkey, logic and common sense are not always the rule.

The family is incontestably the most stable and trustworthy institution in the country. It is the combination under one roof of the health, social welfare and social security systems, and from time to time may even house the justice system, too. What the government cannot achieve, the family does, compensating for all the flaws in the various systems. Therefore, the significance of this institution, with all the roles it plays in society, should not be underestimated. A great percentage of the population lives under its protective wings: the elderly grandparents, perhaps unable to care for themselves, the widowed uncle, the unmarried aunt, the newlyweds without means to pay rent, the out-of-town niece or nephew who must be lodged for university studies. In brief, there are often a large number of people living under the same roof. In such an environment, when you marry, you don't choose just a husband or a wife, but must adopt and adjust to a whole family! For foreign spouses, it goes without saying that this is one of the most difficult aspects of the society that we must accept and learn to live with.

As a matter a fact, while the concept of marriage for a certain small percentage of the population is based on the love of two different people choosing to share their lives, for a large portion of the country, families choose husbands for their daughters and brides for their sons. In some regions, a serious and costly bargaining phase is the final step in arranging for marriage with a chosen bride, thereby making nuptials an expensive matter. Generally, all girls have a dowry composed of household items which their mothers begin making and acquiring for them at their birth and continue compiling through the years with their own labour. The cost of furnishing the young couple's home is shared by the respective families according to established guidelines that determine which family provides for what. Following the wedding ceremony, a remarkable custom consists of giving the bride gifts of bracelets, necklaces and other gold jewellery that will form, if she is lucky, her personal fortune. These gifts are given openly in front of all guests, that is to say,

---

* The faith shown in pharmacists is touching indeed, but people sometimes fail to understand that everyone working in the pharmacy is not necessarily a pharmacist.

witnessed by many people so that the bride can prove ownership in case of a dispute later. The main idea is to make sure the woman has some wealth in case the marriage fails. For over seventy-seven years, the Civil Code was based on the separation of goods so that, with the husband considered head of the family, in case of divorce, women most often found themselves empty-handed*. The wedding gifts were a way for families to ensure a small amount of protection for their daughters, who were generally left to themselves once they had left their family for the house of their husband. Many foreign spouses, not aware of these procedures and without the support of their own families to conclude such arrangements, have often found themselves destitute when the dream is over, that is, without a husband.

Sociological studies show that this country lives under a patriarchal system while the Civil Code, finally modified in the year 2002, granted men the title of "head of the household"! In a country where the main deity, Kibele, was female and where the homeland of the Amazons is located, I would say that the men hold rather the pretension–not the certitude–of being the masters of their homes. When one notices the deep respect shown to elderly mothers and grandmothers, it would appear that this male leadership is a myth perpetuated by women for their own interest and the best interest of the family. While men do have their own sphere of authority and activities, women have long learned the fine art of diplomacy. Their kingdom without any doubt is their home, a setting they run with great care. Great complicity exists between mothers and daughters and there is a very particular bonding between mothers and sons. This very exclusive relationship is a very surprising, in fact, almost shocking social phenomenon for us, who are totally unaware of its existence. One of the most fatal errors committed by a foreign bride in Turkey is to try to force her husband to make a choice between his mother and his wife. Even if the wife is right one hundred-fold, her husband will never contradict his mother, will never think of inflicting on her the ultimate offence of taking his wife's side. This golden diplomatic rule should be carefully applied by a new foreign

---

* The Civil Code was finally modified in 2002. By law, spouses now equally share the responsibilities and the assets of the family

bride in order to maintain happiness in her marriage.

The relationship in Turkey between Mars and Venus is quite different from what we see in our own countries. To begin with, society imposes such restrictive rules on young couples that they hardly have the chance to meet, let alone be on their own. Such a rendezvous demands great planning and synchronizing similar to that seen in spy films. Being seen by a family member or acquaintance means that you have been caught red-handed in the process of committing a heinous crime. The resulting fear and panic paralyses both parties, so that thereafter they refrain from any demonstrations of affection or any displays of love. Such behaviour is unthinkable since it would be regarded as a great insult to the honour of the family. The word "namus" has the double meaning of honesty and virginity, or virtue, and the preservation of the virtue of women is a national obsession.

In this country, there are more murders committed to save the honour of the family following an insult or affront to the virtue of a woman than for any other reason. If you see a couple embracing on the street or in a public place, chances are they are brother and sister, or members of the same family. Only a few rebels would dare to commit such an offence in public. Daily life, literature, poems and songs are filled with heartbreakingly tragic love stories, lovers meeting secretly, dishonouring their families and deserving death. The Turkish penal code is more tolerant than the families themselves in such circumstances. The themes of love songs are usually themes of separation, suffering and impossible love stories. Love is not a happy event, but one filled with sadness and sorrow.

Another aspect of the Turkish family difficult to comprehend is how it goes about raising children. We, mothers from another culture, are reluctant to accept the educational principles maintained and applied by our Turkish mother and sisters-in-law. This difference of opinion brings about dramatic occasions during which the foreign spouse may find herself facing the entire clan in a grand clash of opinions! Generally, children are granted a great deal of freedom, which for us would be more correctly qualified as spoiling the child. The mother becomes a slave to the child and must organize her life according to the thousand and one whims of her child. Meals become everlasting fights to try to get the child to eat. Of course, they are not taught to eat by themselves, even when four or five years old. You really must witness the scene where a mother, fork in hand, runs after the child to have him swallow one by one every bite. They claim that the child will dirty everything trying to eat by himself, or that he will be undernourished if left to his own. This attitude usually causes great dramatics since the children then require more and more assistance from their mothers for everything they do. Since no child in the world voluntarily goes to bed, bedtime rapidly becomes a nightmare and can be transformed into a torture for all participants. Many things are promised to get the child to eat or go to bed. Finally, patience comes to an end and a totally uncalled for reaction takes place. I have never heard such awful threats addressed to children as those heard in this country: "I will kill you... I will cut you to pieces... I will cut your ears off... tear your fingers apart"–threats that are exaggerated and have no effect upon the children whatsoever, since they understand intuitively that nobody will actually perform such acts!

Education is a serious problem for Turkey. After many years of experience as a mother, as a civil servant in the health system and as a teacher at both the secondary school and university levels, I have had plenty of time to observe, study and suffer from the national schooling system. After so many years of effort, how do they still manage to produce such ignorant graduates and so many youngsters with no sense of initiative and a total lack of responsibility? The country is totally overwhelmed by this serious problem. The key to democracy is education.

Thanks to the very outdated, strange public school system, intellectual curiosity is discouraged, thinking is prevented and a huge amount of unrelated, useless knowledge is memorized. The result is an output of unhappy, overworked students who, despite their tremendous efforts, often wind up studying a profession they don't really like and have no desire to practise. I have been astounded by high school graduates who do not know how to look up a name or a word in an encyclopaedia or a dictionary. They cannot draw a map of Europe or even easily locate a country on a map. Worse of all, they cannot manage to decide which career they would like to follow. Those with adequate means choose to study in the very well organized private sector which offers a better education. The deplorable results of the public school system are reaching frightening proportions: an army of mediocre graduates, filled with exaggerated pretensions regarding the value of their diplomas, is flooding into the market.

Graduates and proud owners of a university degree have a tendency to overestimate their capacities, and suddenly adopt a prima donna attitude. See them perform! Having no knowledge to share, they never teach anything to anyone and the little they know remains a well-guarded secret. As a matter of fact, "the" diploma becomes a passport for the sinecure or secure job where a small hierarchy is established to protect the title and the position. Very few people work to the maximum of their capacities and these rare and precious engines must, unfortunately, pull too many wagons in the process. At the same time, they must fight the sophisticated methods used against them to hamper their functioning, methods that all too often succeed. Fighting a system where mediocrity reigns, where the less tiring "status quo" is preserved with great care, requires boundless energy, unending resistance and a never-ending battle for survival. These lazy individuals, like "Oblomov" from the novel of Ivan Gontcharov, cannot tolerate innovation, progress or change; as a matter of fact, they hate work!

> Meyve veren ağacı taşlanır.
> Trees filled with fruit are stoned.

The Turks have developed the habit of popularizing personalities from various sectors. They spoil and flatter them, and then with the passage of time, tend to develop a strong aversion towards these competent, innovative, hardworking individuals and outstandingly brilliant people. They then proceed to do everything in their power to discredit and destroy them. A short study of political history will help one grasp this truth immediately. The best example can be found in the attacks against Atatürk, the founder of the Turkish Republic, born in Thessalonica, a city now in Greece but previously part of the Ottoman Empire. Some Members of Parliament insinuated that since he was not born within the current frontiers of the Turkish Republic, he was not eligible to become President of the Republic! Fulfilling at the same time both his duties as head of the State and also of the Turkish Army, he was accused of neglecting his political duties in Ankara. In fact, those events occurred during the critical period preceding the last offensive of the Turkish Army during the War of Independence. As he was at the time very busy with the last crucial preparations of the army, Atatürk's whereabouts were naturally kept secret at the time.

Several more events also serve to illustrate this destructive tendency. In 1923, General Ismet Inönü, head of the Turkish delegation during the Lausanne peace talks, experienced great difficulties because at that time the Prime Minister refused, for some reason, to answer the messages of his general who, out of despair, therefore had to contact Atatürk directly. Another sad example deals with one of the most important Ministers of Education, Hasan Ali Yücel. This great reformer of the education system, founder of the National Library, ordered the compiling of the first national encyclopaedia. Strangely enough, his own name was never mentioned! That remarkable minister also initiated the work of the translation office in order to introduce the masterpieces of world literature to Turkish readers. He approved the establishment of the Village Institutes,* only to see himself become the target of a defamatory campaign that resulted in the loss of his post. This behaviour has not changed with the years. It still continues to destroy men of value, especially if they gain a better reputation then their own political leaders.

Following the "coup d'état" of 1980, a reform modified the laws governing the universities. This was followed by the establishment of many new universities in various regions of Turkey. They rapidly earned the nickname of "provincial universities". Behind their well-protected legal front, they became ideal regrouping centres for the members of various Islamic factions in search of a legal status. They also became excellent "lodging places" for the mediocre elements turned down by better universities. These centres of high education are almost without financial means since the government cannot meet the necessary expenses for their various needs: libraries and laboratories are far from reaching the standards required for such important institutions. This situation is, of course, reflected in the teaching quality of the staff and the training of the graduates.

---

* Village Institutes were established to train students from the villages to become primary school teachers and return to their respective villages to teach. Teachers from cities did not favour going to the villages at thàt period.

To me, one of the great enigmas of my adopted country remains the indolence, the lack of reaction, the non-productivity of the whole population in the face of disasters and basic social problems. The Turks, very self-centred and individualist, are endowed with a strong tendency to adopt a prima donna, egocentric attitude, with all the negative aspects the term implies. This is why they never succeed, except in very rare instances, in agreeing or work together and build a united front. It thus becomes impossible to organize anything in an efficient manner, to prepare a rapid action plan so a crisis can be faced or to establish logical demands to accomplish such changes. As a result, they are always taken by surprise, unprepared and overwhelmed by recurring events and problems. The famous saying, "Help yourself and God will help you" has absolutely no meaning for them and surely does not arouse any desire for action.* An even less popular concept in this country is, "Unite for strength". It is totally foreign to their nature. Following the example of the "divas" who cannot tolerate competition, they only achieve further division. NGO's with ideal programs are founded only to find themselves dismembered or split up in record time because everyone wants to become the leader and exhibit what they consider their great talents. The disastrous experience of the 1999 earthquake was not sufficiently destructive to wake the people up from their torpor, their deep sleep or their unconsciousness. How can we raise their awareness, suggest they require a better sense of responsibility from their leaders, clearer explanations, reasonable measures and actions rather than great demagogy? Where do the roots of this unforgivable negligence, which leads them to not require basic security norms for the welfare of their community and for their own property, lie?

Faced with such a lack of action from their government and civil authorities, the population did not exert the necessary pressure to obtain the required radical changes in this time of need. The only visible reactions observed following the disaster were great waves of panic and feeble non-productive, sometimes harmful activities. No one knew what to do to protect or save their own lives, how to behave in order not to hamper the work of local and national authorities. As a result,

---

* The motto of the country appears to be "This is God's will".

the conventional phone system and our two GSM systems ceased functioning. It was impossible to establish any form of communication with the stricken area for at least the first three days after the earthquake. People jumped into their cars and blocked all the vital roads. All you can think of that should not have been done in such a case was done. After such suffering, one would think that the next step would be to require everyone to take the necessary precautions to avoid a needless repetition of this string of heartbreaking events. But therein lies the core of the problem, for everyone prefers to behave as the ostrich does and bury their heads in the sand. The approach seems to be: avoid seeing or hearing anything, behave as if such a problem never existed and will never occur again. But in the meantime, anxiety crises, depression, fear, harsh criticism and endless discussions continue, solving no problems, instead only making everyone feel even more nervous and helpless in the process!

So where is the action in all this confusion? There are a few NGO's and a few responsible individuals desperately trying to set up an education program in order to stimulate the population and raise their awareness. Unfortunately, however, our NGO's are deplorably weak and so restricted that no energy is left to exert any pressure on the authorities.

The attitude of the Turks towards foreigners established permanently in their country is difficult to interpret. Even though, thanks to our spouses and our children, we become an integral part of the Turkish family, we remain foreigners to them and will remain so all our lives. The notion of a foreigner being permanent is non-existent in the mentality of the people and in their bureaucracy. To begin with, despite the great love they have for their own country and the great sensitivity they display when it comes to this subject, they are always very surprised to hear that we have deliberately chosen to leave our own countries to live in Turkey, while they themselves are dreaming of the possibility of emigrating to our countries. They are convinced that, in case of a divorce or in the event of the death of the Turkish spouse, our main concern would be returning to our native country. But returning to *what*? After so many years in a country we now consider as our own, where we have our children, our family, our friends, why would we be tempted to go back to our birth country, where so little of our lives is left? This surprising attitude can sometimes be offensive. Unfortunately, I think that the Turks do not nourish great confidence towards what their country can offer or the quality of life available here. One thing is for sure, theirs is not the mentality of a country open to immigration.

Describing the Turkish woman is a very difficult task for the simple reason that the world of women is far from being homogenous and is thus difficult to characterize. In order to give a correct idea on the status of women, one should first proceed with an analysis of women in different parts of the country.

Women living in the eastern part of the country are by far the most unfortunate group. Their living conditions, compared to those of their sisters in the larger cities further west, are much more primitive and laborious. They are constantly under the pressure of the customs and traditions prevalent in that region, traditions which strictly dictate their daily routine and general lifestyle. How many young girls, sentenced by the inhumanely harsh judgments of the males of their clan, have been killed for acts that are considered to harm the so-called "honour of the family"? In Québec, those "dishonourable acts" would be considered normal.

In 1998, on the 8th of March, we took a trip to Urfa, a region very close to the Syrian border, to celebrate Women's Day. We had joined a group of Turkish women's associations to bring the many problems of the area to the attention of the media and to offer some form of support to those oppressed women. The treatment of women in that area is unworthy of the century we are living in. We especially wanted to focus attention on the violent death of a young teenaged girl who had been murdered in cold blood on the street in the middle of the city. Ours was an effort to raise the awareness of the authorities since they have a tendency to consider actions such as the latter to be everyday normal cases and respond accordingly. During the trip I noted that, in this area, the notion of "Women's Day" did not exist. Also non-existent was the slightest idea as to why we had come to Urfa and what we were doing there. As a matter of fact, most women never even knew we were there! And to the few women who saw us, we were simply tourists!

Ms Işılay Saygın, who was at that time State Minister responsible for the Status of Women, was also travelling in the area. She was on a trip to encourage legal marriages, supposedly compulsory since the adoption of the Civil Code in 1926! Legal marriage is a formality few bother with in this corner of the country, where a religious ceremony suffices. The consequences of this behaviour are disastrous: the wife is not legally married and must often accept the presence of a second or third wife. She has no right to the inheritance

First camel ride in the South

of her husband; the children are not officially registered* and so lack identity cards. Here is a complete society which in the eyes of the administration does not exist because it lives outside of the system, seventy-seven years after the acceptance of the Civil Code and the proclamation of the secular state! Where are the authorities? A well-known Member of Parliament escorting the Minister on her visit is himself living in polygamy. During the few days she was in the area, she performed civil marriages for entire villages, distributed official documents and gave identity cards** to hundreds of children.

For the most part, these women are illiterate, have no social security whatsoever and live under the bondage of their husband or the feudal lord of the region. In certain villages, we could not even approach our sisters to exchange a few words. Many of them cannot even speak Turkish, knowing only Arabic or Kurdish. Despite the efforts demon-

---

* A change in the law now allows the registration of children born from such religious marriages.
** Without an identity card, you're officially non-existent. You cannot, for example, be admitted to a public hospital, a school, get a driver's license, establish a business, open a bank account, get legally married.

strated by various associations to try to modify the sad customs so wide-spread in the region, none have succeeded in changing the brutal attitude of men. In 1997, a fourteen year old young girl wrote a letter to a young boy and was executed by her brother, in the street, in accoradance with a decision reached by her family. Our group organized a small ceremony in the market square, scene of the crime, to commemorate the death of this young victim. During this silent gathering, men observed us with stupefaction as we placed flowers on the ground. One politely asked what we were doing there and then proceeded to explain that he did not understand our concern, since the young girl in question had been found guilty by her family and deserved what had happened to her.

While their working conditions may be equally as harsh on the whole, women in central Anatolia, the Black Sea and the Aegean Sea regions enjoy a better fate then their sisters in the east. In general, they have the opportunity to attend at least a few years of primary school. Life can be merciless; marriage comes at an early age; their work in the fields is heavy and exhausting. Added to this is the housework, the care of children and in-laws who often live in the same house, all of which entail exhausting tasks. Young girls in good health, chosen to be good labourers at all levels, become the servants of the whole family and often the drudge of their mothers-in-law. They cook, dye wool, weave rugs, work in the field gathering cotton, tobacco, olives, nuts or tea, and must also take care of the animals. In short, they work constantly. They are courageous, devoted, helpful and endowed with great endurance. They have an inborn talent for handiwork; as young children they first begin to embroider, weave and crochet, with great talent producing small masterpieces they often include in their dowries that they prepare with utmost care and great love. Reserved and shy, they claim nothing in exchange for themselves, but their reliable and serious character is such that they form the backbone of the country. Their labour and devotion confers stability and indispensable continuity to the proper functioning of the country.

Our sisters in the cities can be divided into a few distinct groups. The elite, a minority of cultivated and very well educated women, coming usually from old families, generally speaking two or often three languages, hold key jobs in all sectors. The university world and academic careers are most suitable for them. A great number of important functions in various schools, mostly in medicine and law, are their lot. The posts of rector at both the Istanbul Technical University and Marmara University are held by women. It is among the ranks of this remarkable group of women that can be found the courageous pioneers of women's NGO's. Besides the excellent work they do and despite the strict restrictions imposed by the authorities, they also manage to exert some pressure on the government and to influence public opinion. Together with this group, a great number of women work in various sectors, perhaps with less academic titles, but with endless devotion and generosity. Thanks to this anonymous group, honest, devoted and of exceptional quality, the education system and the public service system is able to maintain an acceptable level of activity.

On the other hand, there is a small, comfortable, lazy middle-class, more concerned with killing time then being useful and participating in projects designed to improve society. They spend their money and energy for their own pleasures and pastimes. A lot of dynamism and unchannelled potential is being lost in the pursuit of useless aims. One wonders if the desire to lead a more interesting and more enriching, worthwhile life would ever occur to them!

The last, but not the least, group is made up of women usually from the rural areas of Anatolia, uprooted from their villages to be brought into the cities where a better life supposedly awaits them. These women must live in one- or two-room accomodations in the slums where they have to squeeze in four or five children, a mother-in-law and perhaps even a sister-in-law or a daughter-in-law together with her children. Often these primitive homes with earth or concrete floors do not even have running water. In these most primitive conditions they must assume responsibility for the survival of their families. Very often they must work outside the home to ensure a stable income for the family, which is often headed by an unqualified, unemployable husband. Younger children are in school, while teenage boys work for next to nothing, learning a trade in a garage or at the hairdresser's around the corner. Teenage girls may be working in a textile factory or as a seamstress and are often married very young. The oldest boy of the family may be doing his military service or, if he has some talent and the meagre means, may try to complete some university studies.

Lacking any formal education and barely able to read and write, these women will work in private homes five or six days a week helping with the cooking, the care of the children and the cleaning. Others manage to find work in industry. Many of these women lead sad, difficult lives without hope and are faced with a multitude of problems in addition to leading a deeply isolated life. The slum areas have become a source of aggressive behaviour and frustrations as they reflect all the social unrest of the country. Their numbers have greatly increased; the differences between the social groups are so tremendous that they have succeeded in modifying the cities themselves. Their political inclinations so profoundly influenced elections that suddenly for the first time ever, Turkey found itself with members of an Islamic party governing the cities of Istanbul and Ankara. This was followed by a national election in which the same movement obtained a majority, thereby winning the elections.* At the same time, a large number of Islamic NGO's were founded and began to work very diligently. They were more successful than many other organizations in mobilizing the women of the slum areas. Strongly helped by the religious fervour and unwavering beliefs of the population in question, they managed to bring hope and promised major changes that would lead towards a better society.

Due to a poor economic situation, a rapidly growing population and traditional and religious obstacles, the goals set by the Republic for the education of women have not been attained. In 1991, the illiteracy rate among women over fifteen years old was thirty-one percent. Despite various laws decreeing the equality of women and their right to equal opportunity, 2.1 million girls of primary and secondary school age are not attending school.

On the whole, my observations indicate that all those who visit this lovely country and have the chance to establish some contact with the Turks are usually charmed by what they manage to discover and generally leave the country with everlasting memories of this warm country.

---

* Over 20 parties took part in the national elections. The law requires that a party receive at least ten percent of the total national vote in order to be represented in Parliament. Only two parties fulfilled this requirement. The votes of the disqualified parties were reapportioned to the two qualifiying parties. 40 million people were eligible to vote, 30 million people used their right, 10 million votes were thus reapportioned. This is how an Islamic party with only twenty-five percent of the votes managed to gain control of Parliament.

Chapter XV

Istanbul University, 1967 – 1983

I was now a modest member of a very well known university clinic. Surrounded by a hierarchy of impressive titles that can hardly be translated into any other language, I was delighted to observe that all the members of the teaching staff spoke at least one foreign language. The director of this institution was known by his title of Ordinarius Professor and he was assisted by a large number of professors, associate professors, residents and interns. These highly qualified academicians allowed me, for a few years, to have a glimpse of a slowly disappearing generation of Turkish society. Those men, usually educated in French schools, came from the best families of the country and were examples of the Ottoman gentleman, refined, cultured and polite to almost an excess.

Those most valuable specialists, wizards of the medical field, were the elite of Istanbul University and of our Pharmacology and Therapeutics Clinic. Among the "first accomplishments" of the clinic, I must emphasize the creation of the first department of nuclear medicine, the first heart catheterization and the first medical oncology department in Turkey.

I would like to stress the following fact about this clinic: it was the complete opposite of most of the other departments of the Medical School, like the pathology, microbiology and internal medicine departments, because this clinic reached a high scientific level without the participation of the distinguished Jewish professors who had fled Germany to take refuge in Istanbul during World War II. This is thanks to the accomplishments of the esteemed Professor Akıl Muhtar Özden. A graduate of the Military Medical School, this Turkish scholar obtained his fellowship in Switzerland then worked in the pharmacodynamics laboratory of Prof Major where he earned the title of associate professor. He developed an original method to demonstrate the effects of substances with anaesthetic properties. Returning to Turkey in 1908 and by then an authority on the subject, he was appointed professor of pharmacology at the Clinic of Therapeutics where he contributed largely to the excellent reputation of the establishment.

After five years of work in the United States in the very relaxed atmosphere of the American institutions, I once again found myself in the strict atmosphere of French discipline similar to what I was familiar with from our hospitals in Québec. The regulations surrounding the "morning visits" of patients every day followed a strict protocol no one would dare challenge. No negligence or carelessness was tolerated and the young doctors in training had to explain and defend each decision they made. The great care and attention given to the education and formation of qualified specialists in internal medicine were exceptional. Every laboratory test requested and every decision taken for the treatment of the patient was the fruit of deep reflections in order to arrive at the diagnosis in an intelligent manner. Today this school of remarkable men of another generation has almost disappeared and only nostalgia for those good old days remains.

I was working in the haematology department directed by Dr Bülent Berkarda and his assistants, two specialists in internal medicine, Dr Uğur Derman and Dr Gönül Akokan. A biologist, Miss Sunay, niece of the director of our clinic, worked as a laboratory technician and took care of the routine work while more sophisticated tests were performed by our two specialists. Dr Berkarda had first worked several years in the department of cardiology, but after some time was asked to take over the department of haematology. His great interest in the problems of blood coagulation led him to develop an excellent test in coagulation, subject of his associate professor thesis. When I joined the department, his laboratory already enjoyed an excellent reputation in the field of bleeding disorders.

As at the Laleli Clinic, the atmosphere was similar to the one found in a large family with every member showing great courtesy towards their colleagues and helping each other. A westernizing wind seemed to be blowing in the clinic. Some of the best years of my career were spent in this institution.

The head of the department, Dr Bülent Berkarda, nicknamed B.B., was above all a man of science, a competent researcher and an excellent teacher with infinite patience. A very polite gentleman, he was endowed with a high dose of Ottoman refinement. One of his favourite pastimes was to pick out Ottoman words still in use in the daily vocabulary, then find their roots and derivations. I always remained a lost cause among his students because I had absolutely no knowledge of the Arabic and Persian languages. Like my father-in-law, he gave me a lot of advice that proved very useful through the years of my working career. His most useful tip was, "One patient man is worth ten courageous men." A hard-working individual, he also managed to steer me into writing a technical manual in haematology and later on suggested I should begin a doctorate in pharmacology.

Had Dr Berkarda been from another country, the coagulation method he developed would now be universally applied in laboratories and would have brought celebrity to him, the inventor. As a physician, Dr Berkarda has always been very sensitive and understanding to the problems of his patients, approaching them as human beings, not just medical cases. Rather conservative, reserved and introverted, it was not easy to discover what he thought. Through the years he was fated to become Dean of Cerrahpaşa Medical School and later Rector of Istanbul University, the largest university in Turkey. The years he held these crucial positions were among the most dangerous and critical years in the history of the Turkish Republic. The years he was elected dean of our medical school, 1979-1982, coincided with the bloodiest period of the country. Each and every day was filled with dramatic events, bombings, assassinations, student uprising and battles between various factions. All this anarchy led to the military coup of September 12, 1980.

The years he spent as the rector of Istanbul University, between 1994 and 1998, were difficult ones spent under the coalition government of Prime Minister Necmettin Erbakan, leader of an Islamic party. During this period, very few people had the courage to criticize the government and openly express their apprehensions. He did not hesitate to do so when he felt that the future of the secular state was at stake. During such a critical period, Dr Berkarda did not fail to remind the members of the coalition government of their responsibilities. Happily, pressure from the military sector brought to an end the plans of that dangerous government. During those times, what was needed was a firm hand with a righteous, impartial and incorruptible character and a great faith in both the values of the political system of the secular state and in the reforms of Atatürk.

Under difficult conditions, Dr Berkarda heroically succeeded in ensuring the proper functioning of the Cerrahpaşa Medical School, then later on, continued to steer the university along the true path despite the many attacks of various religious factions that were trying to obtain concessions from the basic principles of the secular state. In the history of every country in time of crisis, an individual capable of maintaining the required equilibrium will rise.

Dr Uğur Derman and his wife Gül, a former student of my father-in-law, soon became good friends of ours. Graduated from the American school in Istanbul, he was less traditional and somewhat less refined then his boss, but was an excellent organiser. Working together through the years, they achieved a level of partnership that led them to build excellent professional and administrative cooperation on all levels. The premature death of this couple in a tragic car accident brought an end to their brilliant careers. After a while, Dr Gönül Akokan, a specialist in internal medicine, had to leave the department because her position was abolished, but she was able to rejoin the department a few years later. During a sabbatical year spent in Germany, she met the love of her life and left both her work and the country.

As far as I was concerned, the first phase of my work was to add to the laboratory the missing basic techniques usually necessary for the proper functioning of a haematology department, then to train a few technicians since there were, as of yet, no schools available. The space allowed for our laboratory was minimal. We had a small room at the end of a long corridor, infested with cockroaches crawling out of everywhere. We had a sink and a long table on which to perform our "marvels". A small desk was available for our occasional needs. Within a short time, in these rather primitive surroundings, we established an excellent morphology and coagulation laboratory. Some time later, an unused section of the corridor was transformed into a room, a more convenient place to receive the patients.

After a year of work at the Laleli Clinic, I thought I was beyond being shocked by events, until at the end of my first week of work I witnessed in great astonishment the very primitive way in which they cleaned the floors of the clinic. Coming out of the laboratory on a Friday afternoon, cleaning day, I noticed a steady stream of water in the corridor slowly coming towards me and flooding every room on its way. I first thought it was an accidental flood so I tried to find the individual responsible for it. This proved to be a difficult task on a Friday since it appeared that everyone had left the clinic early. The notion of full-time at the university was rather different from ours. The personnel I came across on each floor did not seem to be bothered by this flood and continued to work very calmly as if nothing was happening. Searching for the cause of this flood, I noticed that in the top floor restrooms all the water faucets had been turned on full force. All the drains were blocked with pieces of thick cloths, causing the planned flooding. Similar pieces of cloth were used as barriers here and there in order to channel the flow of water. Once the corridor and the patients' rooms were flooded, the cleaning staff wearing "takunya" (the wooden clogs worn in the Turkish bath) would carefully scrub the floors with pieces of rags soaked in detergent and wrapped around a wooden mop head. What absolutely shocked me was to notice, with deep horror, that these cloths were then washed in the toilet bowls! I never manage to understand how the authorities could have tolerated such a system. Once the floor was "cleaned", the barriers were removed and the mass of water was sent to the floor below via the stairway. I was totally shocked by that most unbelievable and indescribable scene. That method was abandoned a few years later but has remained one of my most unforgettable memories!

I must stress that the first days in the clinic were not totally without surprises and emotions. At that time, the proper functioning of the hospitals seemed to rely entirely upon the daily occurrence of nothing less than miracles. The main problems were, without any doubt, the scheduled and unscheduled water shortages and at certain hours of the day the scheduled electricity cuts. You had to be smart, patient and demonstrate feats of organization in order to work under such conditions! I also never understood why patients were never bathed in the clinic. Was it due to a respect for the cultural and religious principles, or related to the lack of personnel, or because of the water shortage or because they were afraid of being caught in a draft? As a matter of fact, the patients were not taken care of by the nursing staff, but by a member of the family found at their bedside and acting as a nurse! That resulted in filling the clinics with unaccounted for individuals constantly searching for someone or for something in the name of such and such a patient.

On each floor was a refrigerator where the food prepared by the family of the patients could be stored. The family members would spend hours telling us how their patient could not eat this or that food, how sensitive their stomachs were and so on and so forth. What I gathered was that our patients were capricious individuals, living in castles where private cooks met all their needs. I also gathered that hospitals must have had the reputation of being establishments where one would likely die of hunger should necesary precautions fail to be taken.

The water shortage was surely a major problem no western hospital administrator would have accepted or dealt with. But what could you do? It was a reality of everyday life in the country at that time. You could build extra water storage tanks, but then they also ran out of water and one simply could not keep building alternate water storage tanks. We had to keep functioning as best we could. I especially recall the orderly in the department of nephrology who would carry buckets of water from the street fountain for the needs of the dialysis patients... and the cholera outbreak in 1970, when our clinic was without water.

I do not wish to criticize the performance and efficiency of the establishments in this part of the world, but I must stress that speed is not a major priority here! The indolence towards certain problems almost made me lose my mind. Their very primitive way of transporting patients would make me indignant. I would wonder if and where the personnel were trained. Hadn't the doctors noticed, when working abroad, how a patient is transferred from a stretcher to an examination table or to an operating table? When my mother-in-law, then eighty years old, suffered a fractured shoulder, I was astonished when I heard the nursing aide tell her to raise herself onto the stretcher that was much too high. The stretcher had no mechanism to lower or raise it according to the needs of the patient. They brought a chair, and asked my mother-in-law, who was wearing a long tight dress, first to climb onto the chair and then to get onto the stretcher. I'll never forget the difficult time we spent trying to find a solution to this ridiculous situation. Finally, we ended up having to cut her dress. She was sent to the operating room where four men, each holding an arm or a leg, transferred her and her broken shoulder onto the table. Twenty years later, in 2001, I was to witness a similar scene when my daughter-in-law delivered her son in a private clinic. She was also asked to climb onto a shaking chair to get on the high stretcher. Every time I see patients carried on the back of an individual from a car into a hospital, my heart aches and I feel like screaming.

I soon realised that such reactions were not very useful and I had to control myself so as to keep myself from losing my mind. Besides being patient, in order to keep a sane mind and survive these events absolutely void of common sense, I decided to incorporate a second rule into my life: to forget all I had seen before in North America and make no more comparisons between the two worlds. It was useless to apply a logical approach where such a concept did not exist. If there are things I can improve on my own, I will work to do so, if not, I will just keep my mouth shut.

Do not believe that following a year of work in Laleli I had reached an integration level sufficient to prevent me from committing new blunders. One of my first awkward deeds was a direct blow to the very strict hierarchy of the academic staff! If you were to compare a country to a huge tree with several large branches, there cannot be much difference between the branches. The conditions of the University were not very different than what I had found in Laleli. The deplorable state of the sterilisation process in the clinic led me to perform a thorough sterility check on the state of the injectors, needles and other so-called sterilized objects of our clinic. The results were most alarming; I was outraged and without thinking I walked decisively towards the office of the Clinic Director, without even bothering to make an appointment. Usually in our society, the head of the laboratories is a clinical pathologist, and since the current director of our clinic was also a pathologist, I considered it my duty to inform him of the situation and give him the results of my research. File in hand, I knocked on his door feeling quite proud of myself.

Ordinarius Professor Sedat Tavat was a rather short man who apparently did not really appreciate the company of women. As I opened his door, he looked rather astonished to see me there and was hesitant to offer me a seat. Very animated, I showed him the results of my research without hiding my astonishment at such pitiful results. I also expressed my concern for a problem I attributed to gross negligence. In the meantime, I noticed that the door had slowly been opened allowing me to see that several members of the staff had gathered. At the end of my presentation, the staff members politely and skilfully escorted me out of the Professor's office. I had no idea that, quite unintentionally, I had just committed a serious protocol error! That earned me a long lecture from Dr Berkarda on how the strict hierarchy of the clinic functioned. Nevertheless, my unorthodox approach worked and as a result the dangerous and primitive methods used to sterilize the material were replaced.

Several years later, while giving a course on the subject of sterilisation to my laboratory technology students, we conducted a check of the sterilisation in an obstetrical clinic, and found disturbing results! Unfortunately, in that particular case, the attitude of the clinic director was not so scientifically oriented and he refused to accept the results and the recommendations we offered. A large part of my career was spent conducting a battle against both the inadequate sterilization methods in use and the teaching of such obsolete methods. The high incidence of hepatitis following hospitalisation was a good example of the extent of the problem.

The high scientific level and the family-like atmosphere of our department made for a pleasant working environment in which both the routine work and the research progressed at a satisfying pace. I was helped by an excellent technician, Sabahat, trained in an almost record period of time. One day I decided to introduce this young, intelligent girl to our family friend, the Turkish composer, Yalçın Tura. It worked!

They were married a short time later. They have three lovely children, and their son Hasan, an excellent violinist, has chosen to follow in the footsteps of his father and pursue a career in music. After twenty-five years of marriage, Sabahat is still a glowing and pleasant woman.

Sabahat was the cause of my second behavioural mishap in the clinic.

On day while working in the laboratory, she candidly asked me about the exact meaning of communism. Why was it prohibited to talk about the subject? I proceeded to tell her that she was not the only one unaware of the meaning of the word. To prove my point, we proceeded to conduct a rapid survey among the personnel of the clinic. A notebook in hand, we questioned a dozen or so people, among whom were doctors, and we had the time of our lives reading the answers over and over. That night at home, I casually informed my father-in-law of our research. Astonished by what he heard, he submitted me to a severe scolding. Of course, I was devastated. I had not fully realised that it was such a taboo subject. Of course, it was more or less normal that such a phobia of communism would exist in a country so close to the Iron Curtain countries and with Russia as a historically threatening, close neighbour. I also had no idea that each institution usually had a member of the secret police among its personnel. His duty was to report events that could lead to the unmasking of people with leftist tendencies or activities of leftist origin. The next day, as I set foot in the clinic, I was given a second scolding by the biochemist of the clinic before having to face Dr Berkarda, who was impatiently waiting for me in the lab. That experience taught me to behave in a more reserved manner in the future.

One of the main objectives of the department was to gain international approval for the "Self Thromboplastine Time" test invented by Dr Berkarda. In an effort to do so, every member of the department worked hard and managed to attend several international congresses or meetings on the subject. The most important of such meetings, The Asia Pacific Haematology Congress, was held in Istanbul and gathered together the world authorities on the subject of haemostasis. An historical reunion, it brought together the defenders of the four important coagulation test systems used to follow patients who were under anticoagulant treatment: In addition to Dr Berkada, there was Dr Owren of Sweden with his own commercialized test, Dr Poller of Manchester,

England with his commercialized thromboplastine and the Americans with their commercialized "plasma reference" used for the standardisation of commercialized thromboplastine. The Turkish test, "Self-Thromboplastine", presented the advantage of using the patient's blood as a source of thromboplastine, did not require a system of standardization and did not require commercialized reagents. That approach was cheap and offered the great advantage of giving comparable results anywhere in the world, while the other systems required some standardization and costly biological reagents. The reunion proved to be most flattering for our clinic and for Turkey. The value of the test was stressed and no one criticized or opposed the test. Yet we could not succeed in imposing the method on the scientific world! Had this test had a commercial value, I am convinced that many well-known laboratory products firms would have made generous offers to obtain rights. I must also sadly remark that this very simple and useful test is not even routinely used in Turkish laboratories. In the hands of informed and qualified personnel with an interest in coagulation this test can be used for many purposes. It can yield precious information without the use of very complicated techniques.

Besides work on coagulation, our department was also busy with the work required in the preparation of associate professor theses. Our responsibilities increased significantly with the addition of chemotherapy for leukemia patients. Some years later, following the return of Dr Berkarda from a two-year residency in the United States, that work finally led to the establishment of a department of oncology.

In those days, one of the greatest advantages of working at the university was the ease with which we could carry out our research since we did not have the handicap of having to search for funds to meet the expenses of our projects. That was a luxury many western researchers would have greatly appreciated. The well-known saying "Publish or Perish!" illustrates the difficulties involved in obtaining funds, a process highly influenced by the number of publications the researcher has to his credit.

In the early seventies, the Medical School of Istanbul University was divided into two medical schools and our department became part of the Cerrahpaşa Medical School. New buildings went up and in 1976 we left the building behind the municipal Haseki Hospital that had been our home for so many years. This marked the beginning of a new era, characterized by the gradual disappearance of our academic elite who had reached the age of retirement. Routine and clinical work increased. Our oncology outpatient department was now well known and we dealt with over fifteen new cases of chemotherapy every day. New methods had to be taught to the personnel and added to the laboratory routine. The era of immunological methods had arrived and so I took advantage of a trip to Canada to attend a course that allowed me to acquire the necessary knowledge to develop new methods for our research work.

Participating in international meetings was not a problem for me since English was the language used in most meetings and I could express myself reasonably well in that language, but my first Turkish congress proved to be quite an unforgettable event. It was the National Haematology Congress held in Ankara. I was so stressed I could hardly close my eyes the night before my presentation. But, as always, luck smiled upon me. A Turkish haematologist who had been working in the United States for many years apologized and informed us she would give her presentation in English. I gave mine in Turkish immediately after hers. I most likely made a lot of mistakes, but I gained the support of all those present. I completed my talk absolutely exhausted, but the fear was gone and from then on, speaking Turkish in public became easier. That was the "premiere" of a series of similar experiences.

In the meantime, several of our research projects were conducted in collaboration with the pharmacology department of the medical school. This department was headed by Prof Alaeddin Akcasu, nicknamed A.A., an expert on the subjects of histamine, opium derivatives, heroin and morphine, all drugs he had been working with for several years. Somewhat overwhelmed by the routine work of our department and at the suggestion of Dr Berkarda, I decided to begin work on a medical science doctorate in haematology and requested the permission to do so from the executive committee of the faculty. My request was refused but, to my great surprise, I was informed I would be starting work on a doctorate in pharmacology! The branch had been changed by A.A. and B.B. during the meeting and, since there was no time available, I had not been consulted.

During this period, Dr Berkarda was appointed Director of the Nursing, Midwife and Laboratory Technician School of our Faculty. The laboratory technician section was not organized and was in very pitiful condition. Aware of both the love I had for my work and the fact that I would be interested in training students for this poorly known and almost non-existent profession, he offered me the job of setting up the required laboratories to be used for the proper training of students. Between 1974 and 1979, besides my work in oncology, that is, my research work for my thesis in pharmacology, I worked with great enthusiasm to establish good biochemistry and haematology laboratories that were to be used for the training of the laboratory technicians. Partially inspired by the structures I remembered from my former school at Laval University, but modifying things according to the facilities and needs of the country, I worked to establish a technical high school for the training of laboratory technicians. No books were available for the students, so we proceeded to prepare a manual of basic techniques in haematology, with Dr Berkarda writing the theoretical part.

During this period, I became the defendant, the older sister and the advisor of the students. Those most pleasant years of work were well rewarded when I saw a large number of young girls awarded diplomas. These graduates were endowed with valuable professional competence, a feeling of confidence in themselves and the capacity that allowed them to defend their knowledge. They would be in need of all these qualities acquired during their schooling when it came time for them to face the numerous battles they would encounter during their years of work in the health system.

As far as I was concerned, the educational system had served mostly to destroy any self-confidence that the students might have possessed. Our aim was then, quite the opposite, to spend tremendous efforts to have the students develop a personality, some initiative and self-confidence. The health system had no place for frightened shadows; what it needed was young ladies capable of some leadership. I expressed my total confidence in their capabilities and proved to them that they could be trusted by having them set up and run an emergency laboratory in the internal medicine clinic and a small blood count laboratory in the radiotherapy clinic.

Both of the laboratories under the responsibility of the students were very successful and helped accelerate the treatment of patients. Unfortunately, I often ran into serious arguments and some interference from the teachers of the nursing and midwifery section. Fortunately, my convictions and my determination were quite strong and I kept doing things the way I felt was proper. Most of those critics focused on the fact that I was "foreign" and I did not know the conditions and the character of the country. Despite their objections, my method yielded better results. I kept in mind the experience gained by the former successful Village Institutes and did my best to apply similar principles. Once the school was well-established and its personnel well-trained, despite the great satisfaction it gave me, the time to pass on my duty arrived and so I sadly left that position. Those years of hard work allowed me to gain some insight into the miseries of our education system. That well-functioning school successfully training young technicians was closed a few years later when the universities went through their share of reform following the military coup of 1980. I never understood why!

From then on, I concentrated mostly on my research work at the Pharmacology Institute. Dr Akcasu, the head of the department and a wizard in this science, had worked for many years on the mechanism of morphine tolerance and developed his own theory. He spent a great part of his career working to have his theory gain acceptance. A.A., as we called him, certainly did not suffer from a lack of self-confidence; he was a fierce critic of any subject discussed, and had a strong sense of satirical humour. He was a great talker and an avid reader, a hard to please head of department. He had not the least tolerance for mediocrity and expressed his opinions bluntly. Besides our individual research subjects, all members of the department were involved in a research project related to the derivates of opium or concerned with morphine tolerance. With no patients to be taken care of, the atmosphere of the department was relaxed and the scientific discussions were animated and very enriching. It was a Mecca of learning. Our team included a few doctors and several pharmacists. The greatest problem was the lack of interest shown by young doctors towards basic sciences. One of our doctors, Prof Eşkazan, a neurologist, was also an expert on epilepsy. His main research projects were the study of sleep and in his work, he used cats implanted with electrodes, a delicate surgical procedure he did himself. The animal would run around the department giving the visitors the impression of walking in some space laboratory on a foreign planet! My good friend Gabriella was working on her doctorate thesis about anaphylaxis, a deadly allergic reaction in the cat as well.

Those were the years of the Cyprus crisis during which we suffered acutely from the American embargo on many products, especially gasoline and fuel oil. Heating the sections of the hospital where no patients were found became impossible and we spent a winter freezing in our laboratories. Many of the country's electrical plants worked on fuel oil and experienced great restrictions in their production. We found ourselves without electricity for many hours every day and the effects on our frozen stock of cancerous cells were disastrous. Those precious cells, originating in the laboratories of our American colleagues and heroically brought back by our co-workers in their hand baggage, had been most difficult to obtain.

In 1977, my research work for my doctorate was completed and I was ready to defend my thesis, "The effects of compound 48/80 on the fibrinolytic activity of dogs". While I felt ready for the exam, I never really felt I had the soul of a pharmacologist, at least at the level of knowledge I usually expect from myself. I was terrified by the idea of what could be asked during the exam and I felt very nervous in front of the jury. I had nightmares in which I forgot my Turkish and wondered what would happen if I really did. At the bottom of my heart, I cursed this brilliant idea I had of doing a doctorate in Turkish, while most Turks went abroad for such a degree. The subject of my thesis being half-haematology/half-pharmacology, I finally recovered my self-confidence and completed the exam earning the mention of "great distinction". I was the first pharmacology doctoral student to be graduated from the new Cerrahpaşa Medical School.

Having obtained a grant from the British Council, I flew to England to begin working on the radio-immune assay of morphine. Following work at St-Mary's Hospital in London, I then proceeded to visit Surrey University, a trip that allowed me to both visit some of the English countryside and get to know the British better. In their own country, the

British are most pleasant and charming, losing a bit of their arrogance and feelings of superiority they so often display abroad. The British Council treats scholars with great deference and we were offered tickets to Covent Garden and to the theatre. One of my great dreams was thus fulfilled as I saw Pelleas and Melisandre at the famous Royal Opera House and then the charismatic Ingrid Bergman at the theatre. That gesture from the British Council was highly appreciated and I only wish that research workers the world over could all be given the same opportunities.

Following my stay in England, I went to Canada to work for a few weeks at Montreal University. I was in the department of Dr Marc Cantin, a former student of Hans Selye, "the world authority" on mastocytes, the cells I was working on. We were trying to demonstrate that morphine was stored in these cells. While discussing the possibility of finding funds to support this research, Dr Cantin mentioned casually: "If only Turkey were a member of NATO, then we could easily find funds for this research." Upon hearing this comment I told him at once that Turkey was indeed a member of NATO, a fact overlooked by most Western countries. I stressed we could, therefore, immediately apply for a research grant for the project.

A few months later, in 1978, our project having been accepted, I returned to Montreal to complete the research. Those were the rough years of anarchy in Turkey. Once in Montreal, when I found myself hiding behind the trees near the bus stop, a self-defence measure developed to avoid becoming the target of a possible sniper, I realized how difficult life had become in Istanbul! The day I went to Montreal University to begin my work I panicked at the idea of going there without any official paper stating my status or identity. Mentally, I prepared all possible answers to the questions they could ask me at the entrance of the building. What a relief: no police at the entrance, not even a person checking the comings and goings of the people, nothing. I felt absolutely ridiculous and realized how conditioned we had become by the many sad events we lived through in Istanbul. I suddenly felt like a deep-sea diver coming back from the depths of the sea and having to stop at different levels for decompression! Day by day, thanks to the well-balanced and orderly life of the Province of Québec, I succeeded in calming my nerves until I eventually recovered my equilibrium.

The research work began. We injected radioactive morphine into mice that we sacrificed a few hours later using a very sophisticated technique to avoid the de-granulation of the very fragile mast cells. Dr Cantin's wife, a researcher working in physiology, was familiar with the very sensitive technique used to detect the presence of morphine in the mast cells. The results would be available two months later. Therefore, I returned to Turkey and waited for the results to be sent. Weeks went by to no avail, no results, no letters, nothing. We began to wonder what was happening. The situation was a touchy one, giving the impression that I had gone to Canada but had done nothing. Then suddenly one day, Mother informed me of the sudden death of Dr Cantin. The silence surrounding the project was more or less explained. During this same period we were visited by a Rumanian neurologist and his wife, both working in Montreal and familiar with the University. They confirmed the sad news and indicated that Dr Cantin's research laboratory had been suffering severe budget problems.

This new theory on the tolerance to morphine, a project everyone was working on, proved most difficult to get accepted for publication. Not everyone looked so kindly upon this new approach to the mechanism of tolerance being proposed by an unknown Turkish group! The editors asked numerous questions and raised several objections. A.A. entrusted me with the job of rewriting the article and finding a new format to introduce the theory, a feat that took me six months to accomplish. Meanwhile, a colleague in the department who had recently suffered a heart attack began to display aggressive behaviour towards everyone. He purposely began to spread most unpleasant rumours about my NATO project trip to Canada. During this unpleasant period I began to develop some doubts about him and even suspected he could intercept my mail. In the meantime, the very important article on the theory of A.A. had been accepted for publication. The head of our department was not taking a firm position against the insinuations I was the target of, so I felt I did not have to cope with such an unpleasant situation and decided to leave the Institute in 1982. I then returned to the Department of Oncology to work with my former colleagues.

The University was then faced with the reforms suggested by the military authorities following the coup of 1980 and within a short time a new law regulating universities was accepted by the transitory Parliament then governing the country. Dr Berkarda had completed his term as dean of the medical school and was seriously considering working only part-time at the university. He was planning on opening a private medical centre for the treatment of oncological patients and asked me if I would consider working with him and be an associate in the firm. In 1983, not quite satisfied with the poor salary offered by the government to health workers and, with the help of Mehmet who offered to pay my share of the investment required for the establishment of our company, I left the university to work in the private sector.

Chapter XVI

Mehmet Returns from Military Service

In the month of April of 1969, Mehmet came back from Erzurum. At last, his military service was over! The first thing we did was to leave the neighborhood of Fındıkzade, so close to my work, and return to live on the Asian side of the city. One of the interesting aspects of living in Istanbul is that everyone has a definite opinion about which side of the city to live in. Some will swear they cannot live on any other side but the European side, while others claim that the only liveable part of the city is in Asia. In those days, the Asian side of the city was mostly a residential area consisting of lovely private homes, or rather summerhouses, in gorgeous gardens. Any true inhabitant of this city had to have a summer residence either on the Princes' Islands or on the Asian side of the city with a main residence on the European side of the city. Slowly, things changed dramatically and those lovely houses with their rose gardens and fruit trees disappeared, leaving room for the construction of apartment towers of dubious taste. Although I was not born here, the thought of those lovely days fills me with nostalgia. Mehmet absolutely could not even consider living in a neighbourhood of concrete without trees and gardens. Finally, we found a large apartment in an area close to my in-laws' home on the Asian side, on a street with the poetic name of "Gülden"–"from the rose". Opposite the apartment building was a huge empty green field where Rahmi was to spend the major part of his youth, playing soccer. This is where we lived until 1976.

Barely a few weeks after Mehmet's return and before our move, we had our first visitors from abroad, my close friend from university years, Lise Héroux. We had studied together in Québec City and worked together in Ottawa. She came with her friend Bernadette. They were the first visitors I had from Canada and I was very moved by their visit. I did my best to make their stay in Istanbul pleasant and interesting and when possible, tried to accompany them wherever they went. Our most interesting and memorable outing was without doubt our visit to my neighborhood's Turkish bath. Our arrival at the bath in that very Turkish section of the city created quite a commotion. Everyone was looking at us and since we were speaking French and were much taller then our Turkish counterparts, it was impossible for us to maintain a low profile. Besides, we could not get ourselves used to the idea of going around naked, while, quite the opposite, Turkish women appeared very comfortable exhibiting their chubby bodies and short legs. We were closely observed because, as good Christians, we had not epilated the strategic areas of our bodies as prescribed by custom here. We became objects of curiosity! This most awkward situation pushed our great storyteller Lise to exhibit her talents. Inspired by the surroundings, she began relating her famous repertory of "stories". How Lise succeeded in maintaining such a rich repertory of stories that she constantly updated was beyond my comprehension; she was so funny. Of course Turkish ladies would never behave in this most improper manner and we howled with laughter! Under the filtered light of the magnificent dome in the most important room of the Turkish bath, languishingly stretched on the warm marble, we listened to the voice of Lise merging with the gentle sound of water softly dripping from a lovely chiseled marble fountain in the background. The heat, the massage... we fell under the spell of the unusual moments of calm and relaxation. After the bath we enjoyed Turkish tea served in the local tea glasses. An unforgettable experience out of the thousand and one nights! The custom of Turkish baths is anchored in the Turkish way of life and many cities of the country such as Bursa are well known for their lovely baths and for spas famed for their therapeutic properties.

During her stay in Istanbul, Lise informed me that she was in love, but that there was a small problem. Intrigued, I waited for her explanation. She proceeded to tell me that her Prince Charming was a

Catholic priest. He had officially petitioned the Vatican to obtain a release from his vows, so he could leave the priesthood. That was both an astonishing and shocking piece of news. A Catholic priest... Still, I was ready to concede that love did have rather unexplainable aspects! They were married and had two lovely daughters, but their marriage came to an end twenty years later.

Once my friends had left, we moved to the Asian side and Mehmet began looking for a job. Thanks to the influence of my then boss, Dr Osmanoğlu, he found work in a Turkish pharmaceutical company. The owner of this firm was a very well known and respected pharmacist, a pioneer in the pharmaceutical industry of the country. A good businessman, he demonstrated a sense of perspicacity by hiring one of the first Turkish marketing graduates. Mehmet immediately was given the task of undertaking a nation-wide market research project on the consumption of medication in Turkey. The aim was to obtain precise information and statistics that were unavailable from the Ministry of Health. It was a huge project and included visits to all existing pharmacies, drug wholesalers and pharmaceutical warehouses, hospitals and outpatient departments of the whole country. In addition to this work load, an exact list of all practicing doctors in each province of the country was to be established since such an updated list was simply not available anywhere, not even with the Medical Association. Statistics has never been and will never be the favourite subject of the Turks! Even today, finding a reliable and exact figure on any subject remains difficult, if not impossible. In eight months with a team of over one hundred people, Mehmet led the project, a first of its kind. Most of his team was made up of retired army officers. Those men knew the country well, having spent many years during their careers in various parts of Anatolia. Showing authority, a lot of ingenuity–and with the help of friends still in service in faraway places difficult to reach–those men accomplished the almost impossible. At the end of the research, a bulky report was presented to the Ministry of Public Health. That work contributed in establishing Mehmet's reputation in the marketing world.

With Mehmet's military service over, we had a very important obligation to fulfill–getting married once more! In a very simple ceremony with two witnesses and in front of my mother-in-law and my son

Rahmi, we were legally married for a second time, on 19 July 1969. I wore the same dress I had worn at my first wedding but without the veil. Following the ceremony, we came back home and Rahmi immediately began running up and down our street shouting, "My parents got married today..." What a scandal! A few days later the event was celebrated with a big party held at my in-laws' home. Mehmet dove into one of his secret spots in the Marmara Sea and gathered more than two hundred huge mussels. Cleaned and stuffed with rice by a family friend and then tied together with string one by one, they were cooked in a huge pan and became a pure delicacy for our guests.

On that particular evening, I wore a traditional long velvet dress covered with gold thread embroidery, like the Turkish brides of former days. The house was filled with guests and the entertainment was absolutely unforgettable with the great singer and saz player Ruhi Su at his best. That excellent performer, a baritone graduated from the conservatory, following a brilliant career in opera had deliberately chosen folk music and was to become one of its most respected interpreters. A member of the Alevi community, he had also been a teacher at the Village Institutes. His repertory included the musical poems of ancient poets such as Yunus Emre and Pir Sultan Abdal. The theme of the poems he chose was generally human rights or criticism of oppressive regimes that deprived human beings of their rights and liberties, which did not make him very popular with the authorities. Sadly, he became one of the most cunningly persecuted personalities in the country. During his lifetime, not one single song of his traditional repertory was ever aired on national television or radio. Suffering from cancer, he was denied a passport and never had the right to consult medical authorities abroad. When the passport was finally issued, it was already too late... Who has the right to deprive a man of his hope?

Now that we had achieved economic stability, Mehmet decided to realize one of his dearest dreams: the construction of a boat, the exact replica of the one destroyed in a storm while he was away studying in the United States. His first boat had a very special meaning for him because it had formerly belonged to the great poet Orhan Veli before his uncle bought it and then passed it on to him. It had been named "Yaprak" ("Leaf") after the literary review published by the poet. A very strong southern wind had blown and the boat was smashed to pieces where it was anchored in Kalamış Bay. It had been a very graceful, slim boat seven meters long, as they built them in Istanbul in former years. Its slender shape allowed it to be easily rowed. Mehmet, with pictures of the boat in hand, went around to the different workshops where boats were constructed to find a craftsman willing to build the object of his dreams. That whole winter we made periodic visits to check on the state of the boat. In front of our eyes, like a slow-motion film, we followed the evolution of our new "Yaprak" through all the various phases of its construction. At each visit I was deeply impressed by the dexterity of our carpenter, Bilal Usta, ("usta" is a term used to describe those reaching the highest level in the practice of a trade), as he managed to transform rigid pieces of wood into elegant curved forms, soon to become our boat. It reminded me of the days during the fifties when my father had built his own boat in his friend's basement. We were living a very similar experience with all the emotions that it involved. You could see Mehmet's happiness in his shining green eyes as we saw "Yaprak" coming alive! In the month of April, the boat was completed and my mother-in-law painted a beautiful fish just under the boat's name.

When the great day arrived and just before the boat was launched into the waters of the Marmara Sea, to my horror, a rooster was sacrificed! Such deeply embedded traditions exert a powerful influence; it is usual in such circumstances to sacrifice an animal so that the blood flows. The rooster had been the smallest token available.

Since Mehmet has always been a great admirer of the sea and a fishing fan, that boat and its outboard motor became two crucial elements of his life. It was useless to ask what we would do on weekends or holidays. The answer never changed. We went to the Islands for fishing or we would sail along the Bosphorus. We thus had the opportunity to swim in the cleanest spots of the Marmara Sea beyond the Princes' Islands. The numerous fish migrating from the Black Sea to the Mediterranean Sea must, to the great pleasure of the fishermen, pass through the Bosphorus and then cross the Sea of Marmara. The wind in Istanbul usually rises in the afternoon, so very often on our way back to the marina, we suffered foul weather and would have to battle against strong waves. Many times we came back soaked to the bones and freezing to death in spite of the warm weather. Quite the opposite of myself, the wetter Mehmet got, the happier he was.

Learning to fish the Turkish way proved to be a memorable experience. I had to forget all the techniques my father had taught me and learn new methods. Mehmet handed me a small rectangular piece of cork with fifty meters of fishing line wound around it. At the extreme end, according to the capacity of the fisherman, ten, fifteen or even twenty hooks were attached every fifteen centimetres. These hooks were covered with feathers and according to the fish we were looking for, were either with or without bait. It required some dexterity before I could even begin not to be caught in all these hooks. If one had the luck to catch seven or more fish at the same time, it was a professional feat to get the line back in the boat and to unhook the fish without mixing up the line or getting hooked in the process.

The boat was both a source of pleasure and hard work since every spring it had to be scraped down and repainted. During this task, what appeared to be a small boat only seven meters long suddenly took on the proportions of an ocean liner. This light and gentle "Yaprak" when taken out of the water and brought back to our garden seemed to be made of lead. In those days, living in Istanbul without a boat seemed unthinkable, but now the water pollution has reached such proportions that swimming and fishing are two activities that are out of question, at least for the moment. Now, in order to enjoy the sea, every year we must relocate for a few weeks to the southern coast. Since the year 2000, our boat has been resting in a corner of our garden, abandoned; it has not seen the sea for some years...

The routine of our life had begun. Both Mehmet and I worked every day of the week, even Saturday mornings. Rahmi was in primary school, and the first three years of his schooling were full-time, from morning until the end of the afternoon. Then the system changed and students were in school for half a day, either in the morning or the afternoon. That complicated things for working mothers and led to the development of a large network of private schools. Their fees were rather exorbitant, but they did offer a full-day education system. Before long, we had to resort to this option.

Since there was yet no bridge over the Bosphorus, our daily routine was to get on the ferryboat at the right time every morning and then again in the late afternoon, otherwise our daily schedule got completely mixed up. I was usually back home by five o'clock while Mehmet arrived close to eight o'clock. That hellish race lasted until 1977 for Mehmet, and until 1991 for me. At that time, that lifestyle seemed normal but now, as I look back, I am beginning to question the wisdom of such a life for a mother. The profession I loved so much, those research projects I used to find so enthralling, they seemed impossible to live without. When I retired, how did I succeed in leaving them behind as if they were nothing, as if they had never existed? Such a change in my attitude actually stunned me. By a strange coincidence, both Mehmet and I at a definite moment in our lives managed to turn our backs on our chosen careers in order to do totally different things! I, who thought that leaving my cherished profession was nothing short of treachery, found myself realizing the fact that it was not as traumatic as I thought it would be! Of course, there are times when I wish I could sit at my microscope and examine a slide of bone marrow, but on the whole, I do not miss working!

In the summer of 1969, my in-laws and Rahmi took a trip to several European countries and then to Romania to visit my mother-in-law's family. They were away for more than two months. When Rahmi came back, he could even speak a few words of Romanian! It was the first trip my father-in-law had made to his wife's country; the dream dating back to 1934 had finally come true. At that time, my mother-in-law had left her hometown of Iaşi to live in Bucharest and had been dreaming of the day when her beloved would come from Turkey to visit. The projects, the dreams and hopes she had lived with during that waiting period had never been fulfilled. It was only some thirty-five years later that her dream became reality.

In 1971, Mehmet left his job at the Turkish pharmaceutical firm to join the large Swiss based firm of Hoffman-Laroche. Thanks to his new job, we finally got a phone at home, a great luxury at that time! He worked two years for that firm before leaving when one of the executives made uncalled-for comments about Mehmet's private life and his relationship with his staff. Mehmet had gone fishing with two of his assistants. This might have been considered strange on the part of one of the managers of an international firm, but it was very much the Turkish way. Within a few hours of the incident, Mehmet was at home. I had never thought it was possible for one to gather personal effects together so quickly.

1970 was the year I lived my first experiences in the turbulent waters of Turkey's political life, for it was the year of the military ultimatum of 12 March and the declaration of martial law. Many countries lived through periods of phobia against communism and even the United States was not spared this fear, despite the thousands of kilometres that separated it from Russia. If you consider the proximity of the Soviet Union to Turkey, it is easier to understand the severity of the phobia crisis felt in Turkey.

To what extent the danger was real or not, no one will ever know, but as a result of it, severe repressive measures were taken and applied through the years. They led to a long lasting persecution of a large number of writers, poets, journalists and intellectuals. As far back as the early forties, the great contemporary Turkish poet, Nazim Hikmet, was imprisoned for many years. Despite close surveillance, once liberated he found a way of leaving the country clandestinely and went to live in Russia. Many years have gone by since his death, yet the diplomats still haven't found an acceptable formula to bring his bones back to Turkey. I presume he must not still be considered a dangerous individual since his works are now legally available in the bookstores of the country. The truth is that a deep distrust was felt against anything labelled as "social-democrat" or as "socialist" and this feeling was exaggerated on purpose for political reasons. This was expressed by a strong obsession and mistrust towards leftist thought and everything was done to intimidate the intellectuals. If one was to compare the trials and investigations in both Turkey and the United States, a fundamental difference can of course be observed: in Turkey, the country was under martial law and our intellectuals were on trial before military judges!

One by one journalists and writers were arrested and on 20 July 1971, we were informed that Uncle Sabahattin and his wife Magdi, together with three colleagues, had been arrested early that morning. That caused a brutal shock in literary circles and the family was extremely upset. My father-in-law desperately tried to find out where his brother had been taken, but to no avail. Sad days filled with deep apprehension followed. Finally, after several transfers in Istanbul, from the headquarters of the National Security department to the headquarters of the army, they were traced to the military prison in Selimiye on the Asian side of Istanbul. During the course of the next eight months, Mehmet followed their trial and all the members of the family took turns visiting the prisoners, who were by then being held in the military prison in Maltepe.

During my youth in my Canadian hometown, while reading Kafka's *The Trial*, it was impossible for me to really believe that such events could happen and especially place myself in the atmosphere described in that realistically written book. My first visit to the prison took me into the realms of a strange world. Following a thorough search of my personal effects, I sat in a military truck with other visitors and some soldiers, trying with great difficulty to understand exactly the reality of what was happening. It was then I discovered the existence of several levels of reality that are based on the various points of view of different people. But I especially felt that a form of well-directed theatre production in very poor taste was unfolding in front of me. On one of our visits, a rather shaken Uncle Sabahattin asked his brother in a sad voice, "Please, I beg you, get me out of here!" That cry of despair was devastating and broke our hearts. Uncle Sabahattin had had but one concern in his lifetime: to do everything possible in order to improve the living conditions and education levels of the people of his country. Witnessing the state in which he as an honest and valuable citizen found himself absolutely revolted us. To see a man submitted to such treatment while his main thought had been to translate properly the masterpieces of world literature and to study the relationships between ancient Anatolian civilizations and the elements of contemporary life heightened the incoherence of the situation. Finally, even the prosecution saw no other way out but to ask the court to release him. Suddenly, our uncle was set free. Everything happened so fast that we barely had time to drive to the prison in Maltepe and bring him back to our home in Kalamış. His wife was only released a few days later.

These dreadful actions were perpetuated in the name of what? No one knows. No positive results were generated, to the contrary, they caused a lot of suffering and engendered a lot of bitterness. All this served rather to tarnish the image of the army and its court of justice, both at home and abroad. I am sure that was not what the army wanted to achieve. Those months of imprisonment marked Uncle Sabahattin deeply and it was with great awe and deep surprise that I heard him utter, some time after his release, the most aggressive and threatening sentence of his life. Every Friday night, all the members of the family would meet at Mehmet's grandmother's home for dinner. It was there that he told us in a harsh voice: "I shall avenge myself on those who imprisoned me!" Alarmed, I asked what he meant... "I shall translate the book of *Gargantua* by Rabelais..." he answered. With great enthusiasm he described the inscription set upon the great gate of Theleme, in the abbey of the Thelemites, which almost became an epitaph...

Here enter not vile bigots, hypocrites,

Externally devoted apes, base snites,
Puffed-up, wry-necked beasts, worse than the Huns,
Or Ostrogoths, forerunners of baboons:
Cursed snakes, dissembled varlets, seeming sancts,
Slipshod caffards, beggars pretending wants,
Fat chuffcats, smell-feast knockers, doltish gulls,
Out-strouting cluster-fists, contentious bulls,
Fomenters of divisions and debates,
Elsewhere, not here, make sale of your deceits.

Your filthy trumperies
Stuffed with pernicious lies
(Not worth a bubble),
Would do but trouble
Our earthly paradise
Your filthy trumperies.

Here enter not attorneys, barristers,
Nor bridle-champing law-practitioners:

Clerks, commissaries, scribes, nor Pharisees,
Wilful disturbers of the people's ease:
Judges, destroyers, with an unjust breath,
Of honest men, like dogs, even unto death.
Your salary is at the gibbet-foot:
Go drink there! for we do not here fly out
On those excessive courses, which may draw
A waiting on your courts by suits in law.

What a difference between the parties involved! On one hand, the accusers depriving a man of his liberty and on the other hand, the noble unjustly accused man, defending himself with his literary culture, his only weapon. He translated the book along with the friends who had been with him in prison, companions in both work and injustice. On the afternoon of 13 January 1973, the day the translation was almost completed, ending with the above-mentioned inscription, he suffered a second heart attack and died. That day, there was a heavy snowfall in Istanbul, as if to blanket the sadness of the events.

That awful news utterly destroyed my father-in-law, closely bound to the brother who had had such a profound influence on his life. That deep unlimited admiration felt for the "abi", the older brother, had been a source of sorrow during the last few years. Their relationship seemed to have cooled down, especially on the part of Uncle Sabahattin, who would avoid visiting his brother even when in the neighbourhood. At times, there had been serious discussions between the two brothers regarding the dual creativity of Bedri Rahmi, in both poetry and painting. The elder brother firmly believed and maintained that his younger brother should have chosen only one form of artistic expression to which he should have been totally dedicated. Defending himself, Bedri Rahmi maintained that he had no control over those two different urges. There were periods when he felt like painting and others when he felt the urge to write. Whatever the reason behind the coolness that seemed to slip between the two brothers, Bedri Rahmi used to complain about it often and it caused him a lot of unhappiness.

During the heavy snowstorm, all the men of the family converged on the home of Uncle Sabahattin to spend the night. Such storms are rarely seen in Istanbul and the city was paralyzed for several days. Nezahat, the elder sister, came from Ankara with great difficulty. After the funeral, the whole family gathered at Mehmet's grandmother's home. Despite her advanced age, she was very lucid, but the news of Sabahattin's death dealt her a terrible blow. Within a short period, she escaped into a world without a past where she lived several years. After having spent a few days with her, everyone had to return to their homes and their own lives.

Our relationship with Uncle Sabahattin had always been warm but tainted with great reserve. He was not a person with whom one could casually talk of this and that. Besides the holidays or the once a week family get together at Mehmet's grandmother's home, we often went to the Monday evening meetings at his house, where everyone would drop by for supper. Personalities of the academic, artistic and literary worlds would be there, everyone having brought something to eat or drink. The meal would then proceed with stimulating discussions. On some lucky evenings, we would be treated to a slide projection presentation of his last trip to Anatolia to some unusual village or archaeological site. Often we were privileged to have a lesson in art history, to listen to a discussion on his latest translation or to be informed about the newest discoveries at various archaeological sites. Whatever the subject, we always left these meetings happy to have acquired some new knowledge on a specific subject. Just like my father-in-law, he had the exceptional gift of passing his enthusiasm on to others.

He was very fond of Rahmi and at every family get together at Mehmet's grandmother's home, he would always bring him a small gift or one of the whirligigs he had carefully built. On the first Christmas we spent in Istanbul, I had no means to buy a tree to decorate for Rahmi. Very innocently, I mentioned the fact during a family dinner. Very discreetly, he gave me the required amount of money asking me not to reveal its source. During his imprisonment, he decorated the common room of the prison in Maltepe with whirligigs he had himself made in all possible colors and shapes. His own garden, which he would with great pride present for our admiration, was filled with an assortment of whirligigs in every imaginable color. Having suffered a heart attack, he was under medical surveillance. One day I learned that his friend, the novelist Yaşar Kemal, had taken him to the American Hospital for his yearly check-up. I do not know what happened to me, but without the least hesitation, totally contrary to my usual reservedness and despite the deep respect always shown to the elder members of the family, I made a most uncalled-for comment. I expressed the surprise I felt when our uncle, known as a great supporter of Turkish culture, chose to be treated at the American Hospital, for which I had no sympathy, while I, his niece, was working with some of Turkey's best doctors. Overwhelmed by my boldness, he first looked at me a bit stupefied, then agreed that I was right. I had been unable to control my Canadian side as it popped up once again!

Our uncle left behind an impressive number of works in various fields: essays, translations of masterpieces of Western world literature, documentary films on various subjects, many photographs and slides of different sites of Turkey, in short, a lifetime of labour to protect. He also left behind Magdi, his companion for over twenty years, without a legal title. She was not even entitled to legally dispose of his estate, a job that fell onto the shoulders of his family. A few editing houses kept printing his works, but over the years, he was slowly buried in oblivion, simply because the members of the family were growing old and no one seemed to have the required energy to handle the formalities involved. Mehmet, showing great respect for his aunts and uncle, did not interfere with their arrangements. But in 1999, when approached by the publishing house of a large bank with regard to the publication of his father's books, he stipulated he would consider their offer only on the condition they would take over the publication of his uncle's works. The director, a very tactful and patient man, succeeded in gathering together the responsible members of the family to obtain their agreement. The entire body of work of our uncle was finally secured.

After living in Turkey for six years, I took my first trip back to Canada in 1972. Of course it turned out to be a very emotional event for me. Taking advantage of the very cheap fares offered by chartered flights, I decided that Rahmi should go with me. Our resources were very limited, and after paying for the tickets and buying a small amount of foreign currency, nothing was left in our funds. I asked my father-in-law if he could help me to pay for Rahmi's ticket, but in a very proper literary form he refused, carefully adding a proverb saying, "You should never extend your foot further than the length of your blanket..." Very comforting words to hear when you have not seen your family for six years!

Many documents had to be gathered: a formal permission document from Mehmet giving permission for Rahmi to travel with me, Turkish passports for Rahmi and myself in order to leave and re-enter the country, an American passport for Rahmi and a Canadian passport for me. Finally, all the paperwork was done and we were ready to leave for New York, the first phase of our trip. The plane was filled mostly with elderly people going to the United States to visit their children established there. By the time our plane left, we were many hours late and when we arrived at our destination, many passengers could no longer find anyone waiting for them at the airport. Since they could not speak English well enough to place a phone call to their love ones, I spent a good half hour calling a few families in order to inform them of the plane's arrival, not to mention calming down more than a few anxious travellers.

Bearing our huge suitcases, once we reached the city we went directly to the 42nd Street Port Authority bus terminal where we were to board a bus to Montreal. We stored our luggage in a locker at the end of the afternoon and decided to take a walk in the vicinity so Rahmi could see a bit of New York. To my great surprise, an African-American policeman very politely approached me and asked where I was going. He warned me that the city had changed a lot since my departure in 1966 and did not recommend I walk around the streets after sunset. I was a bit baffled by this information and wondered what I should do... After a very short walk, we came back to the huge hall and waited for the departure time of our bus. Those were the years when mini-skirts were very fashionable and Rahmi was very surprised to see a few Canadian girls waiting with us, wearing jackets longer than their mini-skirts. He innocently asked me if they had forgotten to wear their skirts. Once in Canada, I found myself forced to buy a few mini-skirts because Mother refused to go out and be seen with a daughter in long skirts! At the end of my trip, once back in Turkey, it was Mehmet's turn to be very surprised by the length of my skirts.... Traveling through the night, we arrived in Montreal in the early morning. Mother had been living in

Montreal, in the northern part of the city, for the last few years. It was rather strange to find my family in a different city, in a new environment, leading a new life. Claude was now married and I met her husband, Alain, and her lovely daughter, Paula. My brother, Jacques, was in a summer camp and I barely saw him until the very end of my stay. That first return to my country after a lapse of six years proved to be a difficult event to live through. In my mind, I had a clear memory of a given period of Canada, but during the six years of my absence, many things had changed! I had also changed and found it upsetting to observe these changes, assimilate them and re-adjust myself to the "new reality" of the country. The main surprise was that I had left the country as a Canadian, but upon my return, I found I was now a Québecer! The once powerful Catholic Church had lost most of its former supremacy, and our society was living a "Révolution tranquille". For a week, I felt a bit disoriented, as if in another world; then the adaptation process took over and everything returned to normal.

Besides my family, I had the pleasure of seeing once more my friends from the University years, the two Lise's. One was living in Montreal with her husband, the "former priest", while the second one was now married and living in Drummondville. The month was over in no time and I went back to New York to catch my charter flight back home. The amount of baggage our good Turkish passengers were trying to bring back to Turkey was something to see! Everyone had more than triple the weight allowed. There was a great deal of confusion at the airport and almost as many languages as the tower of Babel. Once again, we left the American continent some ten hours late. Rahmi's first comment when we arrived in Turkey was to remark, in a mixture of three languages, "Mummyciğim, how dirty Istanbul got while we were away." Six more years went by before I saw Québec again. Fortunately, Mother came to visit us during those years.

Mehmet was then looking for work in another field of activity and finally chose to work for a newly established aluminium firm. Following the quiet, well-planned years at Hoffman-La Roche, his new position was a return to the frantic activities of market research, including business trips to Anatolian cities such as Trabzon, Gaziantep and Maraş. A young and dynamic team trained in America gave their hearts and souls in order to open up new markets for their firm. At the very beginning, the company headquarters were in the centre of the city, in Sirkeci near the train station. The factory was fifty kilometres out of the city, in the small town of Gebze. A pleasant atmosphere and exceptional under-standing had been established among the personnel of the various departments of the company. They worked with such fervour that noth-ing seemed impossible. Encouraged by competent directors, they accomplished miracles in a short time and aluminium began to be sold at an unbelievable rate. Mehmet, who had not lost any of his pioneering and research qualities, worked very hard to introduce the use of alu-minium in the newspaper industry. And this important new market did open, despite the disbelief of everyone.

In the middle of June 1973, Mother came to Istanbul to spend the summer with us and to join us in our annual "Blue Trip". That was the year she learned what it was like to spend days without running water. This was a new and inconceivable element in the life of a citizen of the province of Québec: to live among pails of water spread here and there in the house for daily use. Since I was working during the daytime, she was alone with Rahmi and the dialogue was inevitably limited. Luckily, it was the year the Istanbul Music Festival began, offering a rather interesting program. After long waits for precious tickets, we managed to see Gisele, with the Royal Ballet, at the Open-Air Theater, with its magnificent view of the Bosphorus and the Tower of Leander. A recital in Aya Irina, an old Byzantine Church, transported us back several centuries ago, a most wonderful experience. We were privileged to attend the first-ever per-formance at the Topkapi Palace of Mozart's opera, "The Kidnapping from the Seraglio". Topkapi Palace, classified as one of the most important museums in the world, is the former residence of the Ottoman sultans. During this month of vacation, we went to Marmaris by bus with fifteen other people for our annual Blue Trip. We were to board the boat "Hudaverdi"* for a twelve-day cruise on the Mediterranean Sea. That Blue Trip turned out to be one of the best trips we ever took. Among the participants was an Italian-American haematologist, with whom my boss B.B. had worked for a year in the

---

* Hudaverdi means "God given".

United States, and his American wife, Glenda. He had shown great interest in a postcard I had sent my boss the previous year and expressed his wish to come to Turkey to take the cruise. A colleague from Montréal, Pierrette, was also with us. Before joining the trip, she had worked for a week to set up new laboratory methods in the nephrology department of our clinic. The other participants included two well-known Turkish painters, Turan Erol and Mustafa Pilevneli, and a young amateur astrologist who worked in the finance department of Mehmet's firm, along with his enigmatic Dutch girlfriend.

This lady was awaited with great curiosity and became the source of much speculation up until the hour of our departure. At the bus station, waiting for the same bus as we were, we noticed a foreign woman of a "certain age" wearing a large white hat over a blond wig. We were most surprised to learn that she was the girlfriend of our young economist-astrologist! Also participating in the trip was a "lion hunter" and his wife. That gentleman had earned his nickname thanks to the safari hat he wore and took excessive care of. Destiny planned a sad end to that hat: one night, the chaise-longue I was sleeping on collapsed on the hat which had been safely stored–or so we thought–under the chair. It was crushed flat, beyond repair. Furthermore, his wife, Ismet, had the bad luck of being seriously pinched by a huge lobster when, overcome by her curiosity, she lifted the lid of a pot of boiling water into which we had just placed the creature to cook. This voyage, deprived of any luxury or comfort, was remembered as the best Blue Trip of all times because of the pleasant atmosphere that reigned during the whole cruise. Various contests were organized: bridge, cooking, swimming, diving and even an art exhibit on the boat. Everyone exceeded himself: Giovanni's spaghetti was the most popular dish of the week and, following the trip, our professor decided to take sailing and cooking lessons. We were told by his wife that it was the first spaghetti he had cooked in his life! My father-in-law, also in excellent form, asked everyone on the boat to find oddly shaped rocks on which he would draw either a fish, or a mermaid and perhaps add a few verses from one of his poems. He drew self-portraits on every surface he could put his hands on: shells, sandals, rims of summer hats and even a "petit beurre" cookie Glenda took back to the United States. That edible masterpiece was to cause uproar later on when

Working on the restoration of the fish

Glenda took it to an art shop and asked them to find a way to preserve it for posterity. After having warned everyone about the fragile work of art and the importance of its being protected, she left the gallery. A few hours later, she received a phone call informing her that someone had taken a bite out of the precious cookie and that a corner was now missing with the imprints of the criminal teeth quite visible.

Everyone kept themselves busy in various ways; some slept under the stars at night and others climbed the ruins of old Lycian theaters. Everyone was happy and finding a thousand things to do. We even held an evening dedicated to the colour yellow and witnessed an array of objects transformed into apparel for the occasion. Even our yellow plastic plates were transformed into a bra for Glenda! The soul and star of our trip was of course our brave and modest Captain Kazım. This hard working remarkable man filled with love and care for others was everywhere at once, and could read our desires even before we expressed them. His first goal was not to earn a lot of money but, rather, to have us enjoy a pleasant trip. Experience has taught me that even if you take a trip in the most luxurious of boats, it may very well turn into a nightmare if your captain is not a capable and pleasant individual. You must also have the luck of traveling among pleasant people, because the success of the trip is directly related to the amount of "blue" found in each of the participants. We were to have a few more trips with Captain Kazım until he died prematurely of renal insufficiency. At the end of this first trip, we spent a few days in Bodrum in the small house my father-in-law had just bought and to which my mother-in-law later added the adjacent house. Old Greek houses, they were first restored under the care of my mother-in-law and then under Mehmet's directive for our own use. At the end of the summer, Mother returned to Canada, rested and happy with her trip.

In 1974, my father-in-law began to complain about rashes or allergies, blaming them on the various materials he used in painting. He also had to deal with a serious drinking problem that had been causing him a lot of trouble. It seemed he was unable to overcome the problem. In the aftermath of the military ultimatum, he was under a great deal of stress because he had become the director of the painting department at the Academy of Fine Arts, a position he never enjoyed. In addition, he had to face numerous and endless discussions, deeply encrusted animosity and great jealousy because quite a few of his students had obtained excellent results in the "European Competition". Surrounded by colleagues who did not appreciate in the least his ways of doing things and considered him a deadly rival, most faculty meetings were occasions for venomous discussions. He became especially bitter when he learned that some of his former students formed the core of the opposition. Bedri Rahmi headed an atelier for almost thirty years and he trained seventy-five percent of the best contemporary painters of Turkey. During the last three years of his life, in the midst of such endless battles, his position brought him only disappointment and weariness.

For the opening ceremonies of the academic year during those times of anarchy, he chose to relate the difficulties he, as an artist, had faced while trying to complete a commissioned work from Germany by using material coming from Turkey. During his speech, he was impolitely interrupted by the president of the student federation who insisted on talking about "the problems of the country", rather than the problems Bedri Rahmi had chosen. The aim of that troublesome student was to criticize the political system as if he were taking part in a meeting held by the School of Political Sciences. Exasperated, Bedri Rahmi asked his young interlocutor: "How old a Turk are you? I am a Turk of sixty years. How many years of military service have you done? I did three years of service." Then in the moment of great emotion and eloquence that followed, Bedri Rahmi brilliantly continued to address the interrupter with one of his best poems, "One of each was not sufficient; many others were needed..."

This poem describes the deep sufferings of the country while praising the greatness of the very few individuals who had struggled to improve life, but who were insufficient in numbers. Besides the thousands without names who lost their lives in war or battles, Atatürk, the great architect Sinan and Ismail Tonguç, the great educator and father of the Village Institutes, are mentioned. The poem completed, he abruptly left the amphitheatre of the Academy in the midst of applause, leaving behind him a disconcerted student.

That was the period when Bedri Rahmi had just completed a stained-glass window for the new Turkish Embassy in Bonn, Germany. He had intended to work in co-operation with the large Turkish glass producing company, Paşabahçe. However, due to severe technical problems, he was forced to use glass material from Czechoslovakia, an added source of expense that had to be paid for in foreign currency. Since he didn't feel well, during the spring months of 1975, Bedri Rahmi abstained from alcohol for one month until 1 April when he decided to consult Dr Berkarda. The examination revealed the presence of an abdominal mass and within a few days an obstruction of the bile ducts led to jaundice. X-rays showed the presence of a mass in the pancreas and it was decided he should have palliative surgery to allow the flow of the bile to resume so his jaundice would disappear. We were then informed of the seriousness of his disease and told that his days were numbered.

Following his surgery, I spent the night in his room together with a close friend of mine from the cardiology department. My father-in-law was an easy patient without caprice; the night was quiet, he appeared to be resting quietly following a long day of suffering. Suddenly in the middle of the night, he called me saying, "Gelin! (daughter-in-law) I have just finished writing a poem; kindly find some paper and write it down." We were stunned to hear him speak, thinking he was quietly sleeping. Overwhelmed by my emotions, I felt I would not be able to write in Turkish, so I asked my friend Canan to note down the poem he had been working on since he had left the operating room. The poem related how under anesthesia, just like a bird, his soul had left his body to perch itself on the branches of a tree near the operating room. He described all he had observed in the room and how the bird re-entered his body following the surgery.

The occurrence of all these events coincided with an important exhibition of his work in an Istanbul art gallery. The news of his health problems followed by his operation fell like a bomb on the artistic world. Exact details of his disease were not available but speculation was high and the sale of his paintings increased at once. As soon as he was discharged from the hospital, an incessant flow of visitors began: friends, old flames, buyers and admirers. In the meantime, I had the unpleasant job of reminding Mehmet that he should take the proper measures to find a burial site since eventually it would inevitably become necessary. Mehmet was utterly overwhelmed by my proposition and thought I was very harsh and without pity to dare think of such details. But I knew deep down inside that he understood what I meant. Such a task would be most difficult to accomplish at a later period. Showing great courage, he looked around and found a plot with a great view of the Princes' Islands... at least a superb spot for visitors. The plot was for four people, but conscious of the difficulties related to this unpleasant job and wanting to avoid giving such a task to the future generation, Mehmet returned and bought four more places, adjacent to the first plot. Our problems were solved for a long time!

Bedri Rahmi was an intelligent man and before long he began wondering about his health. Both Mehmet and his mother were firmly opposed to the idea of informing him about his condition. That brought about the beginning of a great theatrical performance on our part. Going through his papers at a later period, I remember finding a sheet where he had made a list of words beginning with the letter K and had written the following heading: "the things I like the most that begin with the letter "k" such as kadın (women), kiraz (cherries)" and so on, while under the heading "the things I hate the most that begin with the same letter", the first word was "kanser (cancer)!"

Since alcohol abuse had been a feature of his life during his final years, he was both terrified and almost convinced that one day he would suffer from cirrhosis of the liver. Very discreetly we exploited this theme and let it be understood that it was most likely what he was suffering from. In order to avoid raising any suspicions about the seriousness of his state, we planned our Blue Trip as if nothing were wrong. Feeling rather well for a while, he enjoyed a short period during which he could do some research and work on his latest and final passion: ceramic plates.

It was during this period that he met a young photographer by the name of Şakir Serengil who had just completed his studies in Germany and was mostly interested in cinema. He wanted to make a film on "Bedri Rahmi, the Poet". Following long hours of discussion and preparation, they finally came to an agreement. A tape recorder was set near Bedri Rahmi's bed and everyday, he would read his poems and add some pertinent information and details about them to make the shooting of the film easier. That very precious document was prepared almost without our being aware of it. After the work was completed, Şakir took a few days off for a boat trip with friends from Germany; they had planned to go to Şile, a small village on the Black Sea. We wished him a nice holiday and begged him to be careful because the sea in that area was known to be dangerous and treacherous even for good swimmers. The weekend passed and soon Wednesday of the following week was upon us, but there was still no news from Şakir. We decided to call his family and find out where he was. To our deep stupefaction we learned that Şakir had drowned in Şile during the weekend and had already been buried. Mehmet was overwhelmed and tried desperately to come up with a way to inform his father of what had happened, but the expression on his face betrayed him. It became impossible to hide the tragedy any longer. The shock was terrible and my father-in-law almost collapsed. What a tragic destiny for such a young man! The reel of tape became a precious relic for the family of the deceased. They expressed the wish to hear the voice of their son on tape and keep it as a living memory of him. Unfortunately, only the voice of my father-in-law was found on the tape! They later returned the reel of tape to us.

Several years later, a Turkish composer and singer living in Paris, Zülfü Livaneli, expressed the desire to compose a melody for one of my father-in-law's poems written for the great poet Nazım Hikmet and entitled, "They carve a prison cell from the stone" and said that he wanted to hear the poem read by the poet himself. The owner of a large publishing house, Mr Erdal Öz, acted as the middleman in the arrangement. With great confidence, we gave the precious tape to him without taking the precaution of making a copy. That naive act proved to be a major blunder that still haunts us today. That big reel of tape was never returned despite several attempts to trace it. Aunt Nezahat, Livaneli's former middle school Turkish teacher, begged his parents to have the tape returned, but to no avail: the tape had simply disappeared. Needless to say, we never even received a copy of the final work from the composer! Several years later, Mr Livaneli decided to enter politics and became a leftist party candidate for the office of mayor of the city of Istanbul. To our great despair, the musical theme of his campaign was the musical version of that poem and it constantly echoed through the streets. Each time we heard his voice and the theme of the song, "This is where my brave one, my lion, lies imprisoned", we were sadly reminded of our mistake. How could we not feel a breach of faith as Bedri Rahmi, author of the poem, and Nazım Hikmet were both grossly exploited? It was sad to realize that a well-known composer, the object of respect he obviously did not deserve, could lower himself to such acts and so grossly abuse the confidence that people had placed in him. Mr Livaneli was not elected then, but he was later elected to Parliament in 2002! Nothing seems to impair his political career! We later learned from our writer and architect friend Şükrü Günbulut that our great composer had also used, without any acknowledgement, a poem of his mother's as well.

At the beginning of September, Bedri Rahmi's health deteriorated and he had to be hospitalized for a few days, mostly to relieve his discomfort and make his life less painful. Visitors with sad expressions came and went in great numbers. This was not very reassuring for a suffering and worried man. Tired of so many visitors and on the verge of exhaustion, he made a genuine effort not to hurt their feelings and dictated a text he signed and asked me to hang on the door of the room:

My good friends,
I am doing well, but I am very tired.
Please excuse me,
Bedri Rahmi

Some visitors are still angry with me, insinuating that I had, on my own initiative, prevented them from visiting my father-in-law. I could never understand this way of thinking; I consider it rather morbid. My father-in-law was very ill and anyone filled with a feeling of love and respect for him should have understood that it was not of prime importance to see him in that state. Some respect must be shown to a man fighting for his life. Peace should be provided, not the satisfaction of curiosity.

Bedri Rahmi died on 21 September 1975. His death has had a deep influence on the course of our lives. He left behind him a huge cultural heritage. It has required an enormous amount of time and effort to sort and classify his legacy and the endeavour to administrate all aspects of that legacy continues to this day.

Chapter XVII

The Blue Trip

T hree magic words, stimulating to the imagination, describe perfectly what our summer vacations were between the years 1970 and 1983. They describe a cruise along the Turkish coasts of the Aegean and the Mediterranean Seas, a journey taking place usually anywhere between the towns of Bodrum, Marmaris, Kaş and Antalya. On two later occasions, in 1986 and in 1997, we were asked to conduct two additional trips for very special reasons.

As the years went by, the concept behind the trip suffered drastic changes, the rental prices of the boats went way up and the various sites where one would stop became so overcrowded that we simply could not adapt ourselves to that new version of the trip. Areas once known for their quietness, clean air and unspoiled nature had given way to intensive sea traffic with noisy boats and the sudden appearance of diversified forms of pollution. The Blue Trip was once an intimate ritual in our lives and it was with great sadness that we abandoned that kind of summer vacation.

For the last two decades, those who have chosen to visit Turkey have been offered this tempting travel option to complete their tour of the country. Evoking a world of fantasy, many visitors have undertaken the trip but they are totally unaware of its history and original purpose. According to the season, the number of days and the budget involved, they are offered a wide variety of options from sail-it-yourself to completely organized cruises.

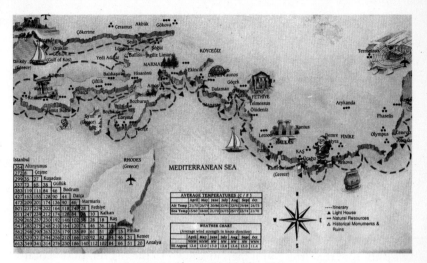

Usual itinerary for the Blue Trip

Since 1983, during our holidays, we have preferred to take short boat trips around Bodrum, where our summerhouse is. Our only activities are swimming and snorkelling in the wonderful blue turquoise bays dispersed here and there.

In 1925, Cevat Şakir Kabaağaçlı, a writer better known by his pseudonym, "The Fisherman of Halicarnassos", was exiled to Bodrum for three years. Bodrum was then a small village famous for its sponges and sponge divers. Besides the native population of the area, there were Turks from the Greek Islands who had come to Turkey during the population exchanges that took place after the War of Independence. An article criticizing the army had been the cause of his exile to that village. Though pardoned in the second year of his sentence, his strong attachment to the people kept him in Bodrum. This village, which at the time didn't have a single road, was built on the remains of the antique city of Halicarnassos, a city with a glorious past. A main city of the Carian Kingdom, it was famed for one of the seven marvels of the Ancient World, the Mausoleum, a tomb built in the memory of King Mausoleus by Queen Artemisia, who was both his sister and his wife. Destroyed by one of the many earthquakes the region has suffered, most of the stones of the monument were used by the Knights of Rhodes in the construction of the fortress of St-Petrum. A deformation of this word gave rise to the word now in use, Bodrum. Because it was so difficult to access, this village became poor and desolated.

Our "Fisherman of Halicarnassos" came from a well-known and established Istanbul family. He had spent his youth in Greece, where his father was a diplomat. Graduated from the American College in Istanbul, he completed his studies in England at Oxford University. Having mastered classical Greek, he had an excellent knowledge of Greek culture and its mythology and was extremely interested in Anatolian cultures, often confused with and referred to as Greek culture. A tireless researcher and passionate writer, he used mythological themes in his books and essays, while describing the harsh life of sponge divers and the natural beauties of the region. An amateur botanist, he managed to get hold of grapefruit seeds and succeeded in introducing the cultivation of that fruit, until then unknown to the region. In one of his books he related a fascinating story of his work on a tree called "bella-sombra". With great emotion, he described how he planted the seeds of that tree and watched over their growth as if they were his children. His happiness when he succeeded in growing the trees was boundless! Tragically, however, one day, the Mayor of Bodrum, for some strange reason decided to construct a new municipality building in the centre of the city close to the harbour, on the exact spot where those trees had been planted and were growing. He ordered the trees to be cut down and removed! That destructive, unnecessary act dealt a harsh blow to the "Fisherman of Halicarnassos" and was one of the reasons why he left Bodrum to live with his family in Izmir.

In those days, travelling in Anatolia was very difficult and very few individuals were aware of the presence of the many archaeological sites, which were largely inaccessible by conventional roads. Our writer, thanks to his fishermen friends, slowly discovered those sites and visited them. Filled with the excitement of his discoveries, he wished to share the result of his explorations and his knowledge with his fellow writer friends who were in Istanbul. The work done in Hattusha and its archives of over twenty-five thousand tablets, deciphered thanks to the work of Hrozny, followed by the reading of the Sumerian-Akkadian archives had yielded new knowledge and had led scholars to develop new theories about the history of the region. Such developments also led

"The Fisherman of Halicarnassos" to become more and more convinced that the source of Western civilisation could be traced to the cultures of Anatolia and Mesopotamia. In 1946, he sent a message to his friends and almost ordered them to come to Bodrum so they could discover both the natural beauties of the area and the archaeological sites, the remains of ancient cultures. He even threatened to bring an end to his friendship with those who even hesitated to accept his invitation. That was how my father-in-law, Uncle Sabahattin, and a few more friends and writers ended up going to Bodrum to undertake the journey he had proposed. Uncle Sabahattin later named it, "The Blue Trip".

Only a few pictures and the magnificent sketchbooks of my father-in-law remain of this first expedition and of the boat of Paluko, the sponge diver. If you consider the fact that those participating in the trip were men highly interested in the origins of Anatolian culture and its elements, you can understand the animation, the emotion and the enthusiasm the trip generated. It was a source of inspiration for all the participants. In the midst of these magical sites, coloured in all shades of blue, the "Fisherman of Halicarnassos" in a deep and stirring voice would narrate the myths related to the various places they visited. And thus was the Blue Trip born! In 1956, despite rather harsh conditions, Uncle Sabahattin, the "Fisherman of Halicarnassos", his follower and disciple, author Azra Erhat, my husband Mehmet and a young lady later to become a well-known ceramist, Alev Ebüzziya, decided to make a second trip. Since there were no cruise boats available at that time–they were built only several years later–the boat of Paluko was chartered. It was not a pleasure boat, just a sponge diving boat, with no cabins, no kitchen and no toilet available. Azra Erhat related the trip in a book, *Mavi Yolculuk*, which soon became a classic, almost a legend.

In time, a few boats, totally void of comfort and used mainly for the transportation of goods between the Turkish villages and the Greek Islands, could be rented for the Blue Trip. Only then could Uncle Sabahattin begin to plan and organize yearly voyages. Every trip was carefully planned and was a source of great enthusiasm for the participants. During the winter, meetings were held, slide projections from previous trips were shown and as time passed, the excitement continued to rise. When Cevat Sakir, the "fisherman", left Bodrum for Izmir,

Uncle Sabahattin with the help of Azra Erhat took over the leadership of those trips. In those days, one of the crucial problems of the voyage was the stocking of a good supply of drinking water and of ice. A boat from Marmaris, the "Hürriyet" (Liberty), became the first boat to be used every year by our uncle and his group for the trip and thus also became associated with the Blue Trip. The boat was sold in 1996 following the captain's retirement. Renovated by the new owner, it still continues to cruise on the blue seas. Until 1980, only the "Hürriyet" and the "Hüdaverdi" were able to do the ten-day cruise. Exactly like my father's hunting trips, after the "Blue Trip", stories would be told and retold for a whole year! The same boat was chartered every year; the trip took place without anyone ever getting tired of the sea, of the archaeological sites, of the magic atmosphere that was generated. Until 1980, the trip could be made at a good price, without great luxury, but in a stimulating atmosphere of friendship among pleasant and helpful individuals filled with a strong desire to learn about the ancient cultures.

My first trip took place in 1970. Mehmet was unable to come with us that year, so Rahmi was with me. The trip was organized by Dr Derman, my colleague at work. Fate ordained that I was never to have the pleasure of taking this trip with Uncle Sabahattin! Following the arrest of Uncle Sabahattin in 1971, the trips that followed were organized by Mehmet and other friends of our uncle who were willing to take over the responsibility. Every year, the trip took us to different places and our itinerary was always very carefully prepared so that our water and ice requirements could be met without difficulty. Depending on our point of departure, food was usually bought in Bodrum or Marmaris. Since the local market could not yet provide us with the required quality, olives and white cheese were always brought from Istanbul. That often caused problems because the cheese containers would leak and soak everything in our luggage.

At departure time, usually fifteen participants with a "minimum of luggage" would board an old run-down bus–no air conditioning, no coffee service, no toilet–to undertake the fifteen-hour trip required to get to our destination. The notion of "a minimum of luggage" always remained a very hazy concept, and I was always amazed to see the amount and variety of baggage piled on the top of the bus. After several stops, we would arrive where the boat would be waiting for us. Since no individual cabins existed, just one big empty space, everyone just piled their baggage wherever they could find a place. After a day or two of utter confusion, a workable system was usually found and everything fell into order. Predetermined teams efficiently took care of the shopping; some bought fruit and vegetables and others purchased the meat, bread and drinks. We usually had to wait for ice on every occasion because of the back-ups caused by electrical cuts. On most trips, we had a doctor in our midst, responsible for the supply of proper medication. Despite the fact that the trip took place in a region infested with scorpions, we never managed to obtain from any medical centre the required anti-serum to be used in case of an accidental sting... While the boat would be ready to leave in record time, we always seemed to have a few passengers lagging behind in the village as if they were tourists... In general, however, the weather got so hot that we all shared the desire to get on the boat as soon as possible. Finally, the boat would leave the port for ten or twelve days.

The itinerary was usually decided on when the trip was planned. You could choose to remain mostly in the Gulf of Cos in close proximity to Bodrum and explore the "Şehir Adaları Islands", finding the ancient city of Kedreai on a small typical island of the area and the gorgeous Cleopatra Beach with its fine sand. That gorgeous beach is now under strict surveillance and has been placed under state protection to avoid its total disappearance. Close to this beach during one of his trips, Uncle Sabahattin had discreetly put up a small memento with the hand imprint of all the participants.

You may choose to travel between Bodrum and Marmaris, staying within the kingdom of Caria, visiting the peninsula of Datça, site of the famous ancient city of Knidos, site of a superb temple to Apollo and the lovely statue of Aphroditis, work of Praxiteles. On your way to Marmaris, a multitude of bays await your discovery, so you can lay anchor and spend the day peacefully in the middle of nature. The bottom of the sea is so nice that you can snorkel an entire day without getting weary. Marmaris is most likely the village that has changed the most during these last thirty years. This once small green and half hidden village with no historical past has been transformed into a huge vacation centre with a large marina and in the process has lost all its charm. Restaurants formerly by the sea are now on a mall of concrete where individuals roam in search of adventure... This spot blessed by the gods, endowed with a rich variety of vegetation offers unique scenery in this dry region. Hotels and buildings now mask the view. This could be anywhere in this world, in one of the many colourless cities built near the seashore... Finding a beach open to the public is almost impossible.

The next place of call is generally a lovely small bay, a few kilometres from the antique city of Caunos, known for its swamps, housing mosquitoes and breeding malaria. Finding your way among the marshes where only small boats can circulate, you reach the edge of the ancient city while enjoying the spectacular view of the Lycian tombs carved in the mountains far away. The boat ride ends at the small village of Dalyan just outside the fishing weir. This particular weir was set up to capture the stripped mullet, extract the eggs of the female, encase them in wax and then sell them for the enjoyment of the connoisseurs.

Since the building of the Dalaman airport, a very popular trajectory is the Fehtiye-Marmaris region with the small village of Göcek. The Gulf of Fehtiye is absolutely splendid and each bay explored proves to be even lovelier then the preceding one. The abundance of evergreen pines rising into the sky or hanging out over the sea with their many shades of green offer a contrast to the turquoise blue of the sea and transform the bays into a real paradise. The seawater is warm and one could swim all day and night, especially when there is a full moon. Deep in one of those bays, during his last trip, Bedri Rahmi painted a huge fish in red, white and black on a large rock. It has now become a guide mark to the fishermen and a popular spot for other visitors. This is one of the rare bays where drinkable water can be found and was formerly known by the name of the "Water of Osman Ağa". The name has now been changed to honour my father-in-law and is called "Bedri Rahmi Bay." In both 1986 and 1997, we cleaned the surroundings and renewed the colours of the fish. In this formerly deserted area, you can now find a shack where cold drinks are sold. On our last visit, the youngsters running the place had no idea who we were and began to tell a most unlikely story about the origins of the fish on the rock! Mehmet patiently listened to their story then proceeded to relate the real story, knowing very well it would eventually be modified once again, into again another legend! In every corner of the Gulf, the bottom of the sea is perfect for divers, but I fear that no shells will remain after thirty years of tourism.

For those who have their sea legs, the best choice is the Antalya-Bodrum trajectory. An absolute dream journey takes you to many marvellous sites. In former, days when the boats used for the trip were small and equipped with weak motors, sailing from Kaş to Kalkan then up to "Ölü Deniz" (Dead Sea), especially if you were battling waves, could last longer than ten hours. The continuous movement of the boat, bouncing from one wave to the next one, for those who can take it, is thrilling. It is delightful to observe the acrobats of the dolphins racing with you and to taste the wind filled with droplets of sea water that sprinkle you in a constant rhythm. At night, no one sleeps in their cabins; everyone stretches out in a sleeping bag and looks up at the stars.

Not a sound to interfere with our reflections, only the vague sound of the waves in the background or the soft voice of one of the passengers suddenly turned poet. How many times I have listened to my Turkish friends recite poem after poem until the early hours of the morning! What strong memories they have... but mostly what a love for poetry in this country! Those moments of rapture were interrupted by swimming sessions in the dark or under the silver rays of the moon. In the daytime, before the hours of torrid heat, but still under a hot sun, dressed lightly but wearing sturdy shoes, we would go to conquer the old civilisations. Here is the beautiful Phaselis, with its two natural ports; there is the eternal flame of Olympos, the ruins of Myra and what remains of the Church of Saint Nicholas. Finally, we would come to Kekova with its grey stones and arid yellow ground. Protected by an old fortress with numerous old olive trees with their tortured and twisted trunks, that is a site I particularly enjoy looking at. I love to examine the many Lycian sarcophagi, witnesses of another age. Forming strange sculptures, they decorate a hill, then abruptly fall into the blue sea that extends a hand to an isolated sarcophagus in the sea near the port.

At sunset, the women of the village, sitting in the cool breeze, usually came either to sell almonds grown in the village or some of their handiwork. That was also the time they chose to consult the doctor they knew was aboard. In a region with no phone and no way of communicating, how did they know we had a doctor with us? In this enchanting place we spent many unforgettable evenings, but we always had to leave in order to visit the small towns of Kaş and Kalkan. On my first trip, Kalkan had no dock, so we had to leave the boat for a few hours and swim to the shore in order to visit the many sites of the area. And there was no transportation available, so we had to rent a truck! Despite the great heat, we managed to visit Xanthos, Patara and Letoon. Xanthos, the Lycian capital, has a very tragic story: the whole population chose to commit suicide rather then to abandon the city and its treasure. We proceeded to Patara, birthplace of Apollo and of Saint Nicholas, and to Letoon, the sacred city so proud of the temples it built to Leto, Artemisia and Apollo. As I visited these places with great difficulties for the first time in the seventies, I wondered how the English, a century ago, managed to carry away the huge stones of the small temple they managed to reconstruct perfectly in one of the huge exposition halls of the British Museum, where they painted the walls in the same blue as that of the Mediterranean sky.

From there on begins the most difficult part of the trip: there are seven capes to bypass before you reach the Island of Gemile near the natural safe haven of the Ölü Deniz (Dead Sea). This stretch of sailing is completely dependent on the state of the Mediterranean Sea: you either go forward slowly battling the elements, rocked and shaken by the waves, or you enjoy pleasant smooth sailing. This is a time when some of the passengers will just sit there and daydream while others will read. Some may sleep a deep sleep caused by the medication they took against seasickness! It is useless to ask the captain how long this part of the trip will last; his answer is always the same: we have approximately one hour left! One hour multiplied by five or six or even ten according to the whims of the wind. In conditions requiring the equilibrium of a circus acrobat, the passengers can be served a light meal or a beverage... We finally make it to the majestic island that, according to the latest archaeological finds, was the location of the remains of St-Nicholas, before being transported to Myra and then to Bari, in Italy. On each of our visits to this abandoned place, we deplore the disappearance of a few more centimetres from the remaining mosaics that had survived the assaults of the last centuries. On our last trip in 1997, the calm and peaceful spot we remembered had become an indescribable hell. It was impossible to put even one foot in the water without risking being cut into pieces on the spot. A great number of outboard motors, showing no respect and no fear, sped by terrorizing everyone. A few weeks later what we had feared the most happened: a young girl lost her life after having been hit by one of those crazy boats. The loss of that small paradise embodies all our fears and is the best example of what the lack of conscience and irresponsibility of man can lead to.

A few hundred meters from the island of Gemile lies a natural refuge, an enclosed bay, an inlet surrounded by a huge sandy white beach, if you can find it. Here, the sand gives the sea a beautiful turquoise colour. The sight of such natural beauty is breathtaking. The entrance to this secret refuge is so well hidden that one has to be very close by to notice it. A legend told in the surrounding villages explains how the name of Ölü Deniz, or Dead Sea, was given. According to the story, a passing captain sent his son to find drinkable water in one of the surrounding bays. The young man on his quest met a nomad girl and fell madly in love with her. From then on, she would sit on the rocks and watch every passing boat to try to see her beloved. One day, caught in a violent storm, the young man, who knew the area very well, suggested to his father that they could hide in a calm refuge, the enclosed bay only he knew about. The captain refused, thinking his son was inventing a reason to see his beloved. A violent man, he hit his son who fell into the water and drowned. The young girl, sitting on the rocks, saw her beloved disappear into the sea and threw herself down onto the rocks... The bay was given the name of "Belcekız" and the secret refuge became the "Dead Sea". In order to preserve the natural beauty of the spot, it is now closed to boat traffic.

The next important stop is the village of Fehtiye, the ancient city of Telmessos. Totally destroyed by violent earthquakes, there are but few remains of the ancient sites. In former times, it was forgotten and neglected by tourists. It has now become such a busy port that it was almost impossible to dock when we arrived during our last trip. In 1970, when we first visited the area our boat, with eighteen passengers aboard it, was the only one at the dock when we arrived . We had to split into three groups to eat, because no restaurant could accommodate all of us. We were also unable to buy meat or bread because it was past noon and all the provisions had already been sold. Times have changed!

The city is proud of the imposing Lycian tomb dominating the area. One must climb many steps in the heat in order to reach it... In former days, while walking to the area it was possible to admire village women weaving lovely silk shawls in their gardens. From such a woven piece, a good seamstress could easily fashion a beautiful blouse ideal to wear on hot days. The artisans have disappeared and the new generation didn't even have an idea of what we were talking about when we inquired about that handiwork!

The Blue Trip has suffered a strange destiny. The reason it was conceived and the people who established it have long been forgotten. Very little is said about Uncle Sabahattin while Azra Erhat is always mentioned because of her book on the subject and Bedri Rahmi has almost become its symbol, with his fish... Here is the poem he wrote on the voyage:

The Blue Trip is a tree with branches of sea
The Blue Trip is a garden with roses of sea
The Blue Trip is a bride with a veil of sea
The Blue Trip is a cradle with a child of sea
My child with sea eyes, sea hands and teeth of sea
The Blue Trip is a dream never seen
The Blue Trip is a paradise, never touched never told
The Blue Trip is a fable unpublished, never written, never drawn.

My intentions are not to curb the desires of those wishing to discover the Blue Trip in this new century. You may have apprehensions or hesitations, but when you are aware of the problems that you may face, you will never be deceived because the legend is indestructible, whatever happens. It will offer you unforgettable moments of rest, allowing you to discover one of the loveliest sides of Turkey. The success of this trip is entirely related to the quantity of "blue" each passenger has in his heart and the aptitude you have to bond with the great beauties of nature.

productive artist! Mehmet called upon two of the last students of Bedri Rahmi and asked them to put everything they found of his father's under mat: drawings, gouaches, acrylic paintings. Once classified, they were wrapped up in order to be protected from the dust and prying eyes. An archive was created, each painting photographed and coded. This information was then transferred to computer. While this work slowly progressed, we had to continue planning painting exhibitions, an activity we managed to keep to a strict minimum.

Mehmet then had to gather the works of Bedri Rahmi, the writer, including what had previously been published and what had not yet been published, and then make a list of all of them. In the process, we discovered a series of diaries Bedri Rahmi had kept from the age of eighteen. To our dismay, it was written with the old Arabic characters, the first alphabet he had learned and continued to use his whole life. Here was a form of writing we could not read, let alone decipher! Thus began the long and patient process of "transcription" from the old Arabic characters to the new Latin alphabet. The reform of the alphabet carried out by Atatürk in 1928 was a major move in the history of the nation. Bringing a totally new system to the written language had far-reaching repercussion and to some degree it made it difficult for the younger generations to bind the two periods together. This deep change led to a profound modification of the Turkish language. By discarding words of Arabic and Persian origin and finding new words to replace them, the language changed to such an extent that the younger generation can hardly read and understand texts written before 1950.

Such a critical job required the help of someone we could trust, who had time to spare, knew the family well and was able to read Bedri Rahmi's very particular style of handwriting. The well-known writer, Vedat Günyol, a friend and collaborator of Uncle Sabahattin, took up the challenge and twice a week came to our house to do that work. Seated in the kitchen in front of a small tape recorder, he would read the various articles, passages from the diaries, the letters exchanged between Bedri Rahmi and his father and brother, in short, everything that we gave him to read. The numerous cassettes were then given to a secretary we trusted and she patiently proceeded to type out all she heard on the tapes. A second reading was required to replace the old

Ottoman and Arabic words, unknown to the younger generations, with the newer, more appropriate Turkish ones. This work lasted a few years and led to the publication of several books such as: "Letters between Two Brothers", "While Painting" and "Unpublished Poems".

In the meantime, even though we had a fairly good collection of the magazines, reviews and newspapers where Bedri Rahmi had published his writings and articles, we still had to conduct a thorough search of the archives of various libraries in order to make sure that we had a copy of all he had written from the year 1929 until his death. That was an extremely slow and demanding process that lasted until the early nineties when finally Rahmi and I were able to help complete the research. This compilation of more than one thousand articles is now being published, in chronological order, by Iş Bankası Kültür Yayınları, the publishing house of Iş Bank. In 1999, Mehmet translated the entire correspondence of his parents, over 300 letters, from French into Turkish. The first three volumes contain their correspondence before their marriage, their love letters. The fourth volume is composed of the letters between 1936 until 1950, written after their marriage, during their travels, periods when they were far from each other. These translations were published in lovely books with reproductions of the drawings and pictures found in their letters. A good part of our life and energy has been devoted to safeguarding the work of Bedri Rahmi.

Deeply affected by the death of her husband, her partner of a lifetime, my mother-in-law suffered several months of deep sorrow. Despite his unfaithfulness, he was still the great love of her life. Her greatest loss was, of course, that of a great friend and a fellow painter she trusted. Despite their tumultuous relationship, he was the one she could talk to and discuss art with in all confidence. Their union was in art and for art. Alone in her huge, beloved but very empty home, she was very depressed and one day finally acknowledged that she could no longer live by herself. There was not much to discuss in such a situation besides a few details about how to organize living together. In order not to invade her privacy and to not change the style of the house, it was decided to make a few changes that would allow us to continue our lives in an autonomous manner without interfering with each other's territory. Knowing just how devoted she was to her house, we modified it in such a manner that we were living with her without actively invading her house.

In 1976, we left our apartment to settle on Magnolia Street in the district of Kalamış in Kadıköy. In order to honour the memory of my father-in-law, in 1991 the name of this street was changed to Bedri Rahmi Eyuboğlu Street. This was done in an official ceremony by the mayor of Kadıköy. The respective busts of both Bedri Rahmi and Eren Eyuboğlu were placed with a commemorative plate on a wall in our garden, in remembrance of the years they had spent in this house. It was a touching gesture to immortalize the two great painters.

Mehmet, caught between his market research work on aluminium and the safeguarding of his father's work, was then faced with the problem of a lonely mother, seriously complaining about being in her large house by herself all day. After giving it serious thought, in the autumn of 1977, he left his job without having any definite idea of what he would be doing at home all day. Of course, that lovely huge home required continuous care. We were faced with a serious heating problem and the central heating option was very costly; we had to find some alternatives. The basement of the house had a great flaw: despite a modern system of water pumps, as soon as there was a heavy rainfall and an electric failure, as was often the case, water flooded the basement. Very often it reached levels of twenty centimetres, causing a direct threat to our central heating system and all the material stored in the basement. Every rainfall, besides being a source of stress in and of itself, found us listening carefully for the sound of the pump motor or had us running downstairs to check if the level of water was rising.

It was during such a catastrophe that Mehmet had an inspiration which led him to discover his new profession. On that day, in the cellar covered with thirty centimetres of water, he saw the wooden blocks his father had used for block printing several years before floating towards the stairway where he was standing. In 1950, the blocks of Bedri Rahmi's own designs had been carved by an Armenian craftsman. Block printing was a traditional craft practised in various regions of Turkey. Originally from China, that form of art is still extensively practised in India and was once very popular in Turkey. Its use has slowly declined since the appearance of the silkscreen technique, a process that greatly increased production.

During his stay in Paris in 1950, Bedri Rahmi had become familiar with the African Art he saw exhibited at the "Musée de l'Homme". He was most impressed by what he saw: beautiful and useful objects used in daily life. That concept brought him a new source of inspiration, and from then on, he decided to use block printing, a craft found in Turkey, to reproduce his designs and make them available to everyone at a much lower price then original paintings.

Mehmet, familiar with the technique, had just found his new profession. The beginnings were modest as mother and son worked together on a limited number of pieces that they printed, then hand-painted to finally be exhibited in our garden. That limited production raised interest among art fans and Mehmet was encouraged to plan a larger production. He worked and managed to develop a new process to carve the blocks from a material different from wood. That method was cheaper and could be used for the first time with larger motifs. With the treasury of designs his father had left and the help of his mother, very familiar with this technique, he could print any design he wanted. Gradually his production increased and as the years went by, he managed to train many hands that learned the craft while working with us.

The Kalamış Block Prints were born. After centuries of geometrical designs and flowers, here was a breakthrough, a different approach to an old craft. In addition to being a rich choice of designs, the second important innovation brought to that form of art was the use of much larger blocks than the traditional ones. Hand painting each print gave them an additional value, transforming them into unique art pieces. Our home, as an art studio perpetuating a form of art, opened its doors to anyone wishing to learn and develop this craft.

Through the years, the relationship between Turkey and Romania had improved and several members of my mother-in-law's family were able to come and visit us on various occasions. Mehmet and I had the pleasure of meeting Aunt Mina, the beloved eldest sister of my mother-in-law, and three of her brothers. Two of these brothers, Alexander and Maxim, were particularly devoted to their sister and did their best to help her during the year following the death of her husband. Since they all spoke fairly good French, we had no communication problems. One by one, many of her nieces and nephews also came to Istanbul to visit their aunt and slowly we got to know most of the family. My mother-in-law was from a family of ten children, so there were quite a large number of people to meet! She was the only painter in the family, but three of her brothers were talented pianists, two of whom were composers and professional musicians, while the third, an engineer by profession, also took great pleasure in musical composition. All the members of this remarkable family had lived very difficult days during World War II. They saw their family home and the business of their father destroyed. The long years of life under the Communist regime were not very good years, but happily, despite numerous difficulties and hardships, they managed to survive. It was only after many years had gone by that my mother-in-law learned about their difficulties.

Two years after the death of her husband, while we were on vacation in Bodrum, just like my father-in-law, she suffered a case of obstructive jaundice caused by gall bladder stones. Mehmet and his mother, under the influence of their great imaginations and still living under the shock of Bedri Rahmi's death, were frightened by those symptoms. We cut short our holiday to return at once to Istanbul for medical care. Surgery was required and the removal of the gall bladder solved the whole problem. No trace of malignancy was discovered and life was back to normal within a short time.

For a short period, we led a quiet, pleasant and peaceful life, but, unfortunately, the country was living through a series of crises, of heartbreaking events that led the nation to a state of complete anarchy and to a military take over on 12 September 1980. I found myself in the midst of my first revolution...

The events that led to this revolution began with the Cyprus crisis, still an unsolved problem despite years of conferences, endless summit meetings, numerous international meetings and arduous attempts to secure a lasting peace. For years, this island has caused such problems to Turkey that only a comprehensive history book could properly relate the situation. I will only relate what it all meant for us and how we lived through the crisis at the time. In 1974, we had just begun our summer vacation and were on a Blue Trip. Anchored in one of the surrounding bays of Marmaris where we had spent the night, we were awaken early in the morning by the sound of a French radio station coming from a boat anchored close to us. The news bulletin was relating the invasion of the Island of Cyprus by the Turkish army. Of course this piece of news came as a total surprise to all of us. We understood that the Turkish government, tired of years of diplomacy yielding no results, had decided to take things into its own hands. This "Peace Operation", as it was called, was conducted to liberate Turkish villages that had been under Greek oppression for many years. I then recalled that, several years before, while living in the United States we had protested in front of the United Nations. At the end of this Peace Operation, a division of the Island into two different regions was achieved with the establishment of The Republic of Northern Cyprus. With Turkey at war, we had to follow the orders of the government and were a bit worried by what was happening in the Mediterranean Sea, where we were sailing. Following hours of deliberation with the harbour authorities in Marmaris, we were told we could continue our trip but should follow certain rules for our security.

The reactions against this Turkish "Peace Operation" were severe and Turkey was highly criticized for its actions. The new Republic of Northern Cyprus has never been recognised by any other country except Turkey. A powerful and well-organized Greek lobby in the United States exerted strong pressure and Turkey found itself hit by an embargo with severe sanctions on various products, especially those related to petroleum. Gasoline was rationed and we found ourselves wondering what fuel to use for cooking or heating purposes. In our daily life this meant that we had to spend long hours in line to fill our car with gasoline and we had to form a car pool so we could get to work every day. We quickly grasped that during the next winter the whole population would have heating problems both at home and at work. Mehmet found a way to set up a wood stove on the second floor of the house and a large coal-burning stove in the living room. Our fireplace was also used when necessary. At the university the situation was more dramatic. Since the building we worked in had no patients, it was simply not heated that winter... Many electrical plants working on fuel oil had to reduce their production. That resulted in electrical shortages, often several hours during the course of the day, bringing our work almost to a complete stop. Working under such conditions required great feats of improvisation. It became most difficult to talk about even a minimal level of production or output. Each day, as the list of missing products got longer, we learned to get in line in order to be able to buy a limited amount of certain food products.

In the meantime, the situation was further complicated by the fact that we had first a minority government soon to be followed by a fragile coalition of two politically very opposed parties, who were unable to exert any authority. A chaotic period ensued during which over twenty individuals lost their lives every day, usually as a result of confrontations between rightist and leftist factions. Universities were paralysed and the students could not pursue their studies. Those institutions were the sites of bombings, battles and attempts on lives to such an extent that most amphitheatres were literary in ruins. I recall how my young medical laboratory students, then fifteen or sixteen years old, threw themselves into these dangerous games, encouraged by the so-called revolutionary spirit of their older "brothers". One fine morning, we found the entrance of the school blocked and were denied access to our classes because these young girls were boycotting! They even tried to drag us into endless discussions on subjects about which they had but very limited or incorrect knowledge. It was total confusion. Since they were legally considered minors at that age, and under our responsibility, we tried to reason with them, but to no avail. Although we were aware that in the case of an intervention, they would not be handled with fine kid gloves, the law forced us to inform the security forces. The students risked being beaten, arrested and thrown into prison, not exactly a desirable situation for young ladies entrusted to the school by their families. At the end of tiring days of work, when it was time to return home, I would find myself checking my car thoroughly fearing it could be booby trapped... Not a very enchanting prospect! After all, I was the only foreigner in the medical school, a good enough reason to become a target! At the end of each day, the whole population would try to get home as quickly as possible and no one felt like going out at night, fearing bomb explosions and attempts on their lives. One evening around eight o'clock, Mehmet and I were driving home and just as we turned into our street, we heard the terrifying sound of a machine gun firing behind us. In our small Volkswagen, we had no place to hide so we simply sped home terrified, arriving more dead then alive. Painful days and time were stupidly lost in a country where it should have been used in a better way.

This was the period during which Claude chose to take her first trip to Turkey, together with her husband Alain and daughter Paula. A couple of friends, Edith and Steven, also joined us some time later. Considering what was happening in the country, they could not have chosen a worse time. Still, excited by the prospect of her visit, I certainly was not going to discourage or scare her. In a period when gasoline was rationed, we had to find ways of saving extra fuel for the trip to Bodrum where we were planning to go for a Blue Trip. Tourists were most welcome during a period when foreign currency was highly appreciated and all means were deployed so they would not be affected by the general shortage of items on the market. We spent ten marvellous days away from the bloody battles of the large cities, in the quietness of the Aegean and Mediterranean Seas.

Claude, until then not particularly considered a great swimmer, had a lot of unplanned opportunities to improve herself, thanks to the mishaps of her husband. Despite his undeniable qualities as a good swimmer and diver, he had absolutely no competence as a seaman. Their first adventure began when they left on their own for an excursion in a small boat, a Zodiac equipped with an outboard motor. We ask them to be very careful, especially around the prominent rocks found near the shore. A few hours had gone by and we were beginning to worry about them when, far away in the sea, we saw two figures slowly swimming towards us. We rushed to meet them and learned that one side of the Zodiac had collapsed after hitting a rock. They had had to swim a few kilometres to get back to the boat. A few days later, in the boat's dingy, we were going towards an excellent spot to do some diving. A bit crowded in the dingy, we warned everyone to very carefully slide down into the sea in order to avoid any accidents. Alain got up and executed a dive worthy of an Olympic competition, a move that sent all eight passengers of the dingy into the sea. The dingy turned over and, together with the motor, slowly began to disappear under the water. With a rapid reflex Mehmet dove and caught the motor before it became lost to us forever. Everyone was in the water searching for their diving material while Alain, without even looking behind, was gracefully swimming toward some unknown destination.

Slowly, we decided to evacuate everyone toward the shore as Mehmet and I continued to recover the rapidly vanishing equipment. The boat and the motor were both saved, but the motor had to be seen by a repairman as soon as possible otherwise it would be damaged beyond repair. We had to swim back to the boat by our own means! Edith could hardly swim, so we surrounded her and helped her along, but after a while, a bit tired, she said she would try to walk to the boat along the rocky coast. Paula and Claude swam side-by-side keeping a close eye on one another; Mehmet and I were behind watching them carefully in case they encountered any problems. We had to swim for one kilometre. This performance helped Claude and that summer, she became a good swimmer and an avid diver with a lot of endurance! Following those adventures, our Québec people returned to Canada, safe and sound. Claude divorced Alain a few months after the trip.

I had been away from my country for some years when I noticed that once you have been living abroad for some time, you can no longer conform to the usual procedures routinely applied in the country. All of a sudden, it becomes almost impossible to accomplish anything while you are visiting your homeland. I had left the country before the establishment of a socialized health system and before social security numbers were introduced. Each of those systems issued a card and it became imperative for me to get those cards, otherwise I would always have various problems. I could no longer write checks because I did not have a social security number and I could not open a bank account without the said number. I could not even dream of consulting a doctor or having a prescription for medication filled without the famous number and the medical care card. I learned that, since I was living abroad, I was no longer entitled to have a medical care card and almost felt like a second-class citizen or one of those outlaw types. Spending only a short time in the country on each visit, I never managed to apply for a social security number. Finally, in October of 1999, I applied for the "number" on the day following my arrival. Filling out the forms did not prove sufficient. My case was so unusual that a clerk wanted to meet me to ask several questions. All of sudden, I felt like some illegal immigrant or a spy trying to cheat the Canadian government. No one could understand, let alone imagine, why I had never applied for the card until then. In reality, the system cannot visualize the state of a citizen living abroad because the system works with cards that we, living abroad, have no access to. A few weeks later, the card was sent to my sister's address while she was in the process of leaving for Africa. She mailed the card to me, without taking the precaution of making a note of the number and the card was lost in the mail! On my trip the next year, I visited the clerk who had questioned me to explain the problem. They couldn't find any trace of the card or the number and I was asked to fill out a new application! This new bureaucratic face of Canada was rather surprising to me.

In 1980, at the end of August, Rahmi left for Canada, just as many young Turks were forced to do in order to avoid the dangers caused by the anarchy reigning in Turkey. This separation, most upsetting for our little family, simply could not be avoided. A few weeks later, on the 12th of September, the army took over the governing of the country and martial law was decreed. We had lived through so many tragic events that we were rather happy and grateful that someone could bring an end to the situation and restore some order to the country. We kept our hopes high for an early return to democracy; at least, such were our aspirations.

The morning we learned about the military coup, the radio and the television stations were broadcasting military marches and folk music. Armed soldiers could be seen everywhere: they were searching, watching and directing various operations. Many individuals were arrested and, although we had the feeling the army were doing its best, we did deplore various uncalled-for excesses we certainly had no wish for. A furious wind of change was blowing in the country, from a revision of the constitution to a planned reform of the universities. No sector was spared and once the transition period was over, we witnessed that, while order had been restored in the country, it was at the cost of serious mistakes. Too many things were being modified at the same time and badly formulated changes led to the sacrifice of some fundamental values. The result was an unusual democracy under constraint, very fragile and without several of its vital elements.

To those living with the conviction that we are oppressing the Kurds: Where were you during the years when our intellectuals and the Turkish leftist movement were literally prosecuted and dispersed? Without doubt, our leaders were filled with good intentions, but the qualities required by a good leader in such circumstances cannot always be found in everyone. The efforts spent in the attempt to imitate the founder of the Turkish Republic did not necessarily yield the expected results.

A year later, to our great happiness, Rahmi came back to Turkey. Order reigned in the country and he could continue his studies in peace. But during those sad years, a generation of youngsters filled with ambition and plans for a better future had either been sacrificed or imprisoned for various reasons.

Mehmet's beloved grandmother, after several years of living in her past, left us in February of 1982. She was over ninety years old. She had lived many years in an apartment near the home of her daughter, Mualla, and her son-in-law, Robert, whom she had come to better appreciate over time. Before her passing, she had been living with her son Mustafa, whom she unfortunately no longer recognised! This remarkable woman, "Honey Grandmother", or "Bal Nene", was gone.

After seventeen years of work at the university and a long period of reflection, I decided to transfer to the private sector. A firm was established where Dr Bülent Berkarda, his wife Dr Nevin Berkarda and I were partners. We began to organize the medical centre we planned to open for the treatment of cancer patients who could be followed during their ambulatory period. We searched for a suitable place, an apartment with at least five large rooms in a central part of the city, in the vicinity of the large hospitals and many of the doctors' private offices. Two rooms were required for Dr Bülent and Dr Nevin, two others for patient care, and the last room was kept for the laboratory. We finally rented an apartment on the ground floor of a building situated on a main street in the Beşiktaş district. It was easy to access and parking was allowed on the wide avenue, a great comfort to the patients, especially those requiring special care. At the beginning, our personnel consisted of a secretary, a laboratory technician, and two nurses. Sabriye, a young refugee from Bulgaria with whom I had been working together at the university, assisted in the laboratory. The nurses, Mine and Nergis, were both graduates of the Cerrahpaşa Nursing School and had both worked with us at the university in the oncology department. A young woman attended to the cleaning and various other needs of the place. Taking care of oncological patient requires highly qualified personnel and could not be left in the hands of the inexperienced.

Setting up your own laboratory is not an event of routine occurrence, but a once in a lifetime dream! Knowing many people from the laboratory world, we were able to buy all the necessary equipment and material without difficulties. We took particular care to furnish our medical centre modestly, quite the opposite of the usual ostentatious layouts found in the medical offices of the private sector. Our wish was to establish a serious centre worthy of the confidence of the patients. We wanted to offer the best care possible thanks to the knowledge and experience we had accumulated through our many years of work. We had no intentions of impressing the patients and their families with the luxury of our establishment, the accessories, the furniture or the curtains. We were not in competition with four-star hotels.

During this organisation period, we had to find a reputable pharmacy in our vicinity; otherwise our work would be difficult. Luckily, our centre was just opposite a small pharmacy owned by a husband and wife pharmacist team, Kemal and Zehra. At our very first contact, we understood

In my own laboratory (1983)

that they had a serious approach to work and wanted to do everything possible to help our patients and us. We gave them an impressive list of medications used in chemotherapy that we wanted to have at our disposal at all times. Those products had to be ordered from abroad through importing firms. The process required the investment of a substantial amount of money since they had to order for several months at a time. We also relied on them to have on hand a fair amount of narcotic painkillers widely used for cancer patients. The bureaucracy involved in the sale of those drugs is so great that, when possible, many pharmacies simply avoid selling them.

I have spent many years in the medical sector and I must say that the Ministry of Health could exercise better authority over the institutions dealing with public health. Our centre was in operation for eight years and, as a laboratory or a clinic, was never inspected or checked by the authorities. This observation is also valid for the laboratory of the Laleli Clinic and other laboratories at the university; I never heard of or witnessed any form of inspection during the eighteen years I worked in the sector. During our training years at the university, an important part of our formation dealt with "quality control", in other words, the supervision of results obtained in a laboratory: their precision and their accuracy. Any professional institution with any respect for its patients must establish an internal control system. It falls upon the Department of Public Health to periodically inspect every institution in order to protect the citizens. Important sums of money are spent for laboratory tests, but no one is absolutely sure of the quality of those results. Accurate results are not guaranteed by the reassuring pleasant words of the laboratory chief or the personnel or the long list of qualifications they have. It is a sector where the presence of qualified personnel is scarce and where an extreme vigilance is required. Errors can occur without anyone being aware of it in the least. A machine may be poorly calibrated, a chemical product altered and variations in the electrical supply can affect the results of a test. No laboratory is exempt from such problems, even in the best of conditions. Thus, it becomes imperative that a system of surveillance be established by the laboratories and by the authorities. They should inspect every establishment by distributing specimens to be analysed. If and when the results obtained are not within the range of accepted values, these establishments should be advised and given a reasonable period of time to make the proper changes. Upon further inspection, if the condition persists, then the license of the establishment involved should be revoked. I think the time has come for Turkey to establish some method of surveillance to protect its citizens.

Within a short time our centre was as busy as a beehive and we had to rent the adjoining apartment to achieve some degree of comfort. Working with cancer patients requires a great amount of patience and stamina. The treatment of cancerous children is a source of endless suffering for the family and the whole medical staff. I have great admiration for the numerous heroic mothers who manage to function and maintain their calm when faced with such an ordeal. I can never forget Özlem, a young girl suffering from acute leukemia. On her birthday, she had to be transfused with a unit of blood, but I am sure, was dreaming of gifts, a birthday cake and most likely some respite from us. The confidence and especially the courage shown by patients as they tolerated their treatment deserve special mention. This pitiless disease most often pursues its course without offering any mercy to the patients or to their families who display so much hope. Cancer destroys its victims only after having exhausted all means, the patient, the family, a good part of their financial resources and all medical attempts. No one can imagine the amount of psychological and physical perseverance required in this profession.

During the last years of her life, my-mother-in law had one of the most productive periods of her painting career. Finally liberated from her housework, she could spend all her time doing what she liked most: painting. The presence of Mehmet at home filled her with an added amount of energy. The constant traffic, the presence of young people helping Mehmet with his block printing, the various painting exhibitions, the annual block printing exhibition held in our garden every June, all these were very energizing activities for her. Her periods of depression were treated with better drugs and her working hours increased to fifteen hours a day, a remarkable workday for a woman of her age. Every year she accompanied us to Bodrum where she could go swimming and finally enjoy the house she had worked so hard to restore before her husband's death. At a later period, this house was further modified and enlarged to bring more comfort to everyone.

In 1986, my good friend Louise and her husband Jean-Marc expressed their desire to visit Turkey and join our annual Blue Trip. We sent a message to Dr Giovanni, our good Blue Trip friend of 1973, and organized what was to be the last one for a long time. Thanks to the acrylic paints kindly brought by our friends, we were able to restore and repair the famous fish painted by my father-in-law his last trip, in 1974. Of course our friends were enchanted with their cruise, but for us, a bell had begun to toll. We witnessed with great sadness how the elements of the trip had deteriorated and how it had been transformed into a different type of adventure altogether. This was most likely the result of a poorly planned approach and policy with regard to tourism combined with a profound change in society. The number of boats had increased unbelievably and there were simply not enough trained personnel available. In order to make our guests more comfortable, for the first time ever we rented a fancier boat. We were most comfortable in the spacious cabins, but our young untrained crewmembers were more a burden then anything else. They were seasick and their every action reflected a complete lack of experience. They were thrown into the sea by the huge ropes every time we manoeuvred to anchor or tie up the boat. The sea traffic was so heavy that finding a proper place to anchor became a feat in and of itself. Just imagine our dismay at finding ourselves forty-second in a line of boats waiting to anchor at a spot, and once anchored finding ourselves practically in the boat of our elderly nudist neighbours. While enjoying our cocktails we were forced spectators of not exactly aesthetic scenes. We didn't know which way to look, so we played a lot of scrabble that evening!

Through the years, the aim of the trip had undergone major transformations. Those who now have the money to take the trip are less interested in the origins of Anatolian culture and even less concerned by the principles guiding efforts for conservation of the environment. We were completely surrounded by luxury boats with powerful sound systems whose immediate duty seemed to be to share their musical tastes with us. Others insisted on terrorizing the swimmers and divers in the surroundings by zigzagging along the shores with their various motorized equipment. The final blow to our patience came when our captain, despite our warnings based on years of experience and on the excellent maps of the British Admiralty, decided to take a short cut between two islands. We soon found ourselves perched on rocks! Thanks to an unexpected wave, we managed to free the boat, only to observe that once we were anchored, our captain did not even have the curiosity to check whether the boat had suffered any damage or not. Mehmet was extremely worried and very discreetly we both dove to inspect the bottom of the boat and evaluate the situation. Some damage had occurred to the hull, but we could continue our trip without any immediate danger. Once in port, some repairs would have to be done to prevent further damage. To our great surprise, the captain did not report the incident, so we were the ones to inform the owners. The golden years of the Blue Trip were definitely over and from then on we planned to take only short excursions around Bodrum.

In the summer of 1987, the International Congress of Chemotherapy was held in Istanbul. It was the largest congress ever held in the city and all eyes were focused on Dr Berkarda, the President of the Congress. Despite various problems, numerous mishaps and difficulties of all types, the Congress was successful and we were proud of the organization. During the week of the Congress I was absolutely astonished by the number of individuals who observed that Turkey was very different than what they had expected after having seen the film *Midnight Express*. Once more, the same story all over again! A small Canadian delegation soon tracked me down and we took some time out to enjoy a visit to the Grand Bazaar where rugs were bought while we had the chance to get to know each other. Istanbul is an ideal spot for such meetings: it offers many sumptuous sites to the visitors. For example, in this case, the banquet offered in the gardens of the former palace of the Sultans in Beylerbey could be classified as an evening out of the Thousand and One Nights. To those interested, we recommended the very popular book of Michel de Grèce, *Les nuits du Sérail*. A magnificent production entitled "I, Anatolia" as interpreted by our great actress Yıldız Kenter was presented at the closure of the congress. Through the eyes of women of various eras, this great play relates the history of Anatolian civilisations. The first woman was, of course, the goddess Kibele. In time she was modified into Aphroditis, to finally become the Virgin Mary.

Some months later, my mother-in-law began to complain about gastric pains. A short time before Rahmi's departure for his military service in Belgium, she underwent a series of tests and an advanced case of cancer of the stomach was diagnosed. This most unpleasant and unexpected news caused deep sadness and great worries in the family. How did we spend the summer of 1988? I have no wish to remember or describe it. It was the third family member I saw dying of cancer and it was painful. The months preceding the diagnosis of her disease were characterized by drastic changes that occurred in the subjects of her paintings. Her drawings and paintings were suddenly filled with figures reflecting deep despair and expressing intense suffering. Many drawings reminded us of those of Goya and stirred up great emotions. For me, the sight of those paintings every morning became an indication of a deep discomfort or a serious disease.

My intuition proved to be correct. Several dramatic moments occurred during the few months of her disease in which she exhibited the type of behaviour often witnessed in patients aware of the gravity of their condition. The worst day was the day when she expressed the desire to sign all her paintings. Conscious of the fact that a signature is what people are buying and looking for, she courageously sat down and signed many of her works. While doing that, she did not refrain from calmly expressing her thoughts on the strangeness of life and the destiny of artists. It was such a sad day for both Mehmet and me, and, I fear, a frightful one for her. Despite her insistence, we did not have the courage, the desire or the heart to sort the paintings so she could sign them. Each signature became the equivalent of money! Each time a buyer expresses his concern over an unsigned painting, I wish the voice of my mother-in-law could be heard to convey exactly her thoughts and feelings on this subject. This work session was the last she had in her studio.

That summer, the son of my good friend Lise Gauthier from Drummondville came for a visit. His aunt had rewarded him with a trip to Europe upon completion of his university studies. At the end of his trip, he decided to come to Istanbul. Happily, during those sad days, the son of a distant relative of my mother-in-law had also chosen the same period to visit Istanbul. Both were put up on the fourth floor of the house where they managed to fend for themselves.

My sister Claude also informed me that she, accompanied by a colleague from work, was planning to come to Istanbul during the month of August. They would be venturing over to Turkey following a tour of the Island of Crete. I felt very sad knowing I could not possibly be with her in Bodrum for a few days as the health of my mother-in-law was progressively deteriorating. The few days that we enjoyed together in Istanbul were the only ones I spent with my sister that year.

My mother-in-law died on 29 August 1988, at the respectable age of eighty-three. She was buried the following day, and to our great surprise, a few hours after the funeral, Rahmi arrived from Belgium. Her death proved to be an irrevocable loss for Mehmet, who was so deeply bound to his mother. While the relationship with his father had always been tense, with his mother the situation was different; he had felt a deep affection for her and they had established a friendship that would leave a feeling of emptiness impossible to fill. During the last years of her life, Mehmet had given her great support on every level, maintaining an atmosphere of work and creativity in the house like that which had existed during her husband's lifetime. He had succeeded in breaking the chains of her solitude.

A new mourning period followed and the responsibilities of protecting a second cultural heritage added an extra load onto Mehmet's shoulders.

Chapter XIX

My Son Rahmi

R aising a child in a multicultural environment requires a great capacity for adaptation and a lot of common sense. Rahmi was always a calm child, joyous and very sociable. Since early childhood, he loved going out every day or being taken for long walks. Instead of sitting passively looking at others, he preferred being on his knees and holding onto the edge of the carriage. Thus perched, he would interact with all the people going by, say hello to everyone and sometimes pull the hair of children coming close to him. I never saw another child riding in a carriage in this fashion. Dressed like a prince in the lovely winter coats covered with designs from our Québec Winter Carnival that Mother would send from Canada, he would attract a lot of attention.

The first two years of his life were spent in the United States and since both Mehmet and I spoke French at home, we were expecting our son to speak French as well. From childhood, Rahmi had never been a great talker. When he finally began to talk, I could not understand much of what he was saying until the day a Canadian friend told me I should listen to him more carefully: my son was speaking, but in English! I had to resign myself to the fact that Rahmi was in fact speaking English. This was of course the result of the many hours spent in the garden playing with his American friends. Just as his vocabulary was getting better, we left the United States for Turkey! Rahmi, then, went into a period of silence and observation. That was accompanied by a period that could be defined as a semi-fasting one; nothing seemed to please him. After we left Holland, where he had enjoyed the good cheeseand ham and had drunk both the good milk and the beer, feeding him had slowly become a problem. Weeks went by before we could find food he really liked and for several years he absolutely refused to drink any milk. In Turkey during those years, milk was sold without being pasteurized. Once bought, it had to be boiled as a precaution, a procedure that modified the taste and especially the texture of the milk. The small prince also had to face a whole family wishing to feed him as if he were still a baby.

A few months after our arrival, I had to start working and therefore also had to find a place where Rahmi could be taken care of. Thus began the long list of day care centers where Rahmi went for several years. It appeared to be the best solution at that time, but when I look back on that decision, I question the wisdom behind that craving to work that we women have.

After years of studies, it appears normal to aspire to use and apply the knowledge acquired; otherwise, what would be the logic behind those efforts? But at one particular point, when we decide to become a mother, I wonder how wise it is to throw ourselves back into the turmoil of a career with such eagerness, especially during the first year of a child. I think the ideal solution to the dilemma will never be known, but at this age and with my experience, I think I should be allowed to admit what my heart always felt: a child should come before a profession. Such devotion to a career is an illusion, the mirage of an oasis not really offering shelter. Reality is much simpler: a child requires all the attention and love it can get. Unfortunately, it is only after long years of experience that we can recognise this fact. By then, when the race is over, we realise that the world has not really drastically changed because of our efforts and very few concrete things remain in our hands. When we are young, we feel invincible, reckless and capable of changing the world. At that time, I loved my work and I would never have considered the possibility of behaving otherwise, could never have imagined doing anything else.

Could that feverish activity be a way of satisfying the ego, a way of filling the emptiness around us or a way of convincing ourselves that we are actually doing something useful and necessary for society? Through the years, usually when my son experienced difficulties in school, I was torn by remorse and really felt a sense of guilt. Every summer, whenever we had to find a place where Rahmi could spend his days, I felt my heart would break. The days of strong winds when the ferryboats would suddenly stop working, no one can possibly imagine the panic I felt at the thought of knowing my child might be in the street, waiting for someone to open the door. Cellular phones were not available at the time and even a simple phone, such a basic and simple convenience easy to obtain in Canada, was impossible to have in Turkey. The waiting lists were over ten years long! It was impossible to make last minute arrangements or to think of modifying a schedule. The drama of a working mother renews itself with every episode of fever her child has, or the appearance of a childhood disease followed by its recuperation period. Since his grandmother was not always available, I–like all the other young mothers I knew–had to call upon a neighbour, the wife of the doorman, or find other solutions close to miracles. For one reason or another, achieving a synchronization between the hours we left the house and the hours children had to leave for school seemed impossible, for they never coincided!

All institutions dealing with children seem to open and close at odd hours. In a world pretending to be well organized, the major problem of working mothers has never been addressed. Even the sophisticated charters dealing with human rights do not seem the least concerned with the inflexible working hours of mothers. At a time when the number of single-parent families is increasing in number, there must be a better solution. How many women today are still in a state of perpetual stress for such reasons?

Some time after our arrival in Istanbul, completely out of nowhere, my father-in-law informed me that he hoped his grandson would speak Turkish well, without being handicapped by a foreign language that would hamper his pronunciation and his Turkish vocabulary. Having joined a well-known family of the literary world, I understood exactly what he meant; besides, there seemed to be no problem since Rahmi always refused to speak French with us, even though he understood everything we said. Needless to say, he learned Turkish much faster than I did. While Mehmet was doing his military service, Rahmi used to talk with me, but I sometimes had no idea what he was talking about. I would note a sentence here and there and the next day would ask my boss, Dr Berkarda, what my son was trying to tell me. One day, I was shocked to hear that the latest sentence I had written down was an expression frequently used, but completely unacceptable in polite society. Children do not necessarily learn bad language at home.

The problems of raising children in two cultures originate in the choice you make in choosing the value systems to be applied. Easier said then done! When we are not yet very well acquainted with the local "way of living", how can we manage to apply it to our lives? Everything is different, from A to Z, and this is the main reason behind the conflicts between mother-in-law and daughter-in-law, conflicts that soon become the source of disputes between couples. Each one of our actions is criticized, rather than analysed: the baby should not sleep on his stomach; the child should be wrapped up like a mummy; he should not be allowed to eat by himself and spill food all over, and the litany continues... Since every mother wishes to raise her child according to her own customs, it becomes a step-by-step battle to fight. A lot of tact, intelligence and compromise are required in order not to hurt anyone. The best results can be obtained if you apply the imperturbable English diplomatic formula: a large smile in front of adversity and the firm determination not to make any concessions. Oh! What joy!

I will never forget the expression on Mehmet's face when he saw his son wearing Adidas sport shoes to go to school. How could I allow such scandalous conduct? Rahmi should have worn conventional leather shoes, but he categorically refused to do so. Turkish schools also required that every student have a clean handkerchief in his pocket, a requirement checked every morning by the teacher. I was always repulsed by such handkerchiefs and instead, provided Rahmi with disposable Kleenex tissues I had brought back from the United States in large quantities. Those were rather unknown in Turkey. Each morning the teacher would scold my son, but to no avail. Rahmi never mentioned it and it was only after a visit to the school that I learned about the problem!

Another interesting subject in the education of a child is the question of religion. Mehmet and I had similar ideas on that subject and, in the beginning, we chose not to discuss religion with our son. We knew that, in time, the question would come up by itself. Sure enough, the occasion arose on the second day of our trip to Canada in 1972. Mother, all excited by our visit, wanted to show Rahmi the city of Montreal as if we were regular tourists. Together, we took a city-tour and our first stop was at one of the numerous Catholic churches of the city. Until then, I had never mentioned the word religion to Rahmi. He was, of course, very upset by the sight of a huge crucifix and a life-size Christ with blood all over his body nailed to it. He immediately asked me: "Who is this man? Did the Canadians do this to him?" Just as I was to answer "No, my child the..." I held back and begged him not to ask me any more questions on the subject. I would explain everything at home that night. Teaching religious stories to a child at a very young age is one thing, but for an eight year old, hearing such stories for the first time is very difficult and bewildering! At bedtime, it took me a few hours to relate and explain while trying not to be illogical in my story. A few days later, we left for a summer camp where Alain and Claude had found work for the summer. A few hours after our arrival, Rahmi came running in and informed me, out-of-breath, that he had just seen a sculpture of the "forest witch" crushing a snake with her foot. First, I was intrigued by this colourful description, but then I slowly understood what he meant. I asked him to take me to see this piece of art. Sure enough, this "forest witch" was no one other than the Blessed Virgin Mary, mother of the man he had previously seen on the cross. I then had to explain the concept of a virgin mother giving birth to a god. (In French her name is Sainte Vierge, Holy Virgin.) Things were getting complicated. I swore never to relate any more religious stories to Rahmi and he never again asked me for any other explanations. I cannot blame him after all he had heard that summer.

While we had closed the chapter on Christianity, we had yet to open the chapter on Islam. Of course, during his high school years, he had lessons in religion. Once when Rahmi had to prepare some homework on a religious subject, he simply had to ask around for some explanations on the subject since we, his parents, were unable to help him.

My son's teenage years coincided with the dangerous years of anarchy in Turkey, before the military coup of 1980. That was a vulnerable age and it was easy to get involved and inflamed by social issues and take part in discussions that could lead to a bloody fight. One day, Rahmi came back from school white as a sheet. Following several questions, he finally admitted he had been threatened by a student with a revolver who had blocked the road on his way back home. He asked Rahmi what political faction he supported, as if all fifteen year olds had active political lives and all belonged to very definite political groups! Rahmi managed to recognise the face of this provocateur and remembered that he belonged to an extreme rightist faction. He concocted an answer that got him out of the delicate situation. I was extremely worried by those developments and that same night, I begged Mehmet to send Rahmi to my family in Canada until the crisis was over. I especially stressed the fact that, until then, I had never asked for anything of the sort, but for the future of our son, it seemed we had to take certain measures. It was a most difficult decision to make because Mehmet really had no wish to be separated from his son. Another serious problem we had to think about was the fact that the province of Québec had just passed the famous French Language Law No. 101, which stipulated that children who had a parent of French origin had to complete their studies in the French language. Talk about human rights! Rahmi wanted to complete his studies in English, but had to pursue his studies in a school for immigrants so he could learn French.

Claude agreed to let him stay in her home and found herself in a house with two teenagers: Rahmi, sixteen years old, and her daughter Paula, thirteen years old. On my first trip to Canada in 1972, we had had ample time to witness the wonderful relationship they enjoyed, nothing short of behaving like cats and dogs! Rahmi, as boys do in Turkey, thought he should control the social life of his cousin, preventing her from being friends with other boys. To add extra flavour to their relationship, they had to take turns doing the dishes every night and both managed to fight each day, trying to escape that chore. Perfect harmony reigned between them! Fortunately this situation has improved through the years and they have become civilised cousins.

As all good parents do, we had a long list of recommendations for our son, the first one being to keep away from the Turkish colony, to avoid speaking Turkish in order to master French quickly and integrate into the lifestyle of the Province of Québec. As a typical obedient child, the first thing he did was to contact the few Turks he knew, get involved with the Turkish group and its various activities and play football (soccer) in the Turkish Club, "Kent Sport". He also made the firm decision not to speak French with my sister and her family, forcing them all to speak English, even the genuine Frenchman, Gilles, Claude's boyfriend. The North American missionary spirit always alive, just like the Americans who in the 1960's had tried to convert his father, Rahmi found a Canadian French teacher with a missionary soul. That completely destroyed whatever desire he might have had to learn some French. Rahmi managed to be one of the few individuals who came back from the province of Québec with improved English. Back in Turkey, he always spoke Turkish with me and the only trace of that French year in Canada was, to my great surprise, a card he wrote to my mother in excellent French.

Back home, Rahmi showed greater interest toward his studies and completed high school without any major problems. His great passion was for athletics, the 100-meter and 400-meter races. It was with tremendous sorrow that I realised that Turkey had no serious organisation dealing adequately with young athletes. He was a member of the famous Fenerbahçe Club, but the club offered no facilities, not even a small corner to take a shower, a chronometer to monitor running times, no definite training program and no staff to coach these youngsters. Rahmi was left completely alone with absolutely no help or support. Today, I understand why he has devoted body and soul to working with the club in order to help young athletes aspiring to perform in a sport other than football (soccer). He has travelled with his own family to support young athletes in competitions abroad, trying to offer what he himself had been unable to find several years before. That was one of the rare moments I experienced some regret for living in an underdeveloped country, instead of living in Canada, where sports and athletic performance are encouraged. Many foreign mothers experience hesitation and regrets when the time comes to submit their children to the mediocre education system of the new country. One cannot help comparing the system with the education we have received in our own country. Many disputes on education have risen between couples and many foreign mothers have chosen to leave the country because of this problem.

Rahmi then reached an important time in his life: he had to decide what profession he was interested in and prepare himself adequately for the university entrance exam, the greatest nightmare of Turkish youth. Conventional studies in a high school don't prepare you for this exam and families must spend a fortune to have their children attend special courses in private institutions that specialize in preparing the students for the university entrance exam. Those who are still in high school go to courses given on the weekend, while those who have completed their studies and are waiting to be able to get into the university go to courses during the week. University studies are almost free, but when you consider the amount of money spent for private tutors and for the private institutions, one can only find the whole system very paradoxical. Those who do not have the financial means to attend these courses find themselves in a situation where they have very little chance of entering a good university. A large proportion of the youth who come from Anatolia never get into university. Every year, over one million students take part in the first entrance examination, a barrier to eliminate the weaker students, and then proceed towards a second exam*. The scores obtained more or less determine which field they will pursue their studies in. With this system only 100,000 students are able to enter what could be qualified as a "serious university". An equal amount of students gain access to lesser universities found in various regions of the country or in the "Open University", a system where students study on their own or by following lectures given on television. The main advantage of the Open University is that it gives male students the right to postpone their military service or, when they do graduate, allows them to do their military service as an officer. Honestly, for all practical purposes, I don't see what else it is good for. It is surely not the type of diploma any employer is looking for.

Choosing a university and a department requires filling out many forms with the help of professionals who see to it that students make the proper selections when applying. Each student must complete a long list of various options ranging from medical school to law school, from tourism school to the Academy of Fine Arts. Most students, to

---

* This system was replaced in the year 2000 by a single exam entrance system.

ensure that they obtain a place in a university, usually also add a school with low admission points, even if they are not really interested in the majors offered. The scores obtained determine the school to which they will be admitted, and this can be in any city in Turkey!

These results are the source of many family dramas, especially for many girls who, for cultural reasons, cannot possibly consider studying outside the city in which their families they live. A similar situation can be found among students who lack the money to go to the university to which they have been accepted. The despair, the sadness felt by those who wind up having to study Chinese instead of going to the law school they were dreaming of is indescribable. Such a system fosters youngsters unable to decide or specify exactly what they want to study because they are never sure they will make it into the school they want. Unfortunately, these frustrated students often find themselves at a university just to please their parents and obtain a precious piece of paper. I often have the feeling that this system is maintained to satisfy parents' egos and their desire of having children with university degrees. In the end, it fulfils a dream they had themselves failed to realise. A large percentage of these university graduates do not even practice their professions and often it is only the elite who manage to study what they wanted. Despite many years spent in this country, there are still things I do not understand, and this university entrance system is one! How parents put up with this situation is beyond my comprehension.

Rahmi completed his weekend courses, took the exam, and succeeded in obtaining a score that allowed him to take the second exam. Since he had never been a very good student, being always more interested in sports and athletics, we were curious to learn which school he was planning to attend. Rahmi wanted to study tourism and, sure of himself, he wrote down, according to his order of preference, the names of ten tourism schools. He took the exam in the month of June and then again in July, and during our vacation in Bodrum, we were pleasantly surprised to learn that he had won a place at the Tourism School of Gazi University. This is a two-year school, located in Bolu, some 150 kilometres from Istanbul. Everything was fine and Rahmi went to Bolu to complete his registration and see where he could find a place to live. The school was newly opened and the residence facilities for the students were very limited, practically nonexistent. At the end of September, we all went to Bolu to find him some living quarters. Thanks to the help of a well-known painter in the city, a friend of my father-in-law, we found a hotel willing to rent us a room for the whole period of his studies.

In Bolu, student life was calm and rather monotonous, a kind of advantage if one thinks of all the problems teenagers had before the 1980 military takeover. Rahmi continued his training in athletics and found a few friends with similar interests. He usually spent his weekends in Istanbul. At the end of his first year of studies, he completed a three-month training period in one of Istanbul's large hotels. By a strange coincidence, it was the hotel where my father-in-law had completed his last work, a large ceramic panel at the entrance of the lobby. It is now called the Hotel Mercure.

As planned, he graduated in 1986 and began to work at the Kalyon Hotel, a well-known establishment situated on the shores of the Marmara Sea, near the old district of Istanbul. During this time, he met Sibel, a young girl from Istanbul. She brought an end to the tradition of foreign spouses in the Eyuboğlu family. I was glad her name was easy to pronounce in both English and French. After a few months, the relationship became serious and Rahmi asked us to take the necessary steps in order to formalise the situation with her family. In Turkey it is not considered proper for a young lady to go out with a young man without informing her family of his intentions. Mehmet and I were completely ignorant of the whole protocol surrounding the engagement and wedding ceremonies. We had to make some efforts to learn and understand what was expected of us in such an event and prepare ourselves for the up-coming social requirements. We asked Şükriye, my mother-in-law's helper for the last forty-five years, to guide us. We were far from being able to imagine all the details that would later come up, but for our son we were willing to do our best.

The first step was, of course, to choose the proper date for the first meeting with Sibel's family. We chose 25 December, a very special date for us. It was exactly twenty-seven years after our first meeting in Ottawa. Mehmet, my mother-in-law and I, with the traditional chocolate, in this instance placed on a ceramic plate made by my mother-in-law, arrived at the home of the Ataç family sometime during the evening.

This was a delicate meeting for both families as they had to evaluate each other and then decide, according to the rules, what the children themselves had already agreed upon. Following a prelude to introduce our family and an interlude to get to know Sibel's family, Mehmet made the official proposal and asked for the hand of their daughter for our son Rahmi. The proposal was accepted and the sequence of events to follow was discussed, everyone expressing their own ideas and desires. Since Rahmi was getting ready to leave for his military service, the engagement was to take place on his birthday, the 27th of February. The wedding would take place after he had finished his military service. I listened with interest and some amazement to all the discussions about each phase of the process. According to custom, the engagement party was organized by the family of the bride-to-be, but the wedding ceremony and reception itself was ours to organize. My mother-in-law informed the young couple that she had bought a small apartment some years before and that was to be her wedding gift to them. We assumed the expense of renovating the apartment to Sibel's taste. The bedroom and kitchen furniture were to be bought by the bride's family and we were responsible for the furniture of the dining room and living room. Mehmet and I had gotten married in such a modest fashion that we were both surprised to learn about the existence of an almost official code of behaviour that governs the marriage arrangements of young people in this country. Many a foreign spouse would have preferred learning about this code not at their children's wedding, but before their own marriage!

The engagement took place in a large hotel and some 200 guests were invited to a dinner following the ceremony. Our family friend Dr Berkarda was asked to place the engagement rings, linked together with a red ribbon, on the fingers of the young couple. That was followed by the cutting of the ribbon and a touching and appropriate speech for the occasion. To the great happiness of my mother-in-law, this successful evening brought together many acquaintances and family members. At the time, such ceremonies may appear useless and vain but, since we don't know the future, they do serve a purpose. Unfortunately, my mother-in-law left us some time before the wedding took place.

On 2 March, Rahmi left for Iskenderun in southern Turkey, where his military service would begin at the naval base there. Following a training period of forty-five days we were informed that since he had been born in the United States, the military authorities wished to evaluate his knowledge of the English language. He was asked to take an exam in Ankara where he was then transferred. The results placed him among the three best candidates chosen to complete their military service in Belgium, in the city of Mons, at the Strategic Headquarters of Allied Forces in Europe (SHAPE).

Doing military service in Europe was a great opportunity that many parents would do anything to see their child take advantage of. However, a few weeks before Rahmi's departure, my mother-in-law, who had been complaining of gastric problems, was diagnosed with cancer. She was eighty-three years old, an age that would not allow a strong and aggressive treatment approach and she refused surgery. We were, of course, shocked to learn of Rahmi's departure for Europe. That difficult period for Mehmet had to be faced without Rahmi's assistance. When the time for Rahmi's departure came, my mother-in-law showed great courage and did not dramatize the event. Mehmet sadly drove Rahmi to the military airport from whence he left for Europe. He never saw his grandmother alive again.

In the spring of 1989, Sibel and I decided to go to Mons to visit Rahmi. We chose to travel by bus and it proved to be quite an experience. When I travel to foreign countries, I leave the country showing my Turkish documents and then use my Canadian passport in other countries because of the great difficulties associated with a Turkish passport in almost all European countries. For a Turk, travelling implies getting visas and they are not easily granted. You must convince the authorities that you will return to Turkey. You must prove you have money in the bank, declare your properties or show proof of work, briefly, produce all types of papers so dear to the bureaucrats. I think it is most unpleasant to have to prove you have the means to travel and then request permission to spend your own money in those countries. Many people have asked Mehmet to open block print exhibitions in Europe, but he has always categorically refused because of the visa formalities involved. Sibel had to get a visa for France where we would also go, a transit visa for Germany where the bus did not even stop, and a visa to enter Belgium.

All formalities completed, we left Istanbul by bus, travelling with a major Turkish bus company. Except for Sibel and myself, the passengers were Turkish workers and their family members residing in Belgium. From the very first hour of our trip it became clear that we would have to endure many long hours of heavy smoke in the bus because almost everyone was smoking incessantly, without the least concern for the non-smokers. We left one or two passengers behind at every border we crossed. They left the bus for reasons unknown to us and were left to their fate, without us being able to intervene. Waiting for them or trying to help them was absolutely out of the question. I had already been given the title of "foreigner" and everyone on the bus was very interested and curious about me and my passport, a document that—unlike theirs—received respect at each checkpoint. I was very sad to witness that a difference in behaviour was exhibited by the custom officers according to the origin of the passports shown to them. The bus driver looked fairly intelligent, but, to my astonishment, knew absolutely no foreign language. How can one be so bold as to carry on with such a job? How can such a large firm take the risk of hiring such a driver?

Except for the compulsory stops at borders, we kept on going straight through to the heart of Yugoslavia where we stopped in a Turkish-speaking village. The facilities were not very comfortable, but we managed. Sibel was already suffering from very swollen feet and was experiencing problems in taking her boots off or trying to put them back on again. We travelled on smoothly through Austria and then crossed the German border. The officers there had not saved their best smiles for us; as a matter of fact, I had the strange sensation of being in a scene straight out of an old World War II movie. It felt like they had a bus loaded with enemies in front of them. What a feeling of human warmth! It was my second experience at a German border and their attitude before had seemed so cordial!

After getting lost in Germany several times and after some forty hours of travelling, we arrived at the Luxembourg border. Within a few minutes, I realised that an important problem had come up. The custom officers were trying to explain something to the driver and their tone of voice was getting harsher and harsher while our driver was just staring at them. He finally called out to me and asked if I could find out what the matter was. I learned that our driver had been issued a single-entry visa and he had already used it the week before. It was, of course, out of the question for the bus to remain at the border and, following a polite exchange, we were given the authorization to proceed to Belgium on the condition that we promise to obtain the proper visa for the driver. Such a well-known firm should have had an efficient person supervise the travelling documents of the drivers going to Europe; a good example of what an incompetent employee can do to a firm.

Rahmi, impatient as ever, was most happy to see us when we finally arrived. We were introduced to and very warmly received by all the young Turkish boys on duty in Belgium. I was very touched to hear them call me "anne", the Turkish word for mother. Following a short stay in Mons and Brussels we finally took the train for a short visit to Paris, then to Nice to visit my good friend Gabriella. The weather was very good in the City of Lights and our lovers were very happy despite the theft of Sibel's wallet in the metro. On this trip, Rahmi could visit more attentively all the museums he had seen on his father's shoulders twenty-four years before! We walked a lot along the wide boulevards and avenues of the city and our curious youngsters, despite some apprehension, finally discovered the metro of Paris.

For Sibel, the highlight of this Parisian visit was the very important shopping day we spent to find her wedding dress. How many stores were visited, how many dresses were admired and tried on! At the end of the afternoon we finally found the dress of our dreams: a silk dress that fitted perfectly and required no alterations. The second step was complementing the dress with various accessories, the veil, the flower to keep it in place, the gloves and finally the shoes. We left the store with the huge box that was to follow me everywhere I went until I finally returned to Istanbul. We then proceeded to Nice where Gabriella in her charming little apartment received us with open arms. Gabriella was working as a tourist guide and using the several languages she is familiar with: English, French, Italian, Portuguese, which she learned in Mozambique while working there for two years, and finally, since she was born in Turkey, Turkish. No one could have had a better guide to visit the Picasso Museum in Antibes or the Chagall Museum in Nice! We also spent a wonderful day in Monaco and Monte Carlo. This jewel of a country on the Mediterranean Sea enchanted us with its buildings, its flowers, its gardens and its great cleanliness. Time flew by and we had to leave that sunny corner of Europe to return to foggy Belgium.

Sibel remained in Mons for ten more days while I, with the precious wedding dress in its huge box, took the road back to Istanbul. The Turks are very sensitive and emotional about all that surrounds a wedding and its ceremony. I had the opportunity to witness the very touching behaviour of the bus driver and then the customs officers when I entered Turkey. As I departed from Mons, Rahmi cautioned the driver as he placed the box in the baggage compartment. Once at the Turkish border, I had no problems, but I was stunned and saddened at the sight of some of the baggage our workers naively tried to get into the country. Also, for some reason, many of our citizens insist on not using suitcases, a practical and simple custom that has gained worldwide acceptance! They still prefer to fill up sacks in a most jumbled way. Having reached the limits of their patience, the officers finally wound up turning the sacks upside down to throw the whole contents onto the ground.

Rahmi completed his military service in the month of August. Amid the joy and the emotion of his return, the last preparations for the wedding, planned for 6 October, were progressing well. The furniture, the rugs and the curtains finally found their respective places in the newly renovated apartment. Invitations were printed and distributed; the long-awaited day was almost there.

On the day of the wedding, as tradition required, we, together with uncle Mustafa, went to fetch the new bride from her home. Her father entrusted her to us with great emotion and, in a long line of cars, we proceeded towards the building where the marriage ceremony was to be held. As previously planned at the time we asked for her hand, a small reception was held in our house after the ceremony, sort of an elaborate cocktail party. We had hors d'oeuvres of all type, but the most awaited delicacy was without doubt the stuffed mussels; a highly appreciated delicacy we had prepared ourselves just as we had done for our second wedding reception. Close to one hundred people were present and, despite the usual confusion and some problems with the zipper on Sibel's dress, the night was a success. For me personally, the mother-in-law and hostess alone among all these guests, the day was extremely sad as no one from my family was present. I had to hold back my tears when Claude called, before the ceremony, to offer her best wishes to the young couple. I don't think I had ever felt so totally alone in my life...

Following their honeymoon, Rahmi had to make a very serious decision about his future: would he continue to work in tourism or should he change his career and work with his father at the Blue Turtle Studio? Mehmet, very busy with the block printing, proposed that Rahmi take charge of the painting exhibitions and establish a good archive for our branch of the Eyuboğlu family. We were very happy when Rahmi agreed to work with us. We have been working together ever since.

In 1991, on 12 February, in the middle of an earthquake, our first grandchild, Eren, was born in Istanbul. I had the pleasure of assisting at her birth, but lived the emotions caused by the earthquake just as she was born by Caesarean section. It proved to be a proper welcome to the world for our granddaughter, a real phenomenon herself! Like many children of her age, Eren suffers from asthma. It is only thanks to the vigilance and perseverance of her mother that she is alive. She was saved by following, to the letter, the orders of her doctor, my good friend Günay, a trained specialist in infectious diseases and in immunology. Now a teenager, Eren seems to be cured of this disease. She is a package of energy who loves music, dancing, reading and animals. She is also a good sketcher and has painted since the age of two. She even surprised us greatly when she was two and half years old and helped her grandfather paint invitations for hours on end. She is a good student and is a bit bossy, which is not at all surprising if one considers her genetic inheritance. Since her birth she has spent her summers on the shores of the Aegean Sea and can fearlessly swim like a fish. When we are together she writes scenarios, telling me what my part is and teaching me what I should say. When she was ten years old, she started to prepare various "gourmet" dishes for us from a mixture of recipes she had gathered while watching TV. Like every grandmother, I find my granddaughter to be an absolute delight, especially since I have no other responsibility than that of loving her. On 15 March 2001, our grandson, Mehmet Rahmi, was born in Istanbul to the great joy of his grandfather whose name he carries...

Rahmi and his family (2002)

Chapter XX

My Travels

Since my arrival in this country it seems I have rapidly joined that large tribe of nomads in perpetual movement–the Turcoman! A year after my arrival, I was already travelling around Turkey and my interest in archaeological sites was rapidly growing. In our old blue Volkswagen, we must have driven all the bad secondary roads of the Aegean region leading to ancient cities and archeological sites. The drive south to various villages in order to join the Blue Trip helped me to learn about and appreciate the most well known region of Turkey. The sites around Istanbul were usually visited with my father-in-law who loved to venture here and there in the surrounding villages. Since at that time there were no proper hotels or restaurants in the area, we usually kept our outings short but pleasant.

Turkey enjoys a great advantage: its geographical position. From Turkey one can visit many countries without having to spend a lot of time and money getting there. In 1977, during the school winter holiday, I joined a trip organized by the Italian Lycee where my good friend Gabriella was teaching and went to Romania on a skiing trip. In a bus filled with youngsters, we drove through Bulgaria where, despite the presence of a local guide, we managed to get lost on the mountain roads before we finally set foot in Romania. We spent several days in Sinaia and Braşov, two fairly popular winter sports centers, and I took advantage of the occasion to go to Bucharest for a one-day visit to see my mother-in-law's family. Despite the abominable administration of the Ceausescu regime, nothing could mask the beauties of that enchanting country, nor diminish the impression left by the tremendous human warmth shown by the people in general. Latin gallantry is present everywhere, a real treat after the Slavic treatment. The brilliant city that was Bucharest in the 1930's may have lost some of its glitter, but will surely recover and become, once more, the small Paris it used to be. Fruit and vegetables were scarce and there was absolutely no comparison with the abundance found in the markets of Istanbul. In return, almost under government supervision, a striving blackmarket in gold and U.S. dollars was thriving. That trip allowed me to meet most of the members of my mother-in-law's family and afterwards, most of them came to visit us in Turkey. Mehmet and his mother had often planned to visit Romania together, but something always came up and they were prevented from realizing their dream. It was only very much later, for the celebrations of the New Year and our entry into a new century in the year 2000, that Mehmet actually managed to set foot in the country. Mehmet was then working on a book, translating the love letters of his parents, written at the beginning of their love affair. In order to complete our documentation, it seemed imperative for us to go there and that was exactly what the whole family did, including my granddaughter Eren.

A primary school friend of Rahmi was then manager of a hotel in Bucharest and invited us to stay there. What a surprise to find we were the only ones in the hotel during that wonderful period of the holiday season. Wonderful for us, but sad for them because the city has not yet been incorporated into the tourism circuits! For a country very much in need of foreign currency, this is a very unfortunate situation. The trip took on the aspect of a pilgrimage for Mehmet, who, thanks to his cousin, succeeded in visiting the cemetery where a grandmother he had never met lay buried. We also could locate and take pictures of three of the four houses his mother had lived in so many years before. We managed to visit the big Çeşmeciu Park, covered with snow and filled with lovely huge trees. She had often mentioned that park in her letters. Our attempt to hunt down the Hasefer Art Gallery, where both of Mehmet's parents had held painting exhibitions in 1934 and 1935, was unsuccessful. That gallery had disappeared some twenty years before and in its place we found a photography laboratory. The owner graciously gave us all the information he had on the past history of the gallery. The old newspapers where we had found clippings relating the exhibitions and articles on Bedri Rahmi had all disappeared during the war. This trip, both interesting and moving, allowed us to better understand certain aspects of the life of my mother-in-law before her arrival in Turkey.

The first long trip Mehmet and I took was in 1977. He had just left his job and returned home to be with his mother and manage the cultural inheritance his father had left upon his passing. It was one of those long vacations connected to a religious holiday and we had been invited by his best friend, Mümtaz, to Adana and Antakya. Driving there, we took time to visit Konya, Kayseri and Cappadocia. In Adana, we were the guests of his wife's family, while in the city of Antakya, formerly known as Antioch, we were with Mümtaz's family for one day. These regions of Turkey are popular with tourists because they embody quite a different aspect of the country and allow everyone to gain a good perspective on the various chapters of the country's history.

Konya, the ancient brilliant capital of the Seljuk Empire, is also the city of Mevlana, the profound thinker universally known for his great tolerance. Strangely enough, this city has been transformed into an ugly, narrow-minded and fanatical religious centre. Kayseri, on the other hand, is an active city, surrounded by villages with names synonymous with quality in the universe of handmade rugs, such as Bunyan, Taşpınar and Yahyalı. Cappadocia is an extraordinary region with very unique and unusual scenery straight out of the fairytales. The strangely carved and hollowed out rocks reveal churches, homes and underground cities where an entire persecuted Christian population would hide from attacks in the seventh century. It is without doubt one of the most majestic sites of the country. Finally, we traveled to Antakya or old Antioch, where we saw the first Christian church of St. Peter and, most importantly, one of the richest and loveliest mosaic museums in the world. The very cordial reception we were given was touching and the refined cuisine of the area, though spicy, was a real discovery.

They say that travelling is learning. That long trip took place while I was very preoccupied with the pharmacology courses I was giving to nurses and midwives and it helped me greatly by allowing me to evaluate and better interpret things. The sight of the villages of Central Anatolia, which are much more primitive then those of the Aegean and the Mediterranean region, was a revelation. I immediately grasped the depth of the abyss separating this part of Anatolia and the Marmara region. This led me to re-evaluate my teaching approach and the techniques I had been using until then. I was forced to realize that poverty and the reality of a daily life void of the basic principles of hygiene and elementary cleanliness was an integral part of my students' existence. I suddenly realized how out of context my teaching had been until then and how strange it must have appeared to my students. Having lived a lifetime without running water, without sanitary installations, without any principles of hygiene in houses of dried mud, with no concept of the existence of health standards, how could the young girls succeed in grasping and maintaining the knowledge they were given in our courses? These connotations also helped me to better understand some of the strange behavior constantly observed in Turkish hospitals. Following this trip, my teaching attitude was radically modified.

In 1982, we were informed by the Turkish Government that they were planning to organize a series of expositions of the paintings of my father-in-law in Europe. A much-respected diplomat, Mr Şarik Ariyak, was in charge of this project and a very nice brochure was prepared for the occasion. The first city of the circuit was Vienna and Mehmet, in order to help with the preparation and the opening of the exhibition, was officially invited to accompany the commissary appointed by the Academy of Fine Arts. For this unique occasion, I took some time off and joined Mehmet for one of the rare trips abroad that we managed to take together. We spent three days in that lovely city then proceeded to London, a city we had never previously had the chance to discover.

The exhibition took place in a section of one of Vienna's main museums and, although we could not speak German, we made serious efforts to communicate with the numerous guests and give them the information they wanted. Aware of my passion for opera, Mehmet spent a small fortune in order to please me and succeeded in finding two tickets for "Norma" under the direction of the great Herbert Von Karajan. Unfortunately, at the last minute, the public was informed that the presentation had to be cancelled due to the indisposition of the diva.

Of course, we did not understand the announcement. To our great surprise, we saw a ballerina on the stage when the curtain opened on the performance of Romeo and Juliet, a ballet by Prokoviev.

Within a short period of time, we succeeded in visiting some of the most important classical sites in the world of music, then the painting museum at the Belvedere Palace, and of course a few of the famous cellars of this refined city. We were very impressed by the care and respect shown to the architecture and the cultural inheritance of Vienna. The more recently built modern buildings offer no daring contrast to the more conservative and older forms of the architecture, but rather seem to melt harmoniously into the environment. Istanbul is a much more ancient city than Vienna, but there appears to be an effort to destroy its appearance by allowing the construction of ugly buildings that simply ruin the panorama and the unity of this great historical city.

To a well-indoctrinated citizen of Québec, visiting London appeared to be something of an incursion into enemy territory: the country of the English! But quite the opposite, this city completely seduced me. The British behave in a much more civilized manner in their own country than when they are abroad. They are helpful, polite and behave in the gentleman-like manner typical of them. Luckily, we enjoyed superb weather. Every day we visited a different museum, usually those very rich in archaeological finds originating from Turkey. At the British Museum, in huge halls painted in the azure blue to remind us of the Mediterranean sky, we saw the small, reconstructed temples of the Lycian City of Xanthos, and frescos from the Mausoleum of the Carian City of Halicarnassos. Every year, we had admired the copies graciously sent by the British for display on the actual site of this marvel of the ancient world in Bodrum. At the Victoria and Albert Museum we were fascinated by a collection of objects originating from both Anatolia as well as various other cultures. We were also very impressed by the Ottoman pieces found in various displays. Mehmet left the museum a bit upset, asking himself, "Who allowed such pieces to leave our country? Who authorized such smuggling? What robbers!" But deep inside he knew that the Sultan himself had sometimes given his consent. When you consider the size of the pieces stolen and the places they had came from, one cannot but wonder how they were discovered, transported and finally loaded onto boats for their long trip without anyone seeing anything....

At that time, English and French books were scarce in Istanbul, and those available were very expensive. Turkish books, on the other hand, were printed on low quality paper so cursory as to almost spoil the pleasure of reading. Reference books were rare and the first extravagance we allowed ourselves was to rush to the numerous bookstores to enjoy the pleasure of playing with books.

The itinerary of the painting exhibition included the cities of Budapest and Geneva and it was my mother-in-law who went to those two countries. The tour of cities was abruptly interrupted when a diplomatic crisis arose between France and Turkey. It was caused by a monument that was erected as a memorial to the Armenian victims of the so-called genocide. The much-respected diplomat and organizer of this exhibition, Mr Şarık Ariyak, was brutally assassinated in Australia, a victim of Armenian terrorism–a very sad coincidence.

The following year, titular of a British Council Fellowship, I left for England on a study trip. I took advantage of the occasion to suggest that Mother meet me in London where we could spend a few days together and then take a short trip to Paris. Mother had been dreaming about visiting Paris for many years. Dressed like a princess, she was radiant as she arrived at the Charles-de-Gaulle airport in Paris, her eyes filled with joy! The weather was atrocious; it was rainy and cold, but nothing troubled her. Comfortably settled in a hotel close to the Opera House, wearing extra sweaters, we began the marathon of visiting the City of Paris. We had to choose among the numerous places to visit and we also enjoyed the luxury of strolling here and there in the corners and places that pleased us. Tired and often with wet, cold feet, we came back to the hotel happy to relax in a hot bath. Those few days went by so fast that the first thing we knew, we were back in Montreal where I had to begin work on my NATO research project.

Through the years, Dr Berkarda was very active in the Mediterranean Society of Chemotherapy. That gave us the chance to participate, as a group, in several congresses held outside Turkey. That was how I participated in two meetings in countries I had always felt attracted to: Greece and Egypt.

Such trips require a double preparation: first, a scientific preparation for the Congress itself and, second, a thorough preparation for the touristic part of the trip so that one can learn and understand all that is to be seen in the visited country. The congress in Rhodes in 1985 took place at a period when the relationship between Turkey and Greece was far from the current honeymoon we are currently experiencing. We left Istanbul by bus, in a small group to go to Marmaris, a well-known summer resort. We boarded a ferryboat and arrived in Rhodes a few hours later. Passport and visa in hand, we found ourselves submitted to a shoe disinfection process, an operation requiring that we step onto a rug soaked with an antiseptic product, to destroy the so-called microorganisms coming from Turkey! That measure of protection provoked harsh remarks from some of the travellers, especially a group of Germans travelling with us. At the passport control desks we Turks were the last to receive our documents!

The Greek Islands and their joyous melodies, though, managed to stir up pleasant feelings. We were there for the sake of science, not for the sake of battles; we therefore tried to look at things with a conciliatory eye. Other than more joyful music and better organization in tourism, there is not much difference between our two countries, both of which share a long history of an almost conjugal life and a sometimes stormy cohabitation.

The trip was most interesting for me, the Canadian, a bit lost in the sinuous paths of history. Worthy disciple of Uncle Sabahattin and of the Blue Trip, I knew the value of preparation and I threw myself into various books describing the region. Visiting sites where the cultural differences are so subtle as to be almost non-existent proved to be quite a revelation. In the meantime, the experts are still disputing the respective origins of both areas.

To the Western World, culture began with Greece: thinking, art, mythology, civilization: the city of Troy, the Odysseus and the Iliad. But archeological findings have slowly revealed that Anatolian cultures existed way before Greek civilization and that mythology, for example, was very much alive in the old Sumerian civilization. Gods such as Apollo and Dionysus and the goddess Aphrodite have been shown to be of Anatolian origin. Were the cities discovered on the Aegean coast really of Hellenistic origin? Was Hippocrates of Cos the fruit of Anatolian or Hellenistic culture? The question deserving to be asked is: "Where does the real cradle of Western culture lie?"

Hoping to find the answers, I decided to consult Uncle Sabahattin's valuable collaborator, the writer Azra Erhat, student of Cevat Şakir, the Fisherman of Halicarnassos. We got together during her illness and talked about the old days before proceeding to discuss what I had in mind. I tried to convey my observations and the hesitations I felt towards some of the statements found in several of the books written by Cevat Şakir and other authors. I expressed my doubts on the scientific value of such articles where practically no references supported the theories advanced. To my great surprise, Mrs Erhat admitted that, in fact, while these books had been written with great enthusiasm, they lacked the required supportive scientific basis. She seemed quite saddened by this fact. Finally, a visit to Mr Iskender Ohri proved to be quite enriching since after listening to me, he suggested the books of Prof A.M. Mansel, a well-known archeologist and authority on the studies of Aegean civilizations. His books on this subject confirmed the view that the diffusion of cultures occurred from the East towards the West, with its roots firmly situated in the civilizations of Mesopotamia and Anatolia.

The congress in Rhodes was attended by some 3,000 doctors. Unfortunately, our delegation encountered a few unpleasant events. The first day of the congress, we noticed that the Turkish flag was not among the other flags of the participating countries, a grave omission since Turkey was to be the host country of the next congress. That was followed by an event taking place in the tour bus especially organized for the congress participants. The guide began to describe with great fervor how the Turks had destroyed the most important sites of the island. We were quite astonished and offended by these assertions, so Dr Derman asked the guide if she could explain how two important cities dating from the Middle Age like Dubrovnic and Rhodes, which we were now visiting, had managed to remain almost intact despite long years of occupation by the Turks.

Masters in touristic organization, the Greeks managed to transport, for one day, all the participants of the congress and their respective buses from Rhodes to Cos. This island was the birthplace of Hippocrates and a ceremony was scheduled to take place in his honor. Under the noon sun, everyone gathered in the ancient open-air theater. A pan flute player and a few young girls dressed in white descended the seemingly endless stairs of the theater scattering rose petals along the way. This procession took quite some time. When it finally came to a stop, the disciples of Hippocrates were asked to renew their oath in front of two "antique stones", which many people presumed to be the original stones. At that particular moment, movie cameras rolled, cameras clicked from all angles, excitement was at a peak. I almost thought we were in Hollywood. Once the ceremony was over and the people had left, I was completely astonished and my mouth fell open as I observed what was done with the precious "antique stones". I began to have real doubts about their authenticity! A simple worker arrived with an ordinary wheelbarrow in which he simply threw in the "oath of Hippocrates" with great noise and took them away without any special care... Later on, during lunch time, while listening to the comments of the others, I was astonished to observe that the participants had really been deeply moved by this simple but cheap performance. I even began to think that we should put on a Hittite show the next year in Istanbul...

The masterpiece of achievements was without a doubt the night banquet. To begin with, try to imagine a hotel hall capable of seating 3,000 people. Then add a Fellini type of food display with an unbelievable variety of meat, pork, chicken and lamb being grilled over open flames, plus a rather sophisticated buffet. Our needs were met by an army of young people flying between the tables; this was the kind of superb organization the Greeks are so well-known for. With Turkey the host country for the World Chemotherapy Congress in 1987, every member of our delegation took advantage of the occasion to gather information on the art of being a host.

Another important congress took place in Egypt in the city of Cairo. Our small group took advantage of that occasion to take a cruise on the River Nile for a few days before the conferences. Following our arrival in Cairo, we rested for the day before flying to Luxor where we boarded a luxurious cruise boat and began our visit to the fascinating city surrounded by the Valley of Kings before proceeding towards Aswan. The atmosphere was such that you have the clear impression of living in another century. The calm found along the Nile, the elegance of the beautiful birds, the silence around us and the various archeological treasures we were slowly discovering all added extra charm to this trip into what seemed like another dimension. Like Turkey, Egypt is a paradise for the amateur archeologist. Despite the heat and the impressive number of visitors, the tourist paths are well-defined and the highest level of comfort is available. Cruise boats are four-star hotels, where they gather visitors into various groups. I can definitely say that on our trip, highly qualified and devoted guides were responsible for each group. Our guide was very happy to serve his first Turkish group and showed great ardor in his work. The history of Egypt and Turkey was closely intertwined at various periods, especially during the Ottoman Empire, and of course in the very old days of the famous Kadesh war between Ramses II and Muwatalli. Writings about this battle, in which both sides claim victory for themselves, can be found in Luxor.

During this cruise we were travelling with a group of young Italians, working members of a tourist agency, some British and a few Australians. The Italians were determined to have fun and enjoy every minute of their cruise. On the last night, a special costume party dinner was organized and every group was encouraged to prepare a small, amusing bit of entertainment for the pleasure of the members of the cruise. A few prizes were promised, so a deep sense of competition and great creative wind blew through the cruise ship. The Italians put on a show about Anthony and Cleopatra, and they had such fun getting ready for their show that I could not help but enjoy observing them. Since a great variety of clothes, material and jewelry could be found in the country at low prices, the whole group was dressed or wrapped in vivid colors, many men dressed as women. A most amusing scene! My cabin was just opposite of Mark Anthony's, so I got to see all the preparations. The British chose as their scenario one of the many unbelievable legends we had heard during the various historical visits of the day. Each god represented a theatrical spirit and the scenes were worthy of Shakespeare's grandchildren. Each scene was accompanied by a narrative of this unbelievable legend.

As a good Québecer, loving fun, I was ready to take up the challenge and compete for our group, but most of our Turkish group of fifteen did not share my enthusiasm. They were such serious people that I realized they would never take part in such a competition. Why the apathy? Was the shyness the result of a very conventional education, or the impossibility of relaxing in such circumstances? I don't know, but no one budged. Only three of us decided to do something, and since all of us were women, we quickly found the perfect plan. Even though my knowledge was quite minimal, we all knew belly-dancing and so decided to introduce ourselves as, "The Princesses of Istanbul" travelling on this boat especially to entertain the participants of the cruise! We were quite a sight in our long dresses, our jewels and our scarves! We had absolutely no idea what music was available for our talents, but our entrance was followed by loud screams, applauses and whistles of appreciation. Belly-dancing for a few minutes is not too tiresome, but because we had to cross the whole dining room to reach the area where the jury was, it didn't take long for us to feel exhausted. Those were the longest minutes of my belly-dancing career! This dance is always appreciated in the Middle East and at one point, everyone likes to join in and have fun. We were eventually joined by some members of the crew and the general manager of the boat! Exhausted, I was very glad when the music finally stopped and we received a great ovation. We won second place in the competition and received bracelets with blue scarabs. I never learned if our group had shared our excitement or if they had frowned at us, but we had fun!

The opening of the congress was held in front of the pyramids and was followed by a sound and light show. Our hosts were certainly doing everything in their power to impress every one of us! Visiting Cairo proved to be a major feat. Hiring a taxi required having the destination registered and bargaining for the fare. Only then would they take us where we wanted to go, wait for us and bring us back to the hotel. An excellent precaution actually, otherwise I think we could have run into trouble. A visit to the Islamic Art Museum on my own was very instructive. I could compare at leisure the work done in various Islamic countries and appreciate the elegance and refinement of the Ottoman work originating from Turkey. Another surprising sight was the first Egyptian

The Turkish delegation in competition while cruising on the Nile (1986)

mosque I saw in Cairo. Used to the elegant domes and the very tall and inspiring minarets of Istanbul, I was surprised by the rather stocky mosques and minarets with no intentions of reaching towards heaven! We are, of course, rather spoiled by the rather spectacular architecture, the tile work and the calligraphy found in Turkish mosques. A most interesting place was the Museum of the Copts, where, unfortunately, no brochure or publication was available. I was not at all impressed by the market of Cairo; it failed to bring back scenes of a Thousand and One Nights. It is not well taken care of, is rather confusing–and the smell! Istanbul's bazaar fares better in all respects.

Conversations we had with the Egyptians about their lifestyle and salaries were very revealing. We found out that the monthly salary they received from the hospital was close to the amount we were spending on taxi fares in their city on a busy sightseeing day. A visit to the local pharmacies showed us just how little medication was available. The vegetable markets of Cairo reflected the poverty of the soil and the difficulties in watering cultivated areas. Very colorfully decorated pastry shops could be found on the sidewalks. They must attract the children, but I wondered what could possibly be consumed without any danger of infection... I had taken the precaution of packing a few bottles of water in my suitcase and some food just in case I needed it. Fortunately, the need never arose. I would love to return to Egypt, such a seductive country. There was enchantment in the history, in its past, in its treasures. The great silence of the desert together with the calm of the Nile fascinated me.

The summer of 1991 proved to be a memorable one. Exactly twenty-five years after his return to Turkey, Mehmet agreed to take a trip to the American continent. The itinerary was such that it almost looked like a pilgrimage! Our plans included a visit to Mother and my sister in Montreal, followed by a visit to her summerhouse near Lake Champlain in the United States. We then planned a short stay in Ottawa, the city where we had met, and another stop in Toronto to visit my good friend Louise. Mehmet hates travelling by plane and it was with little enthusiasm that he oversaw the preparations, including the unpleasant formalities of obtaining visas both for Canada and the U.S. The passport officers couldn't help smiling when he declared that the purpose of his trip was to visit his mother-in-law!

Mother was very happy to receive him as he arrived holding a huge bouquet of red roses. Those flowers caused quite a commotion among the residents of her apartment house, little accustomed were they to such demonstrations! Ottawa City had not changed dramatically since we left and we were filled with nostalgic feelings as we drove around the city. We found our former residence on Sweetland Avenue quite unchanged and well kept. We were informed that the last owner had been Mrs Myner, our former roommate! Our visit to Toronto, a first for Mehmet, was very pleasant. Accompanied by Jean Marc and Louise, who gracefully guided us to the various sights of the area, we enjoyed the natural beauties of the gorgeous scenery. One of Mehmet's dreams was fulfilled when we visited a farm devoted to the breeding of buffalos, like those seen in old western movies. To top off our stay in Ontario, we spent a lovely weekend on the Georgian Bay in Louise's very comfortable "log cabin". Completely under the spell of the area,

Mehmet, seeing the neighbors in the lake in the early morning, decided it would be nice to take a swim. With great enthusiasm he walked towards the shore and stepped into the water... but stopped at once, as if he had suddenly been paralyzed! The water was so cold, he could not even talk and was totally shocked. Too proud to give up, he tried again to take a few steps, but to no avail; it was too cold for him to enjoy swimming. He came back to the cottage a bit upset by his performance, but we knew very well that not everyone can swim easily in Canadian waters in June. That night we witnessed a tremendous thunderstorm with lightning of every possible color in the sky, a spectacle better than the best sound and light show. At the end of the storm, we were surprised to observe that all the neighbors' garage doors had opened during the storm, most likely as a result of the strong electrical discharges.

Having spent so many years in Turkey, I had become used to lovely hot and sunny summers and experienced some surprise when I was faced with our strange Canadian summers again. This feeling was especially strong on the weekend of the 1st of July, Canada Day, our National Holiday. Hundreds of Canadians had come to the shores of Lake Champlain for the long weekend. Everyone was fully equipped with all the possible material required for camping: boats, outboard motors, tents, beds, outdoor kitchens, etc. They had brought everything except the main element required for a summer vacation: the sun. Wrapped in warm sweaters, everyone watched the sky, hoping the rain would stop, and dreamed about the arrival of the sun! I thought of the situation in Turkey, where camping equipment was then expensive and difficult to find, and how, in spite of such obstacles families with very little means would jump into their cars and drive to their favorite seashores. Once at the spot of their dreams, they would find a place on the ground and without the least bit of comfort proceed to happily spend their few days of vacation. They were lucky because they had the heat and the sun on their side! No country in this world is perfect. Another detail I had almost forgotten: at sunset, the arrival of regiments of mosquitoes who did not allow us one moment of peace. We had to build a huge fire to warm and protect ourselves. Where were the warm nights of Bodrum? Back in Turkey, we were more than happy to find the summer once more...

Since my retirement, Rahmi and I have formed the family's mobile crew responsible for exhibitions held outside of Istanbul. Rahmi is usually the one taking care of events related to paintings, while I look after those related to block prints. If necessary, I can also take care of the painting exhibitions. I have no intention of relating all the adventures I have experienced during such assignments, but have chosen two particular instances filled with unforeseen events.

Two exhibitions were planned in the city of Trabzon in the month of February, 1992. This is the month when the city celebrates the anniversary of its liberation from the Russians who had occupied it during World War I. The first exhibition was of the paintings of my father-in-law and took place at the Mahmut Gologlu Art Gallery, which is named after Bedri Rahmi's brother-in-law. The second event was a block print exhibition of Mehmet's work. He had chosen designs with Black Sea region themes: fish, Black Sea traditional dancers and the kemençe (a musical instrument of the region) player. Those colorful designs were highly appreciated by the people of the city.

The Eyuboğlu family originates from Trabzon, a city built on the shores of the Black Sea. This was where my father-in-law spent his youth before leaving, without regrets, following the difficulties he had experienced with his mathematics teacher during high school. He only returned some forty years later on a trip he took with his students from the Fine Arts Academy. Trabzon was also the province Mehmet's grandfather had represented in Parliament during the years of Atatürk.

Inhabitants of the Black Sea region differ from the people of other regions of the country. Lively by nature, they possess a flamboyant character and their strong accent characteristic to the region is easily recognizable. Their folk dances contrast sharply with those of other regions and their music is quite unique. Their favorite instrument is the kemençe, a three-stringed instrument emitting sounds very strange to our untrained ears. At first it seems to lack any sort of melody and it seems as if the same tune is being repeated over and over. On the first morning of my stay, to my great surprise, I woke up at seven o'clock in the morning to the sound of hundreds of kemençes piercing my ears. Rushing to the window of my room overlooking the main square of the city, I learned at once where these sounds were coming from. All the folkloric dance teams of the city

Schoolgirls dancing in Trabzon

and the schools, with dancers of all ages and both sexes, were gathered around the square at this early hour, ready to take part in the celebrations. They were dancing with such zest it created a fascinating scene. Men dressed in white and black with a piece of cloth strangely draped around their heads, heavy silver chains hanging on their chests and their feet wrapped in tight leather boots were doing the Horon, the typical dance of the region. This is a spectacular dance with rapid and abrupt movements performed with stunning precision and, strangely enough, I had the sensation that the dancers had come out of one of my father-in-law's paintings. Obviously he had studied the dance often and had been fascinated by the gracious movements of these light-footed men.

Without losing time I rushed into the square to take pictures of those very colorful scenes and share the enthusiasm found in the street. I could almost forget the sound of the kemençe and find it pleasant to the ear. Looked upon as a tourist, let us say I was the only person of foreign origin in the crowd, a piece of news the children spread around in no time, unaware that I could understand what they were saying.

Following the ceremony, I went to the gallery where the block print exhibition was to take place. The walls were so wide and high I wondered how I would cover all those huge surfaces. Fortunately, I had had some experience in hanging exhibitions under difficult conditions and so was prepared to tackle this difficulty as well. I firmly believed that I could face any and all eventualities until I saw the ladder they brought me for me to work with. I was devastated! How could I ever climb up that primitive ladder? What acrobatic marvels would be required to hang the block prints? As I was contemplating the feats I might have to attempt, I heard a soft hesitant voice asking me: "Do you need help?" Who was making me such an unexpected offer? My guardian angel had sent me a young doctor, an art lover who had some free time. Under difficult conditions, but with infinite patience and some prowess, we succeeded in hanging the exhibition. Suddenly, the hall was transformed and took on a totally new aspect as each piece, reflecting the soul of the region, took life. Those huge panels of various sizes, some more than two meters long, once again gave life to the shepherds, to the peasant and her child, to the young bride, to the kemençe player, to the boats and the numerous multicolored fish, all elements so precious in the daily life of Bedri Rahmi.

We had hardly completed our work when I was informed of the arrival of the Mayor to open the exhibition. I still had a hammer in my hand when he asked if I was ready to inaugurate the exhibition and address the public. Noticing that there were no women in the hall, I naively requested of the Mayor a few more minutes of patience, thinking that surely a few women would come to the opening. Very politely he replied that the women would be there a bit later and without any further delay, he introduced me to a completely male audience. Having to speak in Turkish in public and improvise a talk without any preparation has always been a source of stress for me. As I began to talk, I recovered my self-assurance, but I must admit that it was a laborious and demanding task. As predicted by the Mayor, the men gradually disappeared and the women of Trabzon began to arrive to visit the exhibition. Several art teachers were present and they completed my education on the customs of the region. They proceeded to explain that in such circumstances, men arrive first and are later followed by the women...

The next day, I was to experience a similar "cultural" experience. It was the first painting exhibition of Bedri Rahmi in this area of the country, an important event for a city welcoming back a favorite son she was so proud of! Once again, I had to face a male audience that included judges, bureaucrats, various local authorities and several military officers of various ranks. To my great relief, I was not asked to address the audience, but this time they insisted that I go around the exhibition with them so I could provide some information and explain each painting.

I gracefully agreed to the request. All went well until we arrived in front of a very erotic masterpiece. The title of the work was "BABATOMİ", a word Bedri Rahmi had made up from the French word "anatomy". In Turkish the word "ana" and "baba" respectively mean mother and father. The play on words was very subtle, but how could I, the only woman in the group, explain that to an entirely male audience? Very seriously, mastering my reflexes and in a most academic tone, I managed to explain the painting, wondering what my father-in-law would have done had he been in my place! In exactly the same fashion as the previous day, the men left the gallery after which the women began to arrive. How strange customs can be!

A few hours later, the inauguration of the Bedri Rahmi Eyuboğlu Art Museum took place. A bust of Bedri Rahmi, a copy of the original sculpture found in our home, was placed at the entrance of the museum. It was unveiled during the course of a very emotion filled ceremony. There were only a few paintings in the museum's collection, and in order to honor this city from which his family originated, Mehmet graciously donated a few of my father-in-law's works.

Having completed my duties, I hurried to do my shopping. I wanted to buy some of the famous cheese and butter of the region so I could prepare a local dish when I got back home. Escorted to the airport, I was presented with gifts of nuts and various brands of tea, the famous products of the region. The warm hospitality of the people of Trabzon touched me deeply and I flew back to Istanbul delighted with my trip. I was to return to Trabzon some ten years later with the members of the Eyuboğlu Foundation. They held a large meeting and dinner in the small town of Maçka where everyone appeared to belong to the Eyuboğlu clan!

Mehmet and I took our first trip to Cyprus in 1993 to open a block print exhibition in Nicosia. The exhibition was held in the huge gallery of the Turkish Cultural Center, and the temperature was over 40 degrees. Hanging those huge pieces in such heat was very difficult. Once the block prints were hung, the atmosphere of the gallery was completely changed. Later, we enjoyed a few days of vacation on the warm beaches of the island and some pleasant hours of visiting the area. Six months later, I returned to the island all by myself to open an exhibition of my father-in-law's paintings. The gallery was, in fact, a former church transformed into an art gallery, a first in our long list of galleries. To make things easier, the paintings had been sent from Turkey unframed and so they were to be framed on the spot the day before the exhibition. Besides the paintings, we were also exhibiting, for the first time, a series of hand-painted porcelain plates, copies made from the original designs of my father-in-law.

My visit coincided with the celebrations of the anniversary of the Turkish Republic of Northern Cyprus. Within the frame of good will prevailing on the island, the Greeks deliberately cut off the electricity on the Turkish side. The morning of the opening, we went to the gallery to complete the hanging and add some final touches to our preparations. Quite a surprise was in store for us! To our astonishment, we found that the glass on one third of our framed paintings was cracked and heavily damaged. We had to promptly replace the glass and began to hope and pray for an immediate return of the electricity, in time for the opening. Late in the afternoon, while placing huge candles in the church, we heard a terrible sound of glass shattering and rushed to the entrance of the gallery to find a glass display cabinet in pieces. Was the former church, now art gallery, haunted? It was getting a bit nerve-racking! Of course, we opened in the dark. The exhibition was to be inaugurated by the Honorable Rauf Denktaş the President of the Republic. He duly arrived accompanied by his staff, each carrying a strong flashlight. Most guests arrived with their own source of light, but the surface was so big that we felt more like we were caught in the huge shadows of Eisenstein's film *Ivan the Terrible*. The approach of each guest was announced by the lights of their car seen from a distance. Despite those difficulties, the cocktail party and the exhibition were a success. Very surprisingly, a few paintings were actually sold in this darkness. Late at night, after everyone had left, the electricity came back on! We celebrated the event in a charming restaurant but again we were plunged into darkness...

In 1997, several Turkish NGO's decided to celebrate 8 March, Women's Day, in a Turkish city where the status of women can be described as tragic. Our association decided to take part in the trip and so together with two of my close American friends, we took the road to Urfa, a city in southeastern Turkey, very close to the Syrian border. Built near the Euphrates where Mesopotamia begins, the ancient city had been known as Ur of Chaldea and also as Edessa, an important city during the Crusades. While carefully reading the brochures printed about this city, I was quite surprised to learn that Urfa was referred to as the city of prophets. Among the names of prophets cited were Abraham, Job, Elisha, Jethro, Noah, Moses and Lot, all former residents of the area. Those claims may seem exaggerated, but they are nevertheless interesting.

Abraham is, of course, an important figure in each of the three main religions developed in the Middle East. It appears he came from the Chaldean City of Ur, the ancient name of Urfa. From everywhere, pilgrims come to visit the cave where he was born. He lived there until the age of seven in order to escape the edict of King Nimrod who had ordered the massacre of both all newborn babies and all pregnant women. According to the stars, a newborn child would bring an end to his reign and the cult of idols. This cave can be found within the walls of a small mosque built during the Ottoman period. In later years, when Abraham began to openly denounce the idolatry of his king, he was condemned to be thrown from a high hill into a fire. But the prophet's life was miraculously saved when the fire was transformed into a course of water and the pieces of wood feeding the fire became fish. Two small pools filled with ugly and greedy carp can be found near the cave of Abraham's birth, a site visited by pilgrims from the Islamic World. Extraordinary myths can be found in the basic stories of all religions! Other authorities assure us that the country where Abraham came from was the city of Ur more to the south of Mesopotamia, now in Iraq. But there are indications to the contrary*. Abraham left Urfa in later years to pursue his destiny.

Urfa is very different from any Turkish city I had visited before. This city illustrates very well what the expression "mosaic of cultures" means: a mixture of Turkish, Kurdish and Arab people each speaking their own language. Each group of women dresses according to their own code. Very little difference can be seen between the men. The city

---

* *Ibrahim Peygamber* by Turkish Sumerologist Muazzez İlmiye Çığ, based upon the Akkadian Archives of Nuzi and Hittite texts.

is built on arid ground with very little vegetation and practically no color is seen. In vain does the eye search for some color to break the monotony of the landscape. Seven months a year, the city endures very high temperatures. Turkey is currently developing a gigantic project of dams and irrigation water canals on the Euphrates in order to irrigate the semi-desert like region. This project is, of course, severely criticized by surrounding countries such as Syria and Iraq for whom the water is also vital. This area is becoming more and more important strategically and may become a source of conflict in the near future.

Establishing contact with the women of Urfa proved to be difficult. Except for the Kurdish women, who unfortunately cannot speak Turkish, we hardly saw any women at all. Arab women are well protected behind the walls of their homes and gardens. Among the few Turkish girls we had the chance to meet, some wore Islamic headgear. The University of Harran, a name evoking the first university built during the Seljuk era, is under the strong influence of radical Islam and absolutely no social functions are offered to the students. The traditions of their social life are such that absolutely no contact is tolerated between the sexes. As soon as the sun sets, needless to say, women are no longer seen in the streets.

The auditorium where the meeting took place was filled with people. The meeting opened with the usual speeches by the local authorities, followed by women guest speakers and then by a fashion show organized by the students of a high school. To complete the meeting, a small concert was presented by a group of musicians who had accompanied us for the occasion. They were welcomed with almost a standing ovation and no one wanted the concert to come to an end.

It turned out that this meeting, aimed at enlightening the women of the area, was the area's first and only social program of the year. That is why more then a hundred male university students first sat patiently and even attentively through the first part of the program and then, very happily, enjoyed the musical part of the day. Every evening that we were in Urfa, we sat in the lobby of our hotel and enjoyed memorable musical hours with students from the conservatory of music. This region is particularly rich in folk music and the voices of the men from Urfa have a particular and very moving tone quality found nowhere else in the country.

As an ancient city, Urfa offers a lot of historical sites such as an interesting covered bazaar and an old caravanserai (an ancient hotel where the travellers would stop with their horses or camels) filled with fascinating objects. A few kilometers from the city lies the ancient town of Harran, mentioned in the Bible and now placed under UNESCO protection. Here, the houses, built in the shape of a beehive, offer a unique and extraordinary landscape. A few steps away can be found the ruins of the ancient university dating from the Seljuk period. Research is continuing in the surrounding area to find the famous temple dedicated to Sin the Akkadian moon goddess, since Urfa and Harran were her sacred cities. Urfa is a most interesting city, but filled with anguish and oppression for its women. We learned with interest that a foreign spouse had lived there many years before.

In 1998, I took my first trip to Central Africa to visit my sister who was working in Niger for Oxfam-Québec. How can I describe all I felt at the sight of such misery and poverty? A barren poor country with absolutely no social security, no resources, where eating, even once a day, becomes a crucial problem. How can you not feel shame at such a sight? How could a continent have been left in such a state? Something very essential has failed to be solved in this world...

We were in Niamey, the capital of the country, and we travelled in the surroundings to survey projects financed by Oxfam-Québec. The capital is situated on the shores of the Niger River and offers a majestic view in many areas. The neighborhood where my sister resided included huge, lovely gardens despite the yellow sand prevailing in the city. The population in general lives in thatched huts or in houses made of mud, sometimes aesthetically decorated with mud moldings. The grain storage containers found in each village are usually larger and built more solidly then the houses, illustrating the importance of conserving every precious gram of food.

Observing the mixture of different ethnic groups, each wearing their colorful traditional clothes, was an absolute delight. Young girls in colorful garments were especially beautiful; some had very interesting wrappings around their heads. It is a country of light and color. When I came back to Turkey, it took me quite some time to get used to the gray environment of fall and winter. Since no law on hygiene prevails,

the children of the country walk barefoot on a ground covered with lit-
ter. Education is a problem and despite the fact that it is a French
speaking country, a proud member of "La Francophonie", it is impossible to find a French-speaking woman in most villages. We had to rely
on a translator for our work. Here is another example of a country
where the status of women is very distressing at all levels and where the
customs of society literally crush them. Their adherence to the Islamic
faith, with the practice of polygamy that offers absolutely no possible
security to them, does not help to improve the status of our African sisters. Malaria and the numerous infectious diseases found cannot possibly be eradicated in this environment. The presence of an unbelievable
number of international NGO's is amazing, but great efforts, coming
from all over the world, will be needed in order to avoid the complete
disappearance of this country, condemned to be slowly swallowed by
the sands of the desert.

In March 2000, during the long Moslem holiday following the
Ramadan, I took a short trip to Israel. Totally the opposite of Niger,
the Israelis have managed to literally pull themselves from the desert, an
almost unbelievable feat. What has been accomplished on the technical
level is astonishing, but at the human level, when it comes to understanding what has happened between religions and the people, results
are not very brilliant! While visiting Jerusalem, I was quite stunned to
find absolutely no love emanating from all the various magnificent
churches, synagogues and mosques found there, but rather to feel a
sense of powerful hate directed towards each other. Three great and
very similar religions find themselves in the midst of spectacular
scenery, in buildings where only superlative words could be used to
describe their beauty, yet they cannot succeed in getting to know one
another. Not only do they fail at loving and respecting each other, they
cannot even attain a level where some degree of virulence could be low-
ered. One fact is quite evident: we still have a long road to pursue
before we even begin to understand the messages left by our great spiritual leaders.

Chapter XXI

Life Between 1989 and 2001

Since my arrival in Turkey in 1966, the population of all the larger cities has been increasing constantly. The migrations from Anatolian villages towards the large, filled-with-promise cities have swollen the population of Istanbul in an amazing manner, raising it from three million to some twelve million or more. Despite the construction of two bridges linking Europe and Asia over the Bosphorus Strait, this uncontrolled growth and its repercussions on traffic has made crossing from one side of the city to the other one of the most exasperating problems of daily life. Getting from one side of the city to the other during peak rush hours takes at least an hour and a half in the morning and the same amount of time in the evening, resulting in a senseless waste of precious time and energy. The smallest perturbation in the climate increases this loss period to such a degree that being caught in traffic turns into a veritable nightmare. This situation led me to seriously consider retirement. I was approaching my fiftieth birthday and I concluded that I had done my share. The unceasing contact with cancer patients was also beginning to take its toll. At home, Mehmet's work was increasing and the help I gave him required almost all of my evenings and my weekends. There were always tasks to be done: material to be cut, tags to be sewn, block prints to be numbered, ironed or hand painted. Pieces had to be selected for exhibitions, lists had to be made, records of our stocks had to kept and the bookkeeping had to be done. All this work required time.

Kalamış Manolya Sok. No 10, living and dining room

Thinking about my retirement created serious problems for our medical center. What was to happen to the laboratory? My efforts to find a new laboratory chief or some replacement were hampered by the poor quality of the candidates applying for the job. What a sad fact to face at the end of my career, after so many years of work spent training professionals in my field. I felt worried as I thought about the potential dangers those young graduates, from newly established universities, represented for society. They were totally unconscious of their lack of competence and possessing a university degree gave them a false sense of confidence. It was very difficult to make them understand how insufficient their training had been. I was deeply worried by this problem and understood they could not be blamed for this awkward situation. That responsibility should fall on the shoulders of those who had allowed the establishment of universities that were unable to offer a level of training worthy of the name. I could not leave my laboratory in the hands of an inadequately trained individual, so I decided to close the laboratory and sell all the equipment.

That painful phase was eased when I learned that Dr Berkarda had decided to return to Istanbul University on a full-time basis. He had plans to become a candidate for the position of rector of the University of Istanbul. Scandals and dishonest dealings had shaken that important institution just as they had many other institutions in the country. The current rector was a professor from our former clinic and also the director of the Cardiology Institute. He led a fierce battle to keep the post he had occupied for several years. In December of 1990, I finally turned the last pages and closed the long chapter of my working life. I had worked in the health system of three different countries and after a thirty-three year career, I started a new life. I soon discovered that my home had become a very active beehive with various activities going on and that an important number of people came and went everyday. Since the block printing personnel and students working with us all ate lunch at our house, a tremendous activity reigned in our kitchen, almost as busy as a small restaurant!

Dividing my time between block printing, exhibitions and research work in public libraries, time flew by and I had no time to feel bored. Every year, on the first weekend of June, we hold a two-day block print exhibition in our garden. This event has now become a tradition and

-288-

Mehmet working on a block print

gives us the chance to exhibit Mehmet's work in a pleasant way during the rose season, the nicest month of the year in Istanbul. Over 1,500 handwritten invitations, each with a small sample of our work, are mailed to our friends and acquaintances. On the eve of the event, we prepare homemade cookies to be served with wine and cherries during the two days of the exhibition. A devoted group of young ladies, block print angels, help us every year with the guests and the sales during this event. It is a very colorful but tiring weekend which we enjoy every minute of.

It was during one of these exhibitions that I met a blond American architect, Deanna Erkut, also married to a Turkish citizen and living very close to our home. While chatting with her, I realized to my surprise that, during the many years of my life in Istanbul, I had actually had very few contacts with the foreign colony. Except for a very limited number of foreign spouses in my immediate surroundings, I knew almost nothing about the foreigners in Istanbul. Little did I know at that time that this new acquaintance would bring quite a radical change into my life.

Deanna introduced me to a group known as the American Women of Istanbul or AWI. Quite to my surprise, I learned that this group had over 125 members, consisting mostly of Americans, but including a few Canadians as well. Most of these ladies were ex-patriots living in Istanbul with their working husbands for a determined period of time, while a smaller number was made up of women living here in Turkey with their Turkish husbands. AWI organizes a monthly program focused on a general meeting in addition to excursions of various types in the city, but especially designed for those who enjoy shopping. A monthly newsletter keeps members informed about events scheduled for their entertainment and also contains some useful information for the newcomers. They also have excellent get togethers for their children to celebrate various North American holidays such as Halloween, Christmas and Easter. For the first time since my arrival, I celebrated Christmas among foreigners. Until then, Christmas had been a working day for me since we usually celebrated New Year's Eve with the family.

After joining this group, I discovered a second group, the International Women of Istanbul (IWI). This larger group of some 500 women is open to all foreign nationalities and operates approximately in the same fashion as AWI. A similar monthly newsletter informs the members of the monthly activities of the group, including a monthly luncheon in one of the big hotels of Istanbul or in a fancy restaurant as well as meetings held in the private homes of the members. Both groups are casual groups with no legal structure. I found myself joining IWI without realizing that I was to find myself involved in a new occupation. The founding of an association is regulated by law. The status, the by-laws and all meetings require prior clearance by the authorities. The elections and the annual general meetings are held in the presence of a security officer. Founding a legal NGO requires some courage!

In the spring of 1992, the incoming-president of IWI, Lyne Saka, an American also married to a Turkish national, asked me if I would be interested in taking on some responsibility in the new executive board of the group. Having absolutely no experience in such a field and feeling totally inadequate for such a post, I hesitated before finally, at her insistence, accepting her offer. Finding serious volunteers appeared to be a feat because they are practically non-existent. From that date on, the next ten years were a very active period in the enriching but ungrateful universe of women's associations. From then on, Lyne and I worked very fruitfully as partners in all the future ventures involving association work. We understood very well what we expected from each other and formed a good team.

Having obtained Turkish nationality at my marriage; I had never experienced any of the problems and difficulties usually encountered by foreign spouses who, for one reason or another, do not have Turkish citizenship. In a very short period of time, after contact with such women and with the arrival of new spouses in the association, we discovered the extent of the problem. I remembered my first years of adaptation to Turkey, the isolation felt then, and the very acute feeling that all these upsetting changes were overwhelming. I was convinced that a helping hand should be extended to all those in the same situation and I decided to devote myself to the study of all the problems related to establishing a new life in a foreign country. I concentrated on the problems associated with culture shock, the integration process and its many phases and also on the improvement of the legal status of foreign-born spouses.

Always a passionate one for research, I first dealt with the problem of culture shock, a major problem challenging every new spouse in the adopted country. Not professionally qualified to conduct such research on my own, I looked for and, in the American group, quickly found a psychologist. Since her husband was German, she was also a foreign spouse and was deeply interested in the problem. So we got to work and designed with great care a list of sixty multiple-choice questions covering all aspects of the assimilation process in a foreign country. Several members of the American group were deemed suitable and so the research began with them. Later on, not to limit our research to a single ethnic group, the study continued among the international community of spouses. A total of fifty-seven women took part in our research.

A close friend of the family, a psychology professor at the University of Istanbul and former head of the department, Mrs Nezahat Arkun, heard of my work and showed great enthusiasm for the project, sending me all the foreign spouses that crossed her path. She followed the progress of the study with interest and graciously offered her advice and comments. In the meantime, though, Mary found out she was leaving Istanbul just as our research finished and so I found myself very much alone to work on the interpretation of the study and write the conclusions. I asked for the help of a former colleague from the days of the Therapeutic Clinic, now a professor of psychology at the University of Istanbul. Those two professors helped me. I prepared a paper that I was to present at a seminar in their department. The paper was well received; no serious criticism was formulated so I tried to find a journal where the research and its results could be published. This study remains one of the rare papers devoted to this subject in Turkey. The results clearly indicated that mastering the Turkish language and a very slow adjustment process were the two great hampering factors to the integration of foreign spouses in their new country. Most of those women did not speak Turkish at home and preferred teaching their native language to their children. That is why the usage and the vocabulary of their Turkish always remains at an elementary level, a condition which allows them very little chance of reading or writing the language. It also appeared that a fairly large number of women secretly nourished the desire to return to their own country one day. It was shown that only after having spent some fifteen years in their adoptive country did they appear ready to accept the fact that they were here to stay. A great number of these women also expressed the desire of being buried in their native country. The total dependence on their husbands experienced during their first years is a situation they all seemed to regret and that they perceived as a considerable loss of their autonomy.

As our contacts with foreign spouses living in Turkey increased, we became aware of, and better informed on, the extent of their legal problems. In the case of countries allowing their citizens the right to have double citizenship, the problems were at that time solved if Turkish citizenship was accepted at marriage. This privilege was not given to men.* To our knowledge there are at least some twenty-five countries not giving their citizens the right to dual-citizenship: Germany, Spain,

---

* This law was changed in June 2003. Now Turkish citizenship for both male and female foreign spouses can be applied for after three years of marriage and residency in Turkey.

Belgium, Holland, Scandinavian countries and Portugal to name but a few. For some reason or another, many spouses who had the right to choose Turkish nationality did not take advantage of it and preferred living with the various problems involved. Turkish laws recognized only one description of foreigner: one who is the holder of a foreign passport. With no other classification or sub-groups available, the same procedures are applied to all foreigners. The foreign spouse wanting to reside in the country for more than three months must apply for a residence permit, renewable after three years, then every five years. The cost of such a permit varies yearly and is currently over three hundred dollars. No permit is issued for a permanent stay or for longer periods. The residence permit for a foreign spouse is first given following a petition from the Turkish national spouse requesting residence for his spouse. The validity of the marriage must be established each time a renewal is required. In the event of the death of the Turkish spouse, or in case of divorce, the legal status of the foreign spouse changes and nothing guarantees the renewal of the residence permit of the spouse.

This residence permit does not entitle the bearer to work. A separate work permit must be obtained for this purpose. Only large Turkish or international companies can obtain such a permit from the authorities, on the condition they offer information as to why, under existing conditions, this post cannot be held by a Turkish citizen. Following a serious investigation by the Labor Department, the work permit is either issued or refused. This precious permit is valid for a year and must be renewed accordingly. Several professions, especially those in the field of health, are forbidden to foreigners and so is any type of work for the governmental agencies. To summarize, except for teaching positions in the private sector and secretarial jobs, hope of finding work is almost nil.*

Those two very restrictive formalities offer no security to the foreign spouses who choose to live in Turkey, their adoptive country, without acquiring Turkish nationality. I seriously wonder how they expect a non-working, divorced or widowed foreign spouse with children to survive under such conditions.

---

* This law was changed in February 2003 and foreign spouses have been placed in a special category. Work permits are easier to obtain.

Guest at a television program as the President of the Network of Foreign spouses

Having gathered information about this situation, we decided to develop within the framework of our association a program offering different types of activities to the ex-patriots and foreign spouses. We focused on social activities for the first group and developed a more educational and more informative program for the foreign spouses. We slowly began to understand that no problems could be solved without the frame of a legal association. Inspired by the German spouses who created their own group, Die Brücke, we began to take the necessary steps. We chose seven founding members, four of whom had Turkish citizenship. Lacking the necessary background, we failed to consult a lawyer and simply copied the constitution of the German group. Several years later this negligence proved to be a mistake for our organization. Our file waited a whole year in the office of the National Security where all Turkish Associations are registered and regulated and finally we were advised that our Association was finally legal. For the next five years the Board of the Association was mostly made up of spouses of Turkish Nationals.

The foreign colony traditionally holds a Christmas Bazaar every year, headed for some time by the wives of executive ex-patriots. One day we were informed that, for various reasons, they would no longer organize the event and asked our Association to take over its organization.

However, IWI at that time had yet to be formally approved as a legal group. Lyne Saka, our president, personally took over the administration of the project for one year. After IWI acquired legal status, the complete organization of the event was handled by the association. Working very diligently, we turned the Bazaar into a very good fund raising project for our charity work. The structure was modified and the venue was changed. Until then, all the revenue had been given to the Little Sisters of the Poor to help finance an establishment they run in Istanbul for elderly members of the minorities. Since the earnings had increased significantly, the Board decided to divide the income between the Little Sisters of the Poor and Turkish charitable institutions helping children. A few years later, the Sisters decided to withdraw from the event. This decision was taken during the course of discussions we were having with them in order to obtain free access to a room, at all times, in case a foreign spouse would find herself in need of such assistance. I presume they did not appreciate our request.

During the five years I was on the Board of IWI, I was responsible for the charity work of the association, work I enjoyed tremendously. With the good budget we had, we were able to support important projects such as:

- Helping another association to set up a shelter for homeless children. We helped them buy some furniture and provided funds to help out with recurring feeding problems they were often faced with. We also helped to pay the fees to hire a private tutor for these more or less illiterate children unable to pursue their schooling in the conventional manner.

- We helped buy some of the equipment needed for the proper functioning of a bone marrow transplant laboratory for children suffering from leukemia at the Cerrahpaşa Medical School.

- We donated a respirator to the Surgery Department of the Pediatric Clinic of the Şişli Edfal Hospital. The British group joined in to finance the renovation of the kitchen and the playroom of the department.

- We provided the necessary funds to modernize the Biochemistry Department of the Pulmonary Disease Hospital for Children in Beykoz, Istanbul. Funds were also provided to buy some of the drugs used in the treatment of tuberculosis. That hospital, a charming site on the shores of the Bosphorus, was a former small palace used by the sultan as a hunting cottage. This hospital found itself in a battle for survival and whether or not it would be shut down was the subject of much speculation. This was the period when gambling casinos were allowed to operate in Turkey. Since the lovely site was accessible by boat, it would have provided an excellent location for such a purpose. Our substantial help was noticed by the authorities of the Health Department and our association was invited to Ankara to participate in a ceremony and received a commemorative plaque from the President of the Republic.

- One of Turkey's most important NGO's, led by Prof Türkan Saylan, asked us to help out with a special project. I had met Dr Saylan during my first year in Istanbul at the Monday evening meetings held at Uncle Sabahattin's home. She was also a fervent participant of the Blue Trip. Southeastern Turkey was then suffering from guerilla attacks by Kurdish rebels aiming to paralyze and prevent the state from offering services to the citizens of the area. The city of Idil in the province of Şırnak had been particularly hard hit by those tactics and its very courageous district governor, Mr Parlak, sent out a call for help in the fields of education and health to all the NGO's in Turkey. Being more experienced in medical subjects, IWI decided to help them to establish a small laboratory in a clinic in the city of Idil. This project was completed with great enthusiasm and a special day of ceremonies was devoted to the inauguration of the projects financed by various NGO's.

- The last important health project carried out while I was on the board was one I am very proud of, and was realized thanks to the help of highly qualified members of our association. It was the first pilot project in Turkey specifically designed according to the health needs of a specific community. One of the most important problems of the country is the high infant mortality rate during the first year of life. The high death rate is mostly related to the ignorance of mothers. This huge project was designed and conceived for the specific needs of a specific area of Istanbul and was headed by the Public Health Department of the Pediatric Clinic of the Medical School of Istanbul University. The project was given the name "Healthy Beginnings" and aimed to teach prenatal and postnatal care to pregnant women. Despite strong objections from some of the ex-patriot board members, IWI committed itself to support the project for a period of two years. It was decided to run the project in a very conservative and fundamentalist section of the city, the municipality of Fatih, a low socio-economical area situated near the University. The Mayor of this municipality at that time, Mr. Sadettin Tantan, later to become Minister of Internal Affairs, supported our work as did the pharmaceutical company, Johnson and Johnson. The Egitim Gönülleri Foundation lent us a tremendous hand by allowing us access to the rooms of its awe-inspiring center situated in the area. During the course of our project, at the special request of the future mothers, a course for future fathers was designed and also given to interested candidates. During that period, over 220 mothers and 120 fathers took the courses that had been prepared for them. In October 2000, I was invited to a scientific meeting held to give the results of the research project and to introduce the concept to those interested. To my great satisfaction, this project can now be developed in any Turkish community showing some interest. The educational material has been developed and is available for interested parties. I am most grateful to the group, which is headed by foreign spouse Janet Turan, for the excellent work done and to Renee De Marco, an ex-patriot with great ideals. Both of these women had their own babies during the course of this project!

It was the opinion of the Board that since our association had solidly established itself and since we were living in Turkey and were sharing its difficulties, we should not stand outside of society and of the Turkish NGO movement. We, therefore, decided to establish contacts with the Turkish women's associations. Just then, I was to meet Prof Necla Arat, the head of the Women's Research and Education Center of Istanbul University. This remarkable woman was to play an important role in the movement that led to the modification of the Turkish Civil Code. She headed a campaign, a first in Turkey, whereby she succeeded in gathering over 100,000 signatures for that cause. She also was the woman who brought together over fifty-five women's associations in order to support two very important causes: the modification of the civil code and the necessity and importance of maintaining a secular republic in Turkey.

After informing her of our interest in joining that movement, she very kindly invited us to a meeting where various women's associations were gathered to meet the Minister Responsible for Women's Affairs. She then introduced our association to the members of the group and IWI was welcomed. I shall always be grateful to her for the essential role she played in my integration into the world of women's NGO's. Every year, besides the publication of a review for The Women's Research and Education Center, she edits books on women's research and women's problems. She kindly accepted to include my paper on "The Culture Shock of Foreign Spouses" in a book entitled, *Being a Woman in Turkey.*

As in all countries in the world, the problem of family violence is widespread in Turkey. As a result of the pressure exerted by the women's associations upon the Minister, a small building to be used as a shelter for battered women was finally established in Istanbul. The building could accommodate at the most twenty-five people, women and children. Two social workers were also assigned to help the women and food was provided, but no budget could be assigned for other expenses. Although it was in a deplorable state, that was how, at that time, the one and only shelter for women in Istanbul was established.

We made a plea to all our members who we knew were very sensitive to the cause of battered women. This resulted in a tremendous response and at the luncheon that month we were simply amazed by the number of items our members donated. All basic personal needs were met by this generous response. We were very lucky to obtain from the Renault Company all the furniture and kitchenware left behind by their personnel as they left Turkey. The high quality of the items they donated gave the shelter a pleasant home environment. A similar gift from the Consulate of South Africa helped us provide basic furniture to a few women as they left the shelter to open their own homes. We provided the shelter with a monthly budget of one hundred dollars to cover their medication expenses and to buy fresh fruit for the children. The shelter was without a phone, so we had a phone installed and paid its monthly cost. In very primitive and difficult conditions and with the sole support of IWI, those two social workers did wonders. I visited the center periodically either to bring material and money or to offer some help and moral support to those excellent social workers who were very alone in their work. The many dramas we shared together... That was the last charity project of my term on the Board of IWI.

From the work accomplished at the shelter we were able, during the Habitat meeting of 1996 to share our experiences with international NGO's working in the same field. We participated in a forum gathering groups from the U.S.A., Brazil and Turkey. My first live television appearance was on the subject of family violence. A very popular TV program entitled "Siyaset Meydanı" ("Political Arena") was doing a program on this sad subject and I was invited to describe the situation in other countries of the world. Thanks to the excellent brochures of the Canadian Government on this subject, I was well prepared.

In the meantime, the tragedy of the Bosnian war was taking place and a large exodus of refugees, mostly women and children, began to arrive at the Turkish border. They were received into well-organized camps provided by the Turkish government and previously used for the refugees of Turkish descent fleeing Bulgaria. Again all NGO's were contacted and IWI was able, thanks to its members, to gather a great quantity of clothes and personal care products from several foreign firms. The Turks are always most helpful and generous in such tragic circumstances and the helping hand extended by everyone was most touching. I personally visited the camp on two different occasions and was very impressed by the tremendous organization of the premises.

While we managed to establish the association in the community and create good programs for the membership, we were unable to attempt to achieve any improvement in the legal status of the foreign spouses. We were so busy with the routine monthly program requirements that no time was left for us to concentrate on that subject. After six years of work, we decided to give up our positions as board members and to form within the framework of IWI a committee working exclusively on this subject. Our ex-patriot sisters found our project too "politically" oriented and even admitted they were afraid the Turkish government would retaliate and refuse to extend their residence permits. Despite our insistence, discussions and negotiations, they were determined not to modify their position. They made the decision after consulting a lawyer who recommended that they not deal with such problems because of a flaw in the constitution of the association. We asked the opinion of the Women's Lawyers Association who told us exactly the opposite: our constitution would allow us to do such work. After a year of deliberation, our ex-patriot sisters did not change their opinion and withdrew their support. From the experience gained after having already created one association, forming a second association grouping only the foreign spouses of Turkish nationals would not be so difficult!

Aware that good results could only by obtained by gaining the firm support of the different national groups in Istanbul, we organized a series of meetings with their leaders. The interest was overwhelming and we began our work by creating a network that included Germany, France, Finland, Spanish speaking countries, Belgium, Great Britain, Scandinavian countries, the United States, India and Canada. All the groups interested in the project were welcomed.

Together we studied the laws of various countries and learned about the rights and legal status of foreign spouses in each country. Turkish laws were also thoroughly studied and we attempted to establish and compile a comprehensive list of all the problems encountered by foreign spouses. Co-ordination was established and the first steps toward creating a legal group, The Network of Foreign Spouses, were taken. Having chosen seven close friends who hold Turkish citizenship to be the founding members, we hired a lawyer who prepared our constitution and all required documents. In February of 1998, our association was recognized by the Turkish authorities. I was a founding member of the association and was elected its first president.

Our first step was to visit the Department of International Law at Istanbul University Law School. We wanted to consult with the members of this chair, discuss our problems openly and gain some information on the possibility of modifying these laws and, in the event that such changes could be obtained, how one should proceed and formulate these requests. We were very well received by all the members of the department and they promised their support. A few months later, Professor Dr Aysel Çelikel and Professor Dr Gülören Tekinalp each published an important paper on the problems of foreign spouses; these were to form the base of all our future requests from the Turkish authorities.

In order to introduce The Network of Foreign Spouses to the authorities and in a desire to establish good relations with them, we paid a courtesy visit to the head of the Police Department's division that deals with foreigners. We took advantage of this visit to clear up several matters regarding procedures and bureaucracy involving residence permits for foreigners. That was followed by an official visit to the Provincial Governor, the highest authority of the central government in the province of Istanbul. Besides introducing our group, we placed an official complaint against the Office of Citizenship. The bureaucrats of that office were forcing those who applied for Turkish citizenship to take a Turkish name. We had learned that the law does not require such a change, but that a circular had been published saying that a name change can be suggested to the applicant. Since we felt that a suggestion was not an obligation we discussed this with the Governor. He was very surprised and indignant about this matter and assured us that no one could force us to change our names. Unfortunately, many of our members have been and still are being intimidated during the procedure and change their names. Those who consulted us were supplied with copies of the Governor's written statement along with a copy of the circular. We have found that with these papers in hand, our members could complete their application with ease.

We then proceeded to introduce the association to the foreign spouses in Turkey and tried to raise public awareness of our problems. We began a thorough media campaign, giving a series of interviews to newspapers and organizing television appearances. Our main difficulty was getting members themselves to talk about their own problems. Those who can speak fluent Turkish are few and they are hesitant to talk, fearing they could compromise themselves, while others can barely speak Turkish and thus are more harmful than useful to the cause. We also had to deal with the tendency of the media to distort and exaggerate events.

At that time we had over 200 members originally from thirty different countries, mostly women but including a dozen or so male spouses. While members from the whole country were accepted, the association was based and operated in İstanbul. A file on the important problems of foreign spouses living in Turkey was prepared. The main things we were working for can be summarized as follows:

1 - A permanent residence permit.

2 - A work permit without restrictions.

3 - The permission to acquire real estate without restrictions.

4 - The abolishment of restrictive measures on inheritance for citizens of certain countries.

5 - Solving the burial problems for non-Moslems in the whole country.

6 - Solving the problems related to drivers licenses, credit cards and acquiring a telephone.

A wind of change has been blowing in Turkey for the last few years. The country is working hard to meet the requirements of the European Union in order to be accepted as a possible candidate and join the alliance. We took advantage of this movement and began our lobbying in Ankara. Good relationships were established with the Department of Labor and a dialogue began in order to obtain better, less paralyzing restrictions on work permits for foreign spouses. A new law was being prepared to modify the working permit regulations for foreigners in Turkey and we did our best to put forward the opinion of the Network of Foreign Spouses, the only association representing any group of foreigners residing in Turkey.

Our efforts were rewarded and in March of 2002, I was invited to Ankara to take part in the work of the commission responsible for preparing the final draft of the law to be presented to the Turkish Parliament. The government, however, changed before the law could be presented to Parliament. We were called to participate in another commission in January 2003. The law was finally accepted on 28 February of the same year and the regulations for the application of the law have been in effect since October 2003. This was a most enriching experience for me and helped me to understand an important fact: Many foreigners have a tendency to look down on the Turks, consider them as inferior and adopt a very arrogant attitude towards them. However, I have found that if you show people the respect they deserve, they act in accordance and, within a short time, friendly relations and a mutual feeling of confidence will be established between the parties.

At the beginning of the year 2001, Mrs Müjgan Suver of the Marmara Research Group Foundation extended a helping hand and invited our group to take part in a round table discussion to relate our problems within the scope of human rights.

As far as our complaints about forced name changes during the Turkish citizenship application were concerned, we wondered what results would be obtained. We insisted on the fact that an individual's name is an integral part of his or her identity and that the persistence demonstrated by some bureaucrats to change these names is not a very logical approach. Our diplomas and all other official documents from our native countries are there to bear witness. How can you explain to a passport control officer your possession of two different passports with two different names or the same name spelled in different ways? We consider this a direct violation of our rights.

Our relationship with the Turkish authorities has always been conducted in a cordial atmosphere and I have never perceived intolerance or experienced fanatical feelings in their dealings with us. Many laws dealing with foreigners are over fifty years old and the authorities are more than aware that they should be improved and urgently need to be updated. Up to now, some improvement with regard to the length of the residence permit has been achieved, a drastic change in working permit conditions has been obtained and the burial problems have been partially solved. With both parties showing some patience and good will, I am convinced that better results will one day be achieved. One should remember that the geographical situation of the country is a major cause forcing the authorities to take measures against immigration.

In 1996, The Eyuboğlu Family Foundation was born. The objective of the group was to gather together the members of the family dispersed in various parts of the country in order to promote good relationships between the members and to help one another. The roots of this interesting family can be traced way back to the great Saladin, Selah-el-Din Ayyubi (1138-1193), the ancestor and founder of the Ayyubi dynasty. He is better remembered as the great leader of the Moslem armies who defeated the Crusaders and conquered Jerusalem. As a member of the board of the Foundation, I am mostly busy with cultural activities.

Hughette Eyuboğlu 2004